Old Testament Roots for New Testament Faith

OLD TESTAMENT ROOTS FOR NEW TESTAMENT FAITH

Robert L. Cate

BROADMAN PRESS
Nashville, Tennessee

4212-20
ISBN: 0-8054-1220-4

Dewey Decimal Classification: 221.6
Subject heading: BIBLE. OLD TESTAMENT—CRITICISM,
INTERPRETATION, ETC.
Library of Congress Catalog Card Number: 80-70914
Printed in the United States of America

Dedicated
to the memory of

my parents

who first told me
the stories of Jesus
and those people
from whom he came

CONTENTS

INTRODUCTION

"What is the Old Testament really about?" The man who asked that question sat across from me in the church office. He was a Sunday School teacher who was pleading for help. Such questions have been asked quite frequently by those whose churches have given them the responsibility of teaching others the biblical truths. It has been asked just as frequently by people who are simply seeking to understand God's total revelation. For most of us, the Old Testament is a closed book. We know some of the stories of its great heroes, but we have little idea of how they relate to each other, and less of how they relate to the New Testament.

Since we are Christians, and since the New Testament tells of Jesus and his followers who spread the gospel, many of us wonder why we need the Old Testament at all. Yet, it is included in our Bible. Furthermore, Jesus did refer to it regularly. Therefore we feel guilty for ignoring it. We also feel frustrated when we do not seem to be able to understand it.

We have a definite feeling that God is trying to say something to us through its pages, but we cannot quite understand what. So we struggle through the occasional sermon preached from it, we grapple with the Sunday School lessons based upon it, and we almost always give a sigh of relief when we move back into the New Testament, for there we seem to be on a firmer footing.

It is these feelings and others like them which have motivated me to write this book. I have been in that place of questioning frustration. I know the feeling of knowing little about the Old Testament and understanding less. But I have also had the privilege of hearing God speak through its pages. I have discovered the excitement of learning something of its magnificent message. In its pages I have seen great nations and mighty kings moved by the impulse of the will and purposes of God. I have sat at the feet of Moses and Isaiah. I have wept with Jeremiah, suffered with Job, sung with David, and searched for the meaning of life with Solomon. I have also shared in the mighty acts of God as he worked in the lives of ordinary people like you and me. Most of all, I have discovered that the Old Testament is not a dead book about people of the long ago. It is a living book— about you and me. It tells what God was doing with someone else, in some other place, at some other time. But it also communicates his message to you and me, in the here and now. It is because of this that I am seeking to help you discover the Old Testament roots for our New Testament faith.

The Relationship Between the Testaments

The first problem with which we must deal is, "Why do we have the Old Testament?" While it is true that we have it because God gave it to us, that still really does not answer our question.

It is also true that what we call the Old Testament is the sacred Scripture of Judaism. Some would suggest that since Christianity grew up in the cradle of Judaism, being almost a sect of Judaism at the very beginning, we have kept their Bible to teach us from where we have come. That may be true. We all need a sense of history, so that we can both understand how we got where we are and also know something about where we are going. If that is our only reason for keeping the Old Testament, then it is of antiquarian interest only, with no real bearing upon our lives.

However, we should note that it was the early Christians who preserved the Old Testament for our use. Even after they were cast out of Judaism, they held on to the Old Testament. It surely had some meaning for them beyond its historical interest.

Further, we delight to quote Paul, who said, "All scripture is inspired by God and profitable for teaching, for reproof, for correction, and for training in righteousness, that the man of God may be complete, equipped for every good work" (2 Tim. 3:16-17). When he wrote this, about the only written Scripture which the early churches had was the Old Testament. If he believed it was inspired by God and was profitable, should we not accept it on the same basis?

Also, Jesus himself said, "Think not that I have come to abolish the law and the prophets; I have come not to abolish them but to fulfil them" (Matt. 5:17). He frequently quoted the Old Testament, beginning his ministry by reading from it, claiming that he was fulfilling that to which the Book of Isaiah had looked forward (Luke 4:16-21). This alone should be sufficient reason for our use of the Old Testament.

Related to this is the fact that the early Christians personally believed and publicly proclaimed that Jesus was the fulfillment of the Old Testament. Peter preached this in his sermon at Pentecost (Acts 2:14-36). Philip did the same thing in his witness to the Ethiopian eunuch (Acts 8:30-35). The writers of the Gospels and Paul, in his letters, all note that the Old Testament pointed to Jesus. They saw him as the personal fulfillment of the hope of Israel. Thus, the Old Testament was kept by the early Christians, not because they were conservative, trying to hold on to the past, but because they were daring. They dared to believe that Jesus was the fulfillment of all to which the Old Testament had pointed and for which it had looked with such hopeful longing. They dared to believe that God's great purposes which he had worked out in the lives of Abraham, Moses, David, Isaiah, Jeremiah, and the others, reached their final focus in the life of Jesus, the Christ.

Therefore, in a very real way, the Old Testament is the foundation of the New. In it are the roots from which our New Testament faith has grown and flowered. If we are to understand the full message of the New Testament, we must begin with the Old. This in no way means that you cannot be saved without knowing or understanding the Old Testament. You can be saved even without knowing or understanding much of the New. Salvation is dependent upon Jesus, not the Bible. But you will never come to the fullest understanding of what he has done and is doing without first understanding the message of the Old Testament. Almost every term used to describe Jesus and his ministry has its Old Testament root. It is there that we must begin if we are fully to understand God's revelation in Christ Jesus.

The Authority of the Old Testament

It becomes obvious, then, that the Old Testament has an authority upon those who claim Christ as Lord. He both accepted and proclaimed its authority. We should also. The lordship of Christ Jesus is the fundamental basis for the authority of the Old Testament. But we must next try to understand what the nature of its authority is. How are we to understand and obey it?

A very cursory reading of the Old Testament quickly brings to light several aspects of the problem. How are we to handle the sacrificial system of Leviticus? In what way (or ways) are we to deal with the nature of the so-called holy wars of Joshua? These are not simple problems, and no simple answer will suffice.

Here, also, Jesus has set an example for us. In the Sermon on the Mount, Jesus presented several thoughts related to the authority of the Old Testament (cf. Matt. 5:17-48). Consider the following:

(1) The Old Testament Scriptures will stand with an authority until "all is accomplished" (Matt. 5:18).

(2) No individual has the right to relax or eliminate the authority of the Old Testament (Matt. 5:19).

(3) Mere obedience of the law is not sufficient. There was probably never any group of people who kept the laws of the Old Testament more rigorously than the Pharisees. Yet, we are warned that we must be more righteous than they were (Matt. 5:20).

(4) To explain what he meant by this last idea, Jesus interpreted a number of the Commandments (Matt. 5:21-47). What he did here was to show that there was an underlying principle behind each of the Commandments. Rigorous obedience to the letter of the law while ignoring the deeper principle missed the mark. It still does. Jesus searched for the thrust of each Commandment and accepted that as having a binding authority.

Thus, if we are going to find the authority which the Old

Testament has upon our lives, this is where we must begin. Accepting the lordship of Christ, we must seek to understand the Old Testament against its background. We must search not only for the literal meaning of the words, but also look for the underlying principle, the thrust of any passage or event. Then this thrust or principle must be carried forward under the inspiration of the Holy Spirit, to find its authority upon our lives today.

This is not easy. No one ever said it would be. But it is necessary. It is not enough to give lip service to the authority of the Old Testament. If it has an authority, we must seek not only to understand its message, we must also apply it authoritatively to our lives. Anything less is insufficient.

Foundations for the Study

Since the Old Testament does have an authority upon the life of a Christian, it becomes important for us to know what it says. There is no excuse for believing in its authority and yet failing to find out its message. But this raises two other issues, the problems of text and canon. If we are going to understand and apply the Old Testament to life, we must know exactly what books are in it and we must also know what these books say.

The Canon. The word *canon* comes from a Greek word which means "a reed," or "a measuring rod." From this, it developed into the meaning of "an authority," or "a rule." When applied to the Old Testament, it refers to the authoritative books within it. There is no way by which we can ever understand the message of the Old Testament without first knowing what books actually belong in it. Some Bibles have only thirty-nine books in the Old Testament. Other Bibles, particularly those of the Roman Catholics, have the additional books known as the Apocrypha (usually fourteen books). Still others, notably those of the Eastern Orthodox churches, have an extra three books in the Apocrypha. The question immediately arises as to which is correct. Protestants and Evangelicals have frequently asked why the Roman Catholics and the Eastern Orthodox churches have added books to their Bibles. They, on the other hand, have asked why we leave some books out of the Old Testament. Neither question really gets to the heart of the issue of the canon. What books are authoritative?

The Old Testament was the Bible of Israel. It was originally written in Hebrew, with a few scattered sections in Aramaic. (Aramaic is closely related to Hebrew.) About the second century BC, the Old Testament was translated into Greek. This had become the major language of the world by this time. Many Jews who had been scattered over the known world could no longer read Hebrew. In response to this, their Bible had to be translated into Greek.

It is worth noting that this development made the Scriptures available in the language of the common man. This became a major factor when the early Christians began their missionary activities. There was already a Bible available which was in the common language of the day. This is one more evidence of how God's providence prepares the way for his messengers.

After the Old Testament was translated into Greek, numerous pious Jews continued to write religious books. But these were generally written in Greek. Some of these books came to be added to the Greek Old Testament, while they were rejected by the Hebrew-speaking people of mainstream Judaism. Thus, the Greek version of the Old Testament wound up with more books than the Hebrew original. The Greek version came to be known as the Septuagint, a word which means "seventy." This name was based upon the legend that the translation into Greek was done by seventy elders in seventy days, a legend which has no basis in fact. Septuagint is usually abbreviated LXX.

Since the early Christians scattered around the Mediterranean world spoke Greek, they generally used the LXX as their Bible. When it was translated into Latin by Jerome, near the end of the fourth century AD, this became the official canon of the Roman Catholic Church. On the other hand, Protestants and Evangelicals have felt that, since the Old Testament was the Bible of Judaism, only those books which they accepted as authoritative should be accepted. Thus it is that we have received divergent canons for the Old Testament.

There is one other difference between these canons, and that is the order of the books. Although rejecting the additional books of LXX, we have generally accepted the order in which the books appear. This has made it easier to locate books when a person was using both canons. The Hebrew canon preserves a different order.

The Hebrew Bible is divided into three major sections. The first is the Law, or *Torah.* This is made up of Genesis, Exodus, Leviticus, Numbers, and Deuteronomy, in that order. The second major section is the Prophets, or *Neb-hi'im.* This is further divided into two subsections, the Former Prophets and the Latter Prophets. The Former Prophets contain Joshua, Judges, 1 and 2 Samuel, and 1 and 2 Kings. The Latter Prophets are Isaiah, Jeremiah, Ezekiel, and the Book of the Twelve (the minor prophets, Hosea to Malachi). The third section of their canon is the Writings, or the *Kethubim.* This is made up of Psalms, Proverbs, Job, Song of Songs, Ruth, Lamentations, Ecclesiastes, Esther, Daniel, Ezra, Nehemiah, and 1 and 2 Chronicles. It is important in our further study that we be familiar both with the sections of the Hebrew canon and with the books in each section.

The Text. In studying the message of the Old Testament, it is not enough to know which books are authoritative. We must know what the books say. This is the point at which the study of the text of the Old Testament becomes important. The people who do this kind of work are called textual critics. The work which they do is aimed at seeking to determine the "best" text for each and every verse in the Old Testament.

By "best," we do not mean the one with which we most readily agree. Rather, we are seeking to get as near as possible to the words which the original inspired author recorded. Old Testament text critics have not been blessed with the multiplicity of ancient manuscripts which New Testment text critics have had. When ancient copies of the Old Testament were made, the originals were usually burned or buried, with appropriate religious ceremonies. Thus, what we were eventually left with was a copy of a copy of a copy, and on and on and on. Until quite recently, the oldest full copy of a Hebrew Bible which we had came from about AD 1008. There were a few more ancient fragments, but even these came from centuries after the originals were written.

Thus, the discovery of the Dead Sea Scrolls was met by Old Testament text critics with extreme excitement and enthusiasm. In this one discovery, we were given ancient manuscripts at least ten centuries older than those we were then using. Among these manuscripts we have found full copies of several Old Testament books and parts of every book in the Old Testament but Esther.

The basic impact upon our textual studies which the Dead Sea Scrolls have made lies in the area of accuracy. It had long been assumed that copying and recopying ancient manuscripts for so many centuries would have allowed many errors to have entered the text. This, if true, could have made major changes in our understanding. From the textual study of the Dead Sea Scrolls, two things stood out. First, there were numerous errors of copyists, just as had been expected. Second, not one of these errors which we have identified to the present time has made a major change in any doctrine or basic teaching. Although God apparently left the copyists free to be human and make errors, he apparently overruled even their errors in such a way as to preserve his Word. The Dead Sea Scrolls have given us a renewed confidence in the message of the Old Testament.

Determining which books are authoritative and determining what these books say bring us one step closer to being ready to deal with the message of the Old Testament. There is one more foundation which must be considered, however. This is Israel's history.

The History of Israel. Since the Old Testament is the product of God's dealings with the people of Israel, we must know something about their history in order to understand it. Unlike the New Testament which covers less than a century, the Old Testament experience was spread over many centuries. For us to properly understand the various books and messages, we need a basic historical framework within which to operate. I have found the following to be extremely helpful. The dates are as accurate as I can make them. However, many scholars will disagree with some of the dates. That is to be expected when we are this far removed from the actual events. On the other hand, you will find no disagreement with the basic periods and their sequence.

The Patriarchal Period, ca. 2000 to ca. 1700 BC. This is the period of the migration of Abraham, Isaac, Jacob, and Joseph. It covers the time of Abraham's departure from Ur until the family of Jacob went to Egypt during the famine, while Joseph was prime minister.

The Period of the Sojourn in Egypt, ca. 1700 to ca. 1300 BC. We know very little about the events here. By the end of this time Israel had multiplied greatly and had moved from being guests of Pharaoh to being his slaves.

The Period of the Exodus and the Wilderness Wanderings, ca. 1280 to ca. 1240 BC. These events were those through which Israel was transformed from being slaves in Egypt to being the covenant people of God. The primary focus of this period is the covenant experience at Sinai.

The Period of the Conquest and the Settlement, ca. 1240 BC to ca. 1020 BC. This covers the time of Joshua and the judges. In it Israel was transformed from being a group of wandering tribes to being a settled people in the Promised Land.

The Period of the United Monarchy, ca. 1020 BC to ca. 931 BC. This covers the creation of the Hebrew Kingdom under Saul, the major expansion and consolidation under David, and the decay and dissolution under Solomon. The Hebrew prophets began to make their influence felt here.

The Period of Israel and Judah as Separate Kingdoms, ca. 931 BC to 721 BC. In this period, the two nations separated. During most of this time Israel, the Northern Kingdom, was dominant. The great prophets began to make their impact upon the two nations. The end came when Israel was destroyed and its capital, Samaria, was captured by Assyria in 721 BC.

Judah's Period Alone, 721 BC to 586 BC. Judah's century-and-a-half alone was characterized by great prophets and a final downfall before Babylon. The kings sought for expediency rather than righteousness, as a rule.

The Period of Babylonian Exile, 586 BC to 539 BC. During the time in Babylonian exile, the people of Judah were forced to discover that God had not been defeated by their defeat. Rather, they were given a new faith which was adequate to deal with their personal defeat. This was probably one of the more theologically formative periods since the time of the Exodus.

The Persian Period, 539 BC to 333 BC. When Babylon was defeated by Persia, the Jewish exiles were allowed to return to their own land. This time of relative peace allowed Judaism to begin taking the shape it generally had during the time of Jesus.

The Greek Period, 333 BC to 168 BC. After Alexander the Great overthrew the Persians, Greek culture became the rule of the day for the Ancient Near East. Hebrew resistance to this influence produced persecution from without and rebellion from within. Hebrew religion further developed its intense legalism during this time.

To really understand much of the development of Hebrew faith, we will have to keep the relative relationship of these periods before us during the rest of our study. It is important to remember that Israel's faith was a historical faith. It was based not upon what they thought about God so much as upon what they had experienced with God. Their faith was always rooted and grounded in history.

Approaches to the Faith of the Old Testament

Among the multitude of books which have been written about the faith of the Old Testament, there are several basic approaches which can be identified. The first of these has been to try to reconstruct the development of Israel's faith through the various historical periods which we outlined above. Although this has met with varying degrees of success, when it is completed all that we really have is a history of Israel's religion. This is valuable, and well worth the effort. At the same time, it really does not ever come to grips with the real nature of Israel's faith.

The second basic approach to Israel's faith has been to force some systematic arrangement of doctrine upon the Old Testament. This allows us to carefully examine each doctrine or concept against its Old Testament background, but it falls far short of really dealing with the basic nature of Israel's faith. It is quickly obvious that they never developed anything like a systematic approach to faith. Their faith was based upon living experiences with God, and life is seldom systematic.

A third major approach to Israel's faith has been through the avenue of comparative religion. Here the authors have tried to come to grips with Israel's faith by first studying the faith of her neighbors. Then Israel's faith has been examined against this background in the light of both its similarities and its differences.

A fourth significant approach to the study of Israel's faith has been by the analysis of the common, key theological words. This study of their theological vocabulary has shed great light upon their faith, but it has been too compartmentalized. The great moving sweep of their experience with God just seems to disappear in the dust of multitudinous word studies.

While each of these approaches has added a great deal to our knowledge of Israel's faith, all of them have failed to give us a clear picture of what that faith really was. By utilizing the best results of each of these methods, it appears to me that we can more nearly discover what the real faith of the Old Testament is. As we have already noted, we have an Old Testament canon. Those thirty-nine books were preserved by the Hebrew people, under the movement of God's Spirit, because the books spoke to their needs. We are going to try to come to grips with the common commitments of these books. We are going to try to answer the question, "What is it that binds these books together? What is their common witness, their common message?" By making this approach, we shall obviously leave a great deal out. On the other hand, we shall be able to focus upon the common thread of revelation which binds them together. It is that thread which we are seeking to follow.

We will begin by directing our attention to "the knowledge of God." Here we shall examine the basic concepts of what and how we can know about God. The Old Testament here provides a major root for the New Testament understanding of God's revelation. Until we come to grips with what we can really know about God, we shall never have a basis for any further study. This is foundational.

Next, we shall turn to what the Old Testament understands of the nature of God. To them, God was the fundamental reality of life. So we shall first consider "the God who is." He was a living, personal reality to them. He should be so for us. We shall also deal with their understanding of "the God who acts." The Hebrews were not philosophers. They did not think about God; they met him. Thus what they really knew about God came as a result of

his acts in their lives and in their history. The major feature of his acts on their behalf was his choice of them. They
constantly spoke of themselves as the chosen people. So we
must consider their experience of "the God who chooses."
Each of these areas of study should enrich our understanding of God's acts in Christ and his choices of grace.

The second major reality in the life of the people of the Old
Testament was themselves. But even their self-awareness
was tempered by their experience of God. Thus we will
focus our attention upon their understanding of "man as
God's creature." As we deal with their understanding of
what being human really meant, the next significant development will show up in their growing understanding of
sin, of "man in rebellion." The graphic ways by which they
described their sin experience adds real depth to the New
Testament descriptions of sin. The full awareness that sin
separated them from God left them with a feeling of utter
helplessness. There was nothing they could do for themselves to remove their guilt.

It is at this point that we shall turn our attention to their
growing awareness of the "redeeming God and penitent
man." The Old Testament focus upon God's salvation and
forgiveness serves as the basis for the New Testament
understanding of the mission of Jesus. The fullness of
Jesus' ministry becomes much more real when seen as the
ultimate end of the works which God began in the Old Testament.

When the Old Testament people understood the nature of
God's redemptive acts in their midst, they began to look forward to his ultimate acts of redemption. Because of their
past and present experiences with God, they began to look
forward to a future with him. This draws our attention to
the areas of "God's promises and man's hope." Such a hope
arose out of the firm belief in the absolute sovereignty of
God. Built upon this belief, God gave them a future hope for
the coming of his Messiah and his ministry as the Suffering Servant. This blossomed into their ultimate hope for a
new covenant. All of this provided both the images and the
substance for Jesus' own descriptions of his life and ministry.

We will also need to consider "worship in the Old Testament," which is closely related to Israel's understanding of

God's redemptive acts and of their future hope. The entire New Testament understanding of worship grew directly from these Old Testament roots. Although we no longer use a sacrificial system, since Jesus became our sacrifice, the meanings of sacrifice furnished the foundations for New Testament worship. In fact, the understanding of Jesus proclaimed by the Book of Hebrews cannot be fully apprehended without an understanding of the sacrificial system of Israel.

Closely related to their understanding of worship was their understanding of themselves as "the servants of God." It was at this point that they saw themselves as fulfilling God's purposes in this world. This part of their self-awareness is very significant for the New Testament understanding of ministry and mission.

Next, our study will deal specifically with the developments in their faith "beyond the Old Testament." The faith of Israel divided into two main streams. Part of it moved into Judaism. Here we can see both the both the background of their religion in the days of Jesus as well as its development as one of the major world religions of our day. The other development was Christianity. Here we shall see how Jesus took the faith of Israel and transformed it into New Testament Christianity.

The last section of our study will offer some helps and guidelines in interpreting the Old Testament. It is never enough to know what someone else has said the Old Testament means. We must be able to approach it ourselves and to hear God speak through it.

In pursuing each of these areas, I will try to utilize the best Old Testament scholarship available, including language studies, historical studies, archaeological studies, literary studies, and other areas of knowledge as they bear upon particular questions. Furthermore, we shall also utilize the best of each of the methods which have been used to approach the study of Old Testament theology. Word studies, the history of Israel's religion, comparative religion, and systematization will all play their part. It is not my intent to burden you with the details of these studies, but to present the results of them.

While we are doing this, let us constantly keep before us that we are studying a faith that was alive. Just as a doctor can learn a great deal about a patient by cutting into him at different places, so can we learn about Israel's faith by doing something similar. At the same time, the patient is a living person. He must be examined as a whole, also. The same is true of the Old Testament. If we fail to see the broad sweep of the entire Old Testament, by that much shall we really fail to understand the faith of Israel. And by precisely the margin by which we fail to understand the faith of Israel, we shall also fail to understand the Old Testament roots of our New Testament faith.

The Author's Presuppositions

There is one last introductory item with which we must deal. Before you can fully understand this book and my approach to it, you need to know the basic presuppositions with which I begin this study. They will certainly color my judgments, because it is upon them that I will make those judgments.

My first presuppositions are primarily concerned with the nature of God. I believe that God is love. This is fundamental to me. Furthermore, I believe that his love is not some nebulous feeling on his part, but that it is specifically directed to his human creatures. He loves people. This brings me face to face with the inescapable conclusion that he loves both you and me. This will both color and shape my work in this book. It is foundational to my life and ministry.

My second set of presuppositions has to do with people. I know that I am a sinner. This is not merely a theological belief, it is a practical fact. In addition, I believe that all people are sinners. We have all sinned and fallen short of God's demands and expectations for us. This drives me to the stark realization that both you and I need salvation, redemption. We need to be both cleansed and forgiven. Furthermore, we need a new nature so that we do not slip back into our old sinful ways.

My third set of presuppositions are based both upon experience as well as the biblical revelation. This has to do with the divine-human encounter. God has acted to redeem people, and thus has acted to redeem you and me. He has done this supremely in Jesus Christ. Having so acted, he has graciously made it possible for us to receive the results of his act through our faith. He calls us to submit to the lordship of Christ for cleansing, teaching, comforting, and preparation. He sends us forth to serve him by bearing witness to what he has done. He has not left us, nor any other people, without his Word. He has spoken, revealing himself. His voice may be heard in the world of nature, but most of all in the words of the Bible. His Holy Spirit speaks within our spirits, bearing witness to the truth which he has revealed.

These are, in essence, the basic presuppositions of my life and ministry. It is for these reasons that I am writing this book. I pray that it is for these reasons that you are reading it. My ultimate prayer is that this will serve as an aid so that you will be better able to hear God speak redemptively through the pages of the Old Testament. Then you will be better equipped to serve him in the world in which we live.

1

The Knowledge of God

"Through searching, can you find out about God?" (Job 11:7, author's translation). One of the fundamental questions of the ages, this demands an answer. The testimony of the passing years is simple. No man can find out about God through his own efforts. God is met, not discovered. And he is met when he chooses to reveal himself, not before. The beginning point in any study of faith must be the concept of revelation, God's self-disclosure.

While the Old Testament has very little to say about revelation as such, it focuses a great deal of attention upon several related concepts. Here we come face to face with Israel's understanding of how God reveals himself. Let us beware of forcing our preconceived ideas upon the Old Testament. Rather, we must consider what it says about the revelation contained within it. We should be willing to be confronted by God himself. Our God is neither served nor benefited by people who refuse to see what is inconvenient to their own ideas. He can best be served by disciples who can say with Samuel, "Speak, Lord, for thy servant is listening" (1 Sam. 3:9, author's translation).

The Understanding of Revelation

There are three basic terms or phrases which are used by Old Testament writers in setting forth what they understood about God's self-revelation. These are fundamental to our understanding of Israel's belief in God's self-disclosure. In general, each of these terms focus upon an action. (This is generally true of most basic concepts within the Old Testament. The people of God were far more concerned with what God had done and was doing than with mere ideas about God.)

Revelation. There is no word in the Old Testament for "revelation," as such. However, there is a verb which means "to reveal" or "to uncover." Thus Amos says:

> Surely the Lord God does nothing,
> without revealing his secret
> to his servants the prophets.
> The lion has roared;
> who will not fear?
> The Lord God has spoken;
> who can but prophesy? (Amos 3:7-8).

The prophet from Tekoa began with a statement with which all of his hearers were expected to agree. The people of Israel had a common commitment to the fact that God revealed (uncovered) his purposes to his spokesmen. The word here translated as "secret" actually refers to his "plan," his "purpose." Acknowledging the truth that God will inform his prophets of what he plans to do, Amos then added that since he had received God's revelation, he must proclaim it. There was no other alternative for him. When God reveals his plans, it is for the purpose that they should be shared. This is their very nature.

This basic concept is reaffirmed in the experience of the maturing Samuel, "for the Lord revealed himself to Samuel at Shiloh by the word of the Lord" (1 Sam. 3:21). Immediately following this magnificent affirmation, the Bible says that "the word of Samuel came to all Israel" (1 Sam. 4:1). This was set forth as the reason behind the statement that "all Israel . . . knew that Samuel was established as a prophet of the Lord" (1 Sam. 3:20). Since God uncovered his purposes to Samuel and since Samuel shared this revelation with his people, they knew that God had established him as a prophet.

This same term for the experience of receiving a message from God was used by Jeremiah (33:6), Daniel (2:19,22,28, etc.), and Isaiah (22:14). The prophets were totally sure that

God revealed his purposes to his spokesmen so that they might give them to his people. The basic principle was set forth by Moses in the plains of Moab, just before his death. "The secret things belong to the Lord our God; but the things that are revealed belong to us and to our children for ever, that we may do all the words of this law" (Deut. 29:29). The Old Testament is very clear at this point. God does not leave his people ignorant of his purposes. God reveals them.

The Knowledge of God. To the prophet Hosea, the basic expression for God's self-revelation was "the knowledge of God." He began his messages of judgment by proclaiming:

Hear the word of the Lord, O people of Israel;
  for the Lord has a controversy with the inhabitants
    of the land.
There is no faithfulness or kindness,
  and no knowledge of God in the land;
there is swearing, lying, killing, stealing, and com-
    mitting adultery;
  they break all bounds and murder follows murder
    (Hos. 4:1-2).

Having laid this foundation, he thundered out an oracle of judgment:

My people are destroyed for lack of the knowledge;
  since you have rejected the knowledge,
  I reject you from being a priest to me
    (Hos. 4:6, author's translation).

Then, God voiced through his prophet what his ultimate desires for Israel were.

For I desire steadfast love and not sacrifice,
  the knowledge of God, rather than burnt offerings
    (Hos. 6:6).

To properly understand these words from God's prophet, we must first understand that knowledge in the Old Testament was something learned by intimate experience. It did not merely refer to facts which were comprehended intellectually. Rather, it referred to that which was learned by experience. Thus the "knowledge of God" for which the prophet yearned was not merely that his people should know about God but that they should have *experienced* God firsthand.

That which is learned about God by experience is part of what we mean by revelation. Furthermore, the negative which Hosea used in 4:1 would be better translated, "there is an absence of the knowledge of God in the land." The prophet was actually saying that there was every reason to expect that God's people should be living in, by, and with an experiential relation with their God. The very fact that this was missing was shocking to him. When you raise the hood of your car, you have every right to expect an engine there. When you look at the people of God in any generation, you have every right to expect that they will be living in a daily, experiential relationship with God.

To Hosea, the revelation of God certainly included and may have begun from what his people learned about God through actually living in relation to him. The same should be true of us.

The Fear of the Lord. The third phrase which is basic for understanding the Old Testament concept of God's self-revelation is "the fear of the Lord." In general, this expression has normally been considered as referring simply to awe, terror, or reverence. A brief survey will show that this is far too limited. The psalmist says, for example,

> The law of the Lord is perfect,
>   reviving the soul;
> the testimony of the Lord is sure,
>   making wise the simple;
> the precepts of the Lord are right,
>   rejoicing the heart;
> the commandment of the Lord is pure,
>   enlightening the eyes;
> the fear of the Lord is clean,
>   enduring for ever;
> the ordinances of the Lord are true,
>   and righteous altogether (Ps. 19:7-9).

The "fear of the Lord" is sandwiched in the middle of five other phrases which clearly referred to an authoritative set of rules or regulations. Hebrew poetic parallelism certainly requires that the "fear of the Lord" had some such similar meaning.

Furthermore, when Abraham offered a reason for identifying Sarah as his sister, he said, "I did it because I thought, There is no fear of God at all in this place, and they will kill me because of my wife" (Gen. 20:11). Abraham seems to have feared for his life because he thought that there was no authoritative revelation from God in that foreign setting. Moses later said that he had brought the Ten Commandments down from the mount, "that the fear of him [God] may be before your eyes, that you may not sin" (Ex. 20:20). He obviously saw the "fear of God" as being parallel to the written law, with the purpose of leading Israel away from sin.

Isaiah condemned his people by announcing that,

> This people draw near with their mouth
>   and honor me with their lips,
>   while their hearts are far from me,
> and their fear of me is a commandment of men learned
>   by rote (Isa. 29:13).

Although his people were guilty of believing false teaching, they were identifying the fear of God with a commandment. Jeremiah also equated the "fear of the Lord" (Jer. 32:40) with the law (Jer. 31:33), both of which are to be written ultimately upon the hearts of God's people.

The term really came to the fore in Psalms, Proverbs, and Job. Consider the following:

> Come, O sons, listen to me,
>   I will teach you the fear of the Lord (Ps. 34:11).

> He who withholds kindness from a friend
>   forsakes the fear of the Almighty (Job 6:14).

> Behold, the fear of the Lord, that is wisdom;
>   and to depart from evil is understanding (Job 28:28).

> The fear of the Lord is the beginning of knowledge;
>   fools despise wisdom and instruction (Prov. 1:7).

We must particularly note here that "the fear of the Lord" is equated with knowledge. Lest we miss this emphasis, it was set forth again and again. God's people were told that they would not find God when they began to search for him,

> Because they hated knowledge
>   and did not choose the fear of the Lord (Prov. 1:29).

A future hope was offered to them by the promise,

then you will understand the fear of the Lord
and find the knowledge of God (Prov. 2:5).

The restatements of this idea occur again and again (Prov.
9:10; 10:27; 14:26; 15:16; 15:33; 16:6; 19:23).

That the "fear of the Lord" is equivalent to the authoritative revelation of God is clearly carried forward into the
New Testament by the apostle Paul. In his masterful description of the guilt of all people (Rom. 3:9-17), he summed
up with a quotation from Psalm 36, "There is no fear of God
before their eyes" (Rom. 3:18). For him, this was the basis
of the sinfulness and guilt of all humanity. Lest anyone
should miss his point, he said in the very next words: "Now
we know that whatever the law says it speaks to those who
are under the law" (Rom. 3:19). The "fear of God" immediately turned his attention to the written law of the Old
Testament. Furthermore, in urging purity of conduct upon
the Corinthians, Paul summed up by saying, "Since we
have these promises, beloved, let us cleanse ourselves
from every defilement of body and spirit, and make holiness perfect in the fear of God" (2 Cor. 7:1). When speaking
of the written promises of the Old Testament (which he had
just been quoting), his attention was immediately turned to
"the fear of the Lord."

The "fear of the Lord," then should be understood as referring to the written, authoritative, revealed message
from God to his people. The "fear of the Lord" can and
should be taught (Ps. 34:11). It should be obeyed (Job 6:14).
It can lead to victory over evil, and is the ultimate source of
all wisdom (Job 28:28).

All three of these terms or phrases help us come to grips
with the basic Old Testament understanding of God's self-
revelation. It is always initiated by God. He it is who
"uncovers" or "reveals" himself to us. It is always based
upon experience between God and his people. Ultimately, it
is authoritative upon human life and is the source of all real
wisdom. With this as a background, we are now ready to
consider *how* God reveals himself to his people. What does
the Old Testament have to share with us at this point?

Revelation in the World of Nature

The people of the Old Testament, Israel, believed that
they were confronted by God in a number of different ways.

They knew that God met them in the world around them. God revealed himself in nature. Thus the psalmist could sing,

> The heavens are telling the glory of God;
>   and the firmament proclaims his handiwork.
> Day to day pours forth speech,
>   and night to night declares knowledge.
> There is no speech, nor are there words;
>   their voice is not heard;
> yet their voice goes out through all the earth,
>   and their words to the end of the world (Ps. 19:1-4a).

This magnificent hymn of praise clearly proclaimed that God could be known through the world of natural things. Even without words or a language, the world in its orderliness and in its beauty proclaims God. This is done in such a way that the variety of the languages of the world are no barrier. Anyone can know something about God in the world. This is precisely the idea that Paul picked up and developed in his letter to the church in Rome, where he said, "Ever since the creation of the world his invisible nature, namely, his eternal power and deity, has been clearly perceived in the things that have been made" (Rom. 1:20).

The idea that something of God could be clearly learned from the world of nature was developed by Old Testament writers in numerous places. The Book of Job expanded upon this in chapters 38 through 41. Several of the Prophets and the Book of Proverbs added to the concept. There was a clear recognition in the Old Testament that God was revealed in the world of nature. This was surely underscored by numerous references in the New Testament. However, let us clearly understand that there is a significant difference between what we can learn about God *in* nature and what we can learn about God *in* Christ. In the world, we see God as Creator, Sustainer, and Preserver. In Christ, we know him as Redeemer and Savior.

Revelation in History

The second way by which the Old Testament people believed that God revealed himself was through history, the actual events in which he acted. For them, this was the primary way by which God could be known, or experienced.

The philosophers of ancient Greece tried to learn about God (or the gods) by philosophical thought. The Hebrews learned that God was met in events, in the actual occurrences of the affairs of life. They met God as Lord of nature when he demonstrated that he could part the sea, furnish manna and quail in the wilderness, and provide water in the desert regions. They met God as Redeemer when he delivered them from slavery in Egypt. They experienced him as Sovereign over men and nations when he caused the walls of Jericho to fall before them. Israel learned that God was a righteous Judge when he punished them for stealing some of the goods from Jericho (Josh. 6:16-19; 7:1-26). They also learned that he cared about other peoples when he sent Elijah to Syria and Jonah to Nineveh. Their understanding of God came by what he revealed of himself in the arena of historical events.

At this particular point, the Old Testament is significantly different from all other "bibles" of ancient peoples, in that it focuses upon the whole history of Israel. Rather than merely being a record of the exploits of great people or the record of heroic achievements, the Old Testament directs attention to the unity and meaningfulness of the whole stream of history. Further, it clearly portrays the weaknesses of its heroes and the sinful failures of the nation. Other ancient peoples would never have dared to have recorded such history.

The reason for this appears to have been that no other ancient people ever came to a view of history as a meaningful process on the way to a goal. The underlying cause for this fact was not so much that Israel had a different understanding of history but that they had a different awareness of God. God had met Israel in historical events. He was known by what he did. He had a sovereign purpose that would not be thwarted.

Thus Israel seems never to have recorded history merely as a series of events which had happened. Rather, the Hebrews recorded history because of what the events meant, not because of what the events were. This must be firmly grasped if we are going to understand the Old Testament.

As an example of this, consider two of the kings of northern Israel: Omri, and his son, Ahab. Omri was such an important king that mighty Assyria never forgot him. They referred to Israel as "the land of Omri." Yet, the Book of Kings covers the entire reign of Omri in eight verses (1 Kings 16:21-28). On the other hand, Ahab seems to have made a much lesser impact upon the world, yet, the events of his reign fill 209 verses (1 Kings 16:29 to 22:40). Why should there be this difference? The answer lies not in the two men and their relative importance, but in what God was doing. During the reign of Ahab, God had a prophet on the scene by the name of Elijah. The history which was recorded was written because of its theological importance, not because of Ahab's importance.

Thus, for Israel, history was important because of what God had done. For them, the importance of an event seems always to have rested in its meaning. Their basic question was not, "What happened?" Rather, it was, "What was God doing?" If we merely read Old Testament history trying to find out what happened, we have missed the point entirely.

Therefore, the history found in the Old Testament is never merely the record of history as such, but of significant history. They recorded history as revelation. That is the key to understanding the events recorded in the Old Testament. It is also the basic key to understanding Israel's awareness of the nature of God. He was always known by what he did.

These very same elements are the center and core of the faith of the early churches, as seen in the New Testament. It is for this reason that the advent of Jesus Christ could never be understood either solely or chiefly as the coming of a great teacher of moral or spiritual truths. He was this. But he was more, far more. His coming was a historical event which was the climax of God's redemptive purposes which had guided the divine dealings with man since the creation of the universe. The biblical faith then, was (and is) a recitation of historical events as the mighty acts of God. God is best known as the God who acts.

This is also why it is best to seek to lead people to faith in Christ by telling them what God has done for you and for others. Philosophical arguments may be good for a debate but are seldom effective for winning the lost. God is seldom made known by such arguments. He is more clearly seen by what he has done and is doing. Therefore, we are called as witnesses to report on his historical acts, both past and present. All the arguments of the Pharisees collapsed before the simple statement of the man born blind, when he said, "One thing I know, that though I was blind, now I see" (John 9:25). Argument collapses in the face of a report of what God has done.

Digression: Time and Eternity. Since history matters, time is important. It is the sphere of God's activities. But it is also the arena of human decision and action. Our generation measures time by numbers on a watch or a calendar. We are extremely concerned with the time when things happened. For the ancient Hebrew, this was not so. He was far more concerned with what happened and what it meant than with when it occurred. Therefore we frequently have far less chronological information than we would wish. We are also frequently disturbed over our failure to comprehend some of the chronological information we do have. This is more often than not due to our failure to understand what time meant to them.

To the ancient Hebrew, time was always wrapped up in the event. Thus the author of Ecclesiastes said,

For everything there is a season,
    and a time for every matter under heaven.
a time to be born, and a time to die;
a time to plant, and a time to pluck up what is planted;
a time to kill, and a time to heal;
a time to break down, and a time to build up;
a time to weep, and a time to laugh;
a time to mourn, and a time to dance;
a time to cast away stones, and a time to gather stones
    together;
a time to embrace, and a time to refrain from embracing;
a time to seek, and a time to lose;
a time to keep, and a time to cast away;
a time to rend, and a time to sew;
a time to keep silence, and a time to speak;
a time to love, and a time to hate;
a time for war, and a time for peace (Eccl. 3:1-8).

A further illustration of this concept of time can be found in their names for the months. Rather than just assigning titles, they described what occurred in them, such as "barley harvest," "early planting," "flax harvest," and the like.

Thus, time was important because of what happened in it, not because of its mere passage.

Perhaps the most striking feature of the Hebrew concept of time is that they do not really seem to have had any concept of a timeless eternity. The idea of eternity as something "timeless" was an idea which the New Testament developed. The Israelites do not seem really to have thought of it this way. The basic word which we translate as "eternity" in the Old Testament really means "the dim unknown." It refers to the hiddenness of the distant future or the distant past, rather than to its timelessness. Thus when Isaiah looked forward to the messianic kingdom, he said,

> Of the increase of his government and of peace
>   there will be no end,
> upon the throne of David, and over his kingdom,
>   to establish it, and to uphold it
> with justice and with righteousness
>   from now unto the dim unknown
>   (Isa. 9:7, author's translation).

He was not looking for a timeless kingdom, but for a kingdom within time. It was beyond the boundaries of his vision but within time. He was content to leave that time in God's hands.

A second expression which is also sometimes misunderstood is translated "forever." This, too, leaves us with a sense of timelessness. The actual Hebrew expression is literally "for length of days." Thus the forward look of the psalmist was,

> Surely goodness and mercy shall follow me
>   all the days of my life;
> and I shall dwell in the house of the Lord
>   for length of days (Ps. 23:6, author's translation).

In these expressions stand the roots which the New Testament developed into its concept of eternity. If God could be trusted to care for his people in time, he could also be trusted to care for them beyond time. It is not as if the Hebrews did not believe this, they just never really seem to have thought about it. Their concern was with what God was doing in time. They left the rest to him. This might serve as a warning to us not to become so otherworldly that we forget this world. It was precisely this tendency which Paul was trying to combat in his correspondence with the church at Thessalonica. Some of the Christians there were so eager for the return of Christ that they had gathered in the church to await his return. To them, Paul bluntly said, "If any one will not work, let him not eat" (2 Thess. 3:10). It may be trite, but it is still very true that it is possible to become so heavenly minded as to be of no earthly good. The Old Testament kept its focus upon what God was doing in time, in the events by which God met people in their daily lives. It was in these events that they could and should learn about God.

Revelation Through Interpretation

It is not really enough to recognize that God was seen as revealing himself in the world of nature and in historical events. We must still face the question as to how he did it. It is imperative that we recognize that God always had an interpreter present to interpret or explain what he was revealing. Without the inspired interpreter, the revelation might have been lost.

Physical Means of Revelation. The interpreters of God's revelation experienced his self-disclosure through several different kinds of physical phenomena. They saw his revelation in the normal events of nature such as the rainbow, day and night, or seedtime and harvest (Gen. 9:12-17; 8:22). They also experienced his revelation in abnormal events which were not necessarily supernatural, such as the east wind which parted the waters for Israel to cross the sea out of Egypt (Ex. 14:21-22). While an east wind may be natural, it certainly was abnormal that it parted the waters. That this was done at the right place and at the right time was even more abnormal.

There was also a deep awareness that God revealed himself in the supernatural. This is the area of miracle. To the Hebrew, what we call a miracle was usually described by words which meant "something wonderful," or "sign." Thus, when Gideon was told that the Lord was with him, he responded, "Pray, sir, if the Lord is with us, . . . where are all his wonders which our fathers recounted to us?" (Judg.

6:13, author's translation). Gideon was looking for miracles to prove God's presence. Gideon's failure was in not seeing God in other ways. (Is not this our failure as well?)

Moses was told that God was going to multiply "signs and wonders" in Egypt (Ex. 7:3). Both refer to God's mighty acts. The sign, however, always focused attention upon a meaning beyond itself. If we turn our attention so much upon an event that we miss its meaning, we have failed to understand it. One of Satan's best tricks is to get our attention so focused upon an event that we never hear what God is revealing through it. No miracle is as important as its meaning. We must hear what God is saying.

God also regularly revealed himself to his people through the media of fire and storm. Again, it took his inspired interpreter to see this and explain it. If Moses had not been present to tell Israel that the pillar of fire and cloud was God's presence, they might not have known it. When God descended upon Mount Sinai, he was seen both in fire and in storm (Ex. 19:16,18). Isaiah's vision of God seems to turn our attention to fire (Isa. 6:4). On the other hand, Ezekiel's vision called attention to clouds and lightning, the perfect picture of a storm (Ezek. 1:4). The fire and storm image was carried over into the New Testament, for the Holy Spirit descended on Pentecost in something like a rushing wind and tongues of fire (Acts 2:2-3).

The spokesmen for God also occasionally received revelation through oracular means. On numerous occasions they cast the sacred lots to find the will of God. This was used to determine the identity of the sinner after Jericho, to determine who should be Israel's first king, and to determine whose guilt had brought a storm upon a ship at sea (Josh. 7:16 ff.; 1 Sam. 10:20 ff.; Jonah 1:7 ff.). These sacred lots were known in Israel as the Urim and the Thummim (Ex. 28:30). In addition to these lots, the will of God was also determined by other oracular means, such as Gideon's use of the fleece, or Nebuchadnezzar's shaking the arrows, examining the liver of a sacrificial animal, and consulting the teraphim (Judg. 6:36-40; Ezek. 21:21-22). Each of these was an ancient means of divination, well-documented from archaeological sources.

In addition to these specific means of finding the will of God, there were numerous times when physical revelation was accomplished simply through ordinary experiences. Amos received a major message after seeing a basket of overripe summer fruit (Amos 8:1-3). Jeremiah had a similar experience through a visit to the potter's house (Jer. 18:1 ff.). Furthermore, the use of dreams to reveal God's purposes in the Old Testament is well known. Joseph's rise to power in Egypt came after such a revelatory experience (Gen. 37:5-11; 41:1 ff.).

While these physical means of revelation are not as common in the New Testament as in the Old, they are still present. Peter had a vision or a dream on the housetop at Joppa (Acts 10:9 ff.). The apostles also cast lots to determine the successor to Judas (Acts 1:26).

It appears however that these physical means of revelation had become less significant toward the end of the Old Testament era. Their use in the New Testament period appear to have become almost negligible. With the gift of God's Holy Spirit who was to "guide . . . into all the truth," the use of such other means was really no longer necessary (John 16:13).

Prophetic Revelation. By far the most familiar as well as the most significant means of revelation in the Old Testament was that given to and through God's spokesmen, the prophets. The earliest description of such a man was as a "seer." This would apparently refer to his visionary experiences or his oracular means of discovering God's will. However, the major term used to describe such a man was "prophet." Although we cannot be completely sure of the earliest meaning of this latter term, it apparently referred to "one who poured forth." Thus, such a one would be a proclaimer, one who poured forth God's message.

There are two passages of significance for really understanding what a prophet was. In 1 Samuel 9:9-10, we are told of the transition from the older terminology of seer to the newer terminology of prophet. Even more importantly, we are told that the prophet was a "man of God." It is essential to remember that throughout the Old Testament the prophet was always considered to be a man of God. This referred to the fact that he was God-called, God-motivated, and that he proclaimed God's word.

Also important for understanding the function and ministry of the prophet is Exodus 7:1-2, where God said to Moses,

See, I make you as God to Pharaoh; and Aaron your brother shall be your prophet. You shall speak all that I command you; and Aaron your brother shall tell Pharaoh.

Aaron was to act like a prophet for Moses to Pharaoh. As such, he was to be the channel of communication between Moses and Pharaoh, carrying Moses' message. This described precisely what a prophet was to do. As God's prophet, he carried God's message to the people. The prophet and his people were always clear about where the source of the message was. It was always from God.

Thus the prophet understood himself to be the channel through whom God spoke. It is particularly characteristic of this outlook that the prophets regularly spoke of the "word of the Lord coming to me." He was the channel of God's verbal revelation to his people. But he was more than this.

Looking at the ministry of the great prophets such as Moses, Isaiah, and Jeremiah, we discover that they were also intercessors. They carried their people to God. It would appear that any man who was a great prophet was also a great prayer. Note how Amos interceded for his people in the face of impending judgment (Amos 7:2,5). Never content merely to proclaim God's word, the prophet also sought to lay hold of God's mercy for his people.

The prophets also were frequently involved in symbolic actions. Jeremiah wore a yoke to drive home his message urging submission to the yoke of Babylon (Jer. 27:1 ff.). Ezekiel's ministry was particularly characterized by such actions, where over and over again he seemed to make a fool of himself by acting out his messages (cf. Ezek. 4:1 to 5:12; 12:1-16).

Such actions were a vivid portrayal of the messages which the prophets were proclaiming. More than this, the prophets seemed to have felt that by obeying God in acting out these messages, they were in some way actually releasing divine power to work in those situations. It is quite likely that this concept has some overtones for understanding the New Testament symbols of baptism and the Lord's Supper. These portrayals are more than mere symbols. They are a dramatic and effective witness to the truth of the gospel message which they portray.

The messages of the prophets appear to have been primarily addressed to their specific historical situation. This does not mean that there was no element of prediction in them. However, each message was addressed to the prophet's own people in his own times. This is precisely what makes their messages so timeless. Because they addressed real people in real-life crises, their messages can be translated to other real people in similar real-life crises. It also becomes very important to try to identify the crisis to which a particular message was spoken. In no other way can we be on solid ground as we apply their ancient words to our contemporary times.

It is important that we recognize that the prophets were totally wrapped up in the Word of God. It was his Word which they proclaimed. When they proclaimed it, they expected something to happen. Thus they could say with utmost confidence,

> So shall my word be that goes forth from my mouth;
>> it shall not return to me empty,
> but it shall accomplish that which I purpose,
>> and prosper in the thing for which I sent it (Isa. 55:11).

God's Word was both dependable and effective. It was this fact which allowed the prophets to preach with such boldness. This is still true of God's Word.

Law as Revelation. Modern people have a great deal of trouble accepting the Old Testament understanding of law as God's revelation. We consider law to be binding, restrictive, and generally something distasteful. To the ancient Israelite, the law was one of God's good gifts. Because of this, they could sing:

> I delight to do thy will, O my God;
>> thy law is within my heart (Ps. 40:8).

To this they added,

> But I delight in thy law.
> The law of thy mouth is better to me
>> than thousands of gold and silver pieces.
> For thy law is my delight (Ps. 119:70,72,77).

The basis for this joy in God's law was that it was both true and the bringer of a peaceful relation between man and God and between man and man.

> Thy righteousness is righteous for ever,
>   and thy law is true.
> Great peace have those who love thy law;
>   nothing can make them stumble (Ps. 119:142,165).

The law was such a good source of knowing God's will and receiving his blessings that when Jeremiah looked forward in hope to the New Covenant, he proclaimed God's promise that "I will put my law within them, and I will write it upon their hearts; and I will be their God, and they shall be my people" (Jer. 31:33).

It was upon this foundation that Jesus built, when he said, "Think not that I have come to abolish the law and the prophets; I have come not to abolish them but to fulfill them" (Matt. 5:17). It was the law which let Israel know what God both expected and demanded of them.

But, as Jesus said immediately thereafter, there were deeper meanings to the law than Israel ever understood. As the New Testament makes abundantly clear, the law does not save. But the law did make life livable. It set forth the boundaries of God's expectations. In Christ, we have been made obedient to him as Lord. He has become our law.

One last word about revelation in the law. One of the reasons which make the ancient laws of Israel appear so restrictive to us is the fact that we are so far removed from the culture of the period in which Israel lived. If we are ever going to comprehend the revelation contained in these laws, we are going to have to understand them against their own background, not against ours.

The laws concerning slaves horrify us (Ex. 21:1-11). But in Israel slaves had been little more than property. They were not treated as people, but almost as animals. Thus, in this law, God was saying to Israel, "Slaves have rights, too." This was a tremendous revelation that slaves were to be treated as fellow human beings.

The famous *Lex Taliones* (law of retaliation) sounds extremely harsh alongside of Jesus' words admonishing us to turn the other cheek (Ex. 21:23-25; Matt. 5:38-42). But again, we need to note that, in the world in which Israel lived, vengeance was the rule of the day. Here they were being told that they could exact nothing more than justice.

As we consider these examples, it becomes obvious that

the law was a quantum leap forward in their dealings with others, with one another, and with God. Truly, it was part of God's good revelation. They never doubted that it came from God.

Sacred Story as Revelation. A fourth area by which we can see how God's self-revelation was understood in the Old Testament is seen in the histories which these ancient people recorded. We have already confronted the fact that Israel's view of history grew out of their view of God. No other ancient people ever wrote a history like Israel's. Other peoples created a golden age in their past to which they looked back with pride. Israel looked back to slavery in Egypt, from which God had redeemed them. Other peoples seldom recorded defeats of their national armies. Israel looked to the defeats as their just punishment from God for their sinful apostasy. Other peoples ignored the failures of their heroes or magnified their great men as being above the moral codes. Israel again and again painted its heroes in human terms, showing both their tragic sins and God's gracious forgiveness. Ultimately, other peoples assumed that if their nation was ever defeated, their gods had been defeated as well. Only Israel developed a theology of exile, pointing to their own national defeat as further evidence of God's sovereignty over all nations. The God of Israel could use both Assyria and Babylon as his instruments, whether or not those peoples ever knew him. It was from this basis that Isaiah proclaimed,

> Ah, Assyria, the rod of my anger,
> the staff of my fury!
> Against a godless nation I send him,
> and against the people of my wrath I command him,
> . . . .
> But he does not so intend,
> and his mind does not so think;
> but it is in his mind to destroy,
> and to cut off nations not a few (Isa. 10:5-7).

And when Habakkuk wondered what God was going to do about the sins of Judah, God said to him,

> Look among the nations, and see;
> wonder and be astounded.
> For I am doing a work in your days
> that you would not believe if told.

> For lo, I am rousing the Chaldeans [Babylonians],
>   that bitter and hasty nation,
> who march through the breadth of the earth,
>   to seize habitations not their own (Hab. 1:5-6).

So Israel's history was not just history, it was the sacred story of God's redemptive acts, even in judgment. To God's interpreters, God's historical judgments always had a redemptive purpose. When Amos looked over the catastrophic events of his day, two truths stood out. First, the natural and historical calamities were evidence of God's judgment upon Israel's sin. But there is a recurring refrain that points to the other truth. Four times he pointed to contemporary judgments and each time ended with the refrain, "Yet you did not return to me" (Amos 4:6,8,10-11). It is obvious that God's purpose in those judgments was not merely punishment but redemption. The divine acts were intended to cause Israel to return to God.

Thus, the sacred story of their history became the agent of God's revelation. What we have then is not Israel's history so much as it is the history of God working out his redemptive purposes in and through Israel. It was this sacred story which set the stage for God's ultimate sacred story, the gospel of Jesus Christ. It was also Israel's sacred story which gave us the vocabulary by which Jesus' mission was proclaimed by the New Testament preachers. (These will be pointed out in detail in later chapters.)

Wisdom as Revelation. The Books of Job, Proverbs, and Ecclesiastes, along with a few psalms, are the product of what has been called the Hebrew wisdom movement. Wise men in the Old Testament are frequently listed alongside the prophets and priests as being the major functionaries in the national faith. Jeremiah's enemies deny the validity of his judgment proclamations by saying, "The law shall not perish from the *priest*, nor counsel from the *wise*, nor the word from the *prophet*" (Jer. 18:18, italics mine).

The message of these books focuses our attention upon the practical problems of daily living, the experience gained from life, and the ultimate issues of life. Because so much of their attention seems to be on nonreligious matters, many interpreters simply ignore these books. This misses the point altogether.

The wise men were searching for real wisdom. They

found much practical wisdom in ordinary life, but they proclaimed that real wisdom came only from God. Job asked with simplicity,

> Whence then comes wisdom?
> And where is the place of understanding? (Job 28:20).

He answered with equal simplicity,

> Behold, the fear of the Lord, that is wisdom;
> and to depart from evil is understanding (Job 28:28).

The author of Proverbs underscored this, saying,

> The fear of the Lord is the beginning of knowledge;
> fools despise wisdom and instruction (Prov. 1:7).

Since, as we have seen, "the fear of the Lord" appears to have meant the authoritative, revealed word of God, the wise men of Israel were proclaiming that real wisdom was to be found in God's Word, not in all the philosophical searchings of man. Furthermore, when the author of Ecclesiastes had examined all of human experience, he concluded with the admonition that, "This is the end of the matter; all has been heard. Fear God, and keep his commandments; this is for every man" (Eccl. 12:13, author's translation).

The wisdom writers were simply saying that human experience is important. If it were not, so much attention would not have been given to it. But the divine revelation is more so, for it is the result not merely of human experience, but of human experience with God. Thus, the ultimate revelation is what happens between a man and his God. When Job came to the end of his conflict, he made a climactic statement. He had questioned God, based upon his own experience. He had also questioned God, based upon the experience of others. His questions were finally silenced however, not because God answered them, but because God confronted him. Thus when Job met God, he said,

> I had heard of thee by the hearing of the ear,
> but now mine eye sees thee;
> therefore I despise myself,
> and repent in dust and ashes (Job 42:5-6).

It was only after this that Job could and did pray for his friends (Job 42:10).

In the Old Testament, then, revelation came to man only as he experienced God. He might experience God both in nature and in history. He might experience God in natural, abnormal, and supernatural events. He might experience God as he sought for a response from God or as God confronted him. He might experience God as God revealed his prophetic word or his authoritative law. But ultimately, all of these kinds of experiences were recorded in what we call the Old Testament. It was God's word to Israel in specific historical situations. It is God's word to us in our historical situation. It is our responsibility to let its words lead us from the printed page of a book to our own personal experience with God in daily life.

2
The God Who Is

When the first telephone cable connection was made between England and South Africa, the announcement was made to the House of Commons in England. The usually reserved members of that august body responded with a great deal of cheering and applause. As the noise died down, a member of the House rose to his feet and responded: "Wonderful! Wonderful! Now that we can speak to the South Africans, what shall we say to them?"

The ability to communicate is relatively unimportant unless there is something to communicate. We have seen that the Old Testament has a clear understanding of the fact that God communicates through his Word. That is wonderful. But that fact by itself is of little significance. What is significant is our understanding of what he has communicated. What did God reveal to the people of Israel? What does he reveal through the Old Testament to us?

To understand the answers to these questions, we must remember that the Old Testament was recorded by people who lived in a world that was extremely religious. The men of all ancient nations believed in some kind of gods. They all practiced some form of worship. They all had some type of faith, some system of belief. Unless we recognize this, we shall be very likely to misunderstand a great deal of what the Old Testament has to say to us about God.

With this understanding and with the clear conviction

that God did and does speak through the pages of this ancient book, we are ready to say,

> Morning by morning he awakens,
> he awakens my ear
> to hear as those who are taught.
> The Lord God has opened my ear.
> and I was not rebellious,
> I did not turn away backward
> (Isa. 50:4b-5, author's translation).

We shall not be likely to hear what God is revealing unless and until we allow him to open our ears and communicate with our minds and hearts. We dare not turn away from the truth he reveals about himself. Let us rather listen to his voice as it speaks to us through his Word.

The Living God

"He is alive!" That startling affirmation was the keystone of the preaching of the early Christians. It was the striking affirmation that Jesus had conquered death.

In a very similar way, the keystone of the Old Testament proclamation was that God was alive, living. This was the basic fact of life to Israel. The ancient Greeks described their gods either as colorless, mythological creatures, as static, unmoved beings, or as wholly immoral creatures, almost less than human. The same can be said of most of the religions of the ancient Near East. This was not true of the ancient Hebrews. Their first concepts of God were dynamic, moving, living, and exalting. The ancient Hebrew never tried to prove the existence of God. Rather, he met God through his living actions in history. To him, it was both obvious and fundamental that God was alive.

Anyone could stand in the presence of an idol with no real fear. But after God's meeting with Israel at Sinai, Moses was driven to exclaim,

For who is there of all flesh, that has heard the voice of the living God speaking out of the midst of fire, as we have, and has still lived? (Deut. 5:26).

Hosea, preaching in the dark days just before the fall of Samaria, expressed his hope for the future in similar terms, saying, "In the place where it was said to them, 'You are not my people,' it shall be said to them, 'Sons of the *living* God' " (Hos. 1:10, italics mine). Further, Jeremiah contrasted the idols to which his people had turned with the God of Israel, by proclaiming,

> But the Lord is the true God;
> he is the living God and the
> everlasting King (Jer. 10:10a).

Regardless of what other terms the Hebrews might use to describe God, and they used many, he was always fundamentally the living God. As such, he was active in history. It was his actions which were the primary evidence of the fact that he was alive. As we have also seen, it was his activity which gave ultimate meaning to history. Thus we can truly say that history is primarily "his story."

Without question the Old Testament understanding of God grew and developed with the passage of time. But this must never be considered to be a product of the fact that men thought more about God as time passed. The evidence to the contrary is overwhelming. Their understanding of God grew because they were steadily and consistently being confronted by the God who lived. They knew more about him because he continued to meet, confront, and challenge them. As the years passed, God's acts of redemption, judgment, and love caused them to understand more of his very nature. Thus we cannot really say that their theology developed over the years. (It did, but that was not the point.) What did develop was the insight of faith responding to the experience of the living God. The very mark of their awareness of the living God was the fact that their faith response was also living. It grew and developed in response to their personal experience with God. This is still true.

The very nature of a faith experience with the living God is that it produces a growing faith. Thus the common witness of the New Testament is that the new convert is a babe in Christ, growing and developing into a mature Christian. Paul declared:

But I, brethren, could not address you as spiritual men, but as men of the flesh, as babes in Christ. I fed you with milk, not solid food; for you were not ready for it; and even yet you are not ready (1 Cor. 3:1-2).

The author of Hebrews further underscored this idea.

For though by this time you ought to be teachers, you need some one to teach you again the first principles of God's word. You need milk, not solid food; for every one who lives on milk is unskilled in the word of righteousness, for he is a child. But solid food is for the mature (Heb. 5:12-14).

Peter added an affirmation to this process of spiritual growth through the faith experience, saying, "Like newborn babes, long for the pure spiritual milk, that by it you may grow up to salvation" (1 Pet. 2:2). Such growth in faith comes about through being confronted by a living Lord through a living Word. This was true in New Testament times. It was true in Old Testament times. It is still true today.

So certain were the men of the Old Testament that God was alive that they would swear "as the Lord lives" to affirm an oath (cf. Judg. 8:19; Ruth 3:13). Such oaths were taken only upon the basis of something which was absolutely permanent. There are at least sixty occurrences of this particular oath in the Old Testament.

As the living God, he is concerned with living beings. This concern was focalized in his concern with men's actions. They were expected to respond in obedience. God said through Moses,

You have seen what I did to the Egyptians, and how I bore you on eagles' wings and brought you to myself. Now therefore, if you will obey my voice and keep my covenant, you shall be my own possession among all peoples (Ex. 19:4-5).

When their actions were contrary to his will, then they were called to give an accounting. On the other hand, obedience to God was the way of life.

The living God was the author of all life, both physical and spiritual. Genesis declares that "the Lord God formed man of dust from the ground, and breathed into his nostrils the breath of life; and man became a living being" (Gen. 2:7). But we are also told that God said to Israel:

See, I have set before you this day life and good, death and evil. If you obey the commandments of the Lord your God which I command you this day, by loving the Lord your God, by walking in his ways, and by keeping his commandments and his statutes and his ordinances, then you shall live and multiply, and the Lord your God will bless you in the land which you are entering to take possession of it. But if your heart turns away, and you will not hear, . . . I declare to you this day, that you shall perish; you shall not live long in the land which you are going over the Jordan to enter and possess (Deut. 30:15-18).

Furthermore, all animal life came from God (Gen. 1:20-25). For the ancient Hebrew, the living God was unquestionably the source of life, all life.

Because he is the living God, he is known by what he does, not by what men think about him. As we have already seen, the knowledge of God came to the Old Testament people through God's own self-revelation, not by man's searching or by his thought processes. Thus Amos declared with assurance:

> Surely the Lord God does nothing,
>   without revealing his secret
>   to his servants the prophets (Amos 3:7).

Jeremiah pointed out that the absence of this personal revelation from God was the mark of the false prophet, saying:

> For who among them has stood in the council of the Lord
>   to perceive and to hear his word,
>   or who has given heed to his word and listened?
>   (Jer. 23:18).

So all of the prophets constantly looked at what God was doing, or had done, in history to define the very nature of the God they proclaimed.

But even though God was known by what he did, and even though he revealed that part of himself which he chose, yet he was never fully known. There was always a part of the nature of the living God which was beyond anyone's ability to understand. So the saints could sing,

> Great is the Lord, and greatly to be praised,
>   but his greatness is unsearchable
>   (Ps. 145:3, author's translation).

Thus Job, who arrogantly demanded so much from God, was suddenly hushed when he was confronted by the immensity, majesty, and power of the living God (cf. Job 38:1 to 41:34). He had questioned the things he had been told about God. Having met the living God, he simply confessed,

> I had heard of thee by the hearing of the ear,
>   but now my eye sees thee;
>   therefore I despise myself,
>   and repent in dust and ashes (Job 42:5-6).

No matter how much one learns about the living God, there is always a hiddenness about him. The Old Testament saint knew perfectly well that God was known only when he cared to be known and only to the extent that he cared to be known. The living God was met by a living person only when God chose to be met, not when the person decided to find him. He was met when he acted, not when men thought about him.

The Old Testament prophets described idols as dead—a stark contrast to the living God. Idols were gods without life. The very opposite of the living God, idols were "no-things." This is a common term describing idols in the Old Testament, but it was a favorite of Isaiah's. Note the following.

> Their land is filled with no-things;
>   they bow down to the work of their hands,
>   to what their own fingers have made
>   (Isa. 2:8, author's translation).

> And the haughtiness of man shall be humbled,
>   and the pride of men shall be brought low;
>   and the Lord alone will be exalted in that day.
> And the no-things shall utterly pass away
>   (Isa. 2:17-18, author's translation).

> In that day men will cast forth
>   their no-things of silver and their no-things of
>   gold,
> which they made for themselves to worship,
>   to the moles and to the bats
>   (Isa. 2:20, author's translation).

> For in that day every one shall cast away his
> no-things of silver and his no-things of gold, which your
> hands have sinfully made for you
>   (Isa. 31:7, author's translation).

On the other hand, Jeremiah simply described idols as "no gods." You can almost hear him snort at the folly of Judah who sought to serve such creations.

> For cross to the coasts of Cyprus and see,
>   or send to Kedar and examine with care;
>   see if there has been such a thing.
> Has a nation changed its gods,
>   even though they are no gods?
> But my people have changed their glory
>   for that which does not profit.
> Be appalled, O heavens, at this,
>   be shocked, be utterly desolate, says the Lord,
> for my people have committed two evils:
>   they have forsaken me,
> the fountain of living waters,
>   and hewed out cisterns for themselves,
> broken cisterns,
>   that can hold no water (Jer. 2:10-13).

Even the heathen were loyal to their gods, though they were no gods, gods without life, gods without existence. The people of Judah, on the other hand, were more foolish. In treachery and infidelity, they turned from the living God to no gods! This was both foolish and tragic. Since God alone is alive, God alone gives life.

It was this sense of God as alive that served as the basis for the affirmation of the Fourth Gospel, that "in him was life, and the life was the light of men" (John 1:4). Furthermore, when the Sadducees sought to entangle Jesus about the resurrection, Jesus responded by saying,

> And as for the resurrection of the dead, have you not read what was said to you by God, "I am the God of Abraham, and the God of Isaac, and the God of Jacob"? He is not God of the dead, but of the living (Matt. 22:31-32).

Ultimately, it was this sense of God being alive and being the source of all life that gave rise to the full hope of salvation. The living God not only gave life, he gave eternal life. "For God so loved the world that he gave his only Son, that whoever believes in him should not perish but have eternal life" (John 3:16). Just as he created physical life, the living God also creates spiritual life. Thus Paul boldly proclaimed, "Even when we were dead . . . [God] made us alive together with Christ (by grace you have been saved). . . . For we are his workmanship" (Eph. 2:5-10). The God who is living gives life to whom he will. Apart from him there is no life at all.

The Personal God

God in the Old Testament was not content merely to reveal himself as living. There are lots of things which live. He added to his self-disclosure the fantastic truth that he was personal. This fact was observed by the children of Israel in several ways. We must beware that we do not take this revelation for granted. In ancient times as in modern times there were two basic tendencies which men had in trying to describe their gods. The first was to portray the gods as some kind of impersonal, unmoved forces. This is still with us. Many people who profess to believe in God speak of him in terms so remote and impersonal as to be wholly theoretical, unrealistic, and irrelevant.

The second tendency which shows up in descriptions of gods is to make them so radically persons as to remove any sense of divinity. In modern times this shows up in the image of a gray-haired, old grandfather, or the man upstairs. In ancient times this showed up in the many mythological descriptions which portrayed the gods as something far less than human. The behavior of the gods of Greece, Egypt, and Babylon, while described in human terms, was usually on a far lower plane than that of the typical person in any of those nations. Their gods were usually licentious, immoral, capricious, and generally subhuman. The God of the Old Testament fell into neither of these extremes in the fact of his personhood.

The first step in the ancient Israelites' understanding of the fact that God was personal is seen in his personal name. The divine name was first clearly set forth in the call of Moses (Ex. 3:1-15). When Moses asked for a revelation of the identity of the God who called him, he was given a personal name.

God also said to Moses, "Say this to the sons of Israel, 'Yahweh, the God of your fathers, the God of Abraham, the God of Isaac, and the God of Jacob, has sent me to you': this is my name for ever, and thus I am to be remembered throughout all generations" (Ex. 3:15, author's translation).

The entire experience was recorded in terms of one person speaking to another. It was concluded with the affirmation of a personal name for the God of Israel.

There are two problems related to the name of God. The first is its meaning. It appears to come from the same verb root as that which was expressed in the affirmation, "I AM" (Ex. 3:14). The first person form of the verb form is apparently what God called himself: "I AM." The form which the Hebrews were to use appears to be the third person form: "HE IS." While this is a nontechnical oversimplication, it does appear to offer the best solution. Further, the name could also be translated as: "HE WAS," "HE WILL BE," or "HE CAUSES TO BE." The name focuses both upon the real existence of God and his creative power. Further, it also draws attention to the consistency of God. It is quite likely that it was from this idea that the author of Hebrews later made his glorious affirmation that "Jesus Christ is the same yesterday and today and for ever" (Heb. 13:8).

The second problem related to the name of God is its actual spelling and pronunciation. In ancient Hebrew, vowels were not written down. So the name was recorded as *YHWH* (or, *JHWH*). In the Greek version of the Old Testament (the Septuagint, abbreviated as LXX), the divine name was transliterated and the vowels "a" and "e" were inserted giving *Yahweh*. Although this was done centuries after Moses' call, it is the earliest evidence we have as to what the actual vowels were.

In Israel's later history, the fear of violating the Third Commandment became so strong that they actually ceased pronouncing the divine name at all. Whenever they read the Scriptures, they would pronounce the Hebrew word for "Lord" everywhere the name of God appeared. When they finally started writing vowels, in order to make sure that everyone remembered not to use the real name of God, they added the vowels of the word for Lord to the consonants of the name of God. It was from this that the form *Jehovah* (or *Yehowah*) came. There never was such a word. It was merely a device to protect people from using the name of God in vain.

But the Hebrews were not only given the revelation of a personal name for God, they also understood him in personal terms. The many so-called anthropomorphisms (describing God in human terms) may at the same time be understood as being theomorphisms (describing humans in divine terms). Be that as it may, there is absolutely no question but that God was understood by the saints of the Old Testament as a person.

Man is described as being created in the image of God in the Genesis creation account. For "God said, 'Let us make man in our image, after our likeness; and let them have dominion . . . over all the earth' " (Gen. 1:26). We shall deal with this in detail when we consider Israel's understanding of man. But in regard to their understanding of God, he was in some sense similar to man. This at least includes personhood.

In addition, God was regularly described in terms common to human personality. He walks, he talks, he feels, he is angry, he rebukes, he remembers, he forgives, and he loves. Furthermore, he is described as having a back, a face, arms, hands, feet, and breath. While it is obvious that these may be figures of speech seeking to describe an infinite God so that he can be comprehended by finite people, it should also be obvious that each and all of these terms are terms of personhood.

At the same time, the Old Testament always makes it clear that while God has personal characteristics, he is always above and beyond the human level. That difference was clearly set forth by Hosea.

> How can I give you up, O Ephraim!
>   How can I hand you over, O Israel!
> How can I make you like Admah!
>   How can I treat you like Zeboiim!
> My heart recoils within me,
>   my compassion grows warm and tender.
> I will not execute my fierce anger,
>   I will not again destroy Ephraim;
> for I am God and not man,
>   the Holy One in your midst,
>   and I will not come to destroy (Hos. 11:8-9).

It would be very easy to dismiss the anthropomorphisms of the Old Testament as a crude, primitive, outgrown approach to the understanding of God. But the easy way is seldom the best way. Certainly, Jesus himself spoke of God in similar terms. He spoke of the "Father who sees in secret" (Matt. 6:6), the "Father [who] knows what you need" (Matt. 6:8), and the Father who feeds the birds of the air and clothes the grass of the field (Matt. 6:26,30). At the same time, he also emphasized the differences between God and man.

The anthropomorphisms are neither crude nor outworn. Rather they convey a deep and profound truth which no abstract philosophical description could ever give. Impersonal, philosophical descriptions give no real concept of what God is like. If the message of the Bible in both the Old and New Testaments is clear on anything, it is clear on the fact that God is personal. For the saints of the Old Testament, the living God was truly personal and terms of personal description alone were adequate to describe his relationships with man. Furthermore, personal categories alone sufficed to describe and define God's activity in nature and in history.

In fact, as we said above, perhaps it is man who is described in theomorphic terms. Since we are told that man was created in God's image (Gen. 1:26), we may say that the Old Testament proclamation is that man is like God rather than the reverse. That which really defines what a person is may be God rather than man. God from the beginning was fully personal. Man merely developed personality from his dust. At the same time, whatever God is, he is always over, above, and beyond man. The ultimate evidence of the limitation of anthropomorphism was the prohibition of making any visual representation of God (Ex. 20:4; Deut. 5:8). Such a representation would either have imprisoned him within limitations or would have become a substitute for him. Israel was clearly taught that there was no limit to the being or nature of God.

Ultimately, Israel's understanding of their relationship with God was fully personal. Their relation is always described in terms of a covenant, an agreement between persons. It amounted basically to a command handed down from a great king to his subjects. But its basis was always both personal and ethical. It demanded a response from one person to another.

The God of Israel was a person. Perhaps, it is more accurate to say that he was the Person. As such, he was personally understood and demanded a personal response.

This understanding of God ultimately bore fruit in the life and ministry of Jesus. When God chose to send his ultimate revelation of himself, he sent a person, not a philosophy. Thus it is that John proclaimed with power and joy.

And the Word became flesh and dwelt among us, full of grace and truth; we have beheld his glory, glory as of the only Son from the Father. . . . No one has ever seen God: the only Son, who is in the bosom of the Father, he has made him known (John 1:14-18).

A further affirmation of the fact that God can be best known in personal interrelation was given in the discussion between Jesus and Philip following the Last Supper.

Philip said to him, "Lord, show us the Father, and we shall be satisfied."

Jesus said to him, "Have I been with you so long, and yet you do not know me, Philip? He who has seen me has seen the Father; how can you say, 'Show us the Father'? " (John 14:8-9).

Thus we can say with assurance that God's ultimate self-revelation was in a personal life. The Old Testament proclamation was that God was a living person. He is still best understood in personal terms.

Let us not be dismayed that in some ways the personhood of God in the Old Testament appears to fall so far short of that which was revealed in Christ. This is only to be expected. If the people of the Old Testament could have fully comprehended the total nature of God, the life and ministry of Jesus would have been unnecessary. God does not force more truth upon people than they are able to grasp. Even Jesus said to his disciples,

I have yet many things to say to you, but you cannot bear them now. When the Spirit of truth comes, he will guide you into all the truth; for he will not speak on his own authority, but whatever he hears he will speak. . . . He will glorify me, for he will take what is mine and declare it to you (John 16:12-14).

God's self-revelation was a growing disclosure. If at times Israel's understanding of him is less than that revealed in Jesus, at the same time it was far advanced over that of their contemporaries. Our understanding of God is not limited by God's ability to reveal but by our ability to comprehend. This is true now and it was true then. The growing Christian knows more about God today than he did a year ago. The New Testament knows more of God's personhood than the Old Testament did. But there is no question that the God we meet in both Testaments is a living person. He is never merely the product of rational thought or of a vivid imagination.

The Holy God

The Old Testament understanding of God as personal was always tempered by its portrait of him as the holy God. Our grasp of this image is frequently distorted because of our failure to understand what the Bible means by the word *holy*. Usually this word brings to mind the image of a superpious, otherworldly, self-righteous individual, unrelated to life as it really is. Whatever else may be said, the Old Testament concept of holiness is not at all similar to this image.

The word-picture behind the Old Testament concept of holiness appears to carry two basic images. It would appear that holiness meant to be burning, glowing, and radiant, yet at the same time it meant to be separate, set apart, different. Certainly, in its actual usage, both images are clearly carried by the word. There was that about God which was radiant and burning. In fact, he is frequently described in terms of fire. Moses was attracted by the burning bush (Ex. 3:2-4). The Israelites were led by a pillar of fire and smoke (Ex. 40:38). Even the descent of the Spirit at Pentecost was described in terms of tongues of fire (Acts 2:3).

At the same time, usage clearly points to the idea of separation, of being set apart. "Holiness" and "holy" were used to describe objects and persons who were set apart from secular usage. The term at first clearly had a nonmoral character, for the sacred prostitutes of the Canaanite Baal worship were called "holy ones." As such, they were women set apart for the Baal worship. Holy objects could not be approached or touched by secular people. Uzzah was not allowed to touch the ark nor was Moses allowed to tread on "holy ground" without first taking off his sandals (2 Sam. 6:6-7; Ex. 3:5).

Ultimately, the Hebrews came to realize that only God was holy. Objects and persons became holy because they had been set apart for God's use or because he had taken them over for his particular use. Holiness thus seems to come to describe the very nature of God. The Philistines trembled before his power, saying, "Who is able to stand before the Lord, this holy God?" (1 Sam. 6:20).

By the time of the great eighth-century prophets, the very concept of holiness had come to be a synonym for God himself. Thus God spoke through Hosea, proclaiming, "I am God and not man, the Holy One in your midst" (Hos. 11:9). The most characteristic description of God found on the lips of Isaiah was that he was "the Holy One of Israel." In fact, the basic feature of his call experience was the revelation of God's awesome holiness. As he viewed God in his vision, the seraphim uttered the dramatic refrain, "Holy, holy, holy is the Lord of hosts" (Isa. 6:3). The young Isaiah had gone to the Temple seeking to discover what kind of God Israel served. The revelation he received proclaimed him as a holy God.

At this point, holiness described the otherness of God. God is spirit and man is flesh. Yet at the same time, the term carried a moral dimension as well, when applied to God. Man is a sinner and God is righteous.

We must clearly understand that holiness never meant that God was remote from man. Its emphasis was upon the fact that God was different from man. Because God was holy, the very term itself began to develop a moral connotation. Whatever God is, is holy. Thus Isaiah declared,

> But the Lord of hosts is exalted in justice,
> and the holy God shows himself holy
> in righteousness (Isa. 5:16).

However, the term never lost its emphasis upon God's otherness. Holiness was always that which marked the difference between God and man. Whatever that difference was, it was God's holiness that made it. Thus basically, holiness could be described as the character of God. It placed him in a completely exclusive category. Nothing else was holy by itself. For Israel, only that was holy which belonged to God and had been separated for his use. In simplest terms, holiness was neither more nor less than what God was. This is still so.

This brings us face to face with the glory of God. When Isaiah was told that the God of Israel was holy, the seraphim added another statement to their description of the divine nature.

> And one called to another and said:
> "Holy, holy, holy is the Lord of hosts;
> the whole earth is full of his glory" (Isa. 6:3).

In some way, glory and holiness seem to be related. What is that relationship?

The Hebrew word for glory originally meant heaviness, whatever had weight. It is easy to see how the basic term came to refer to anything of significance. As such, it was used of riches, power, success, and victory. But it also came to be used of a person's response to any of these things. This especially showed up as it was applied to God. God had glory in himself. He revealed his glory to men. But men in responding to him, must also give glory (significance, weight, importance) to him.

In a very real sense, when the Old Testament says that God has glory, it appears to refer to the summation of all the qualities which make up his being. It is at this point that we can see its close affinity to his holiness. Holiness marked the difference between God and man. Glory is that which sums up God's perfect nature. It also appears in some way to be a visible extension of God, with the specific purpose of manifesting God's presence to man. Thus, when the people of Israel murmured against God because of their hunger, "they looked toward the wilderness, and behold, the glory of the Lord appeared in the cloud" (Ex. 16:10). Thus they were assured of God's presence with them by this visible manifestation. At the same time, glory also seems to be merely synonymous with God's presence (Isa. 6:3; Ex. 24:16).

To the Hebrews, the glory of God had a concreteness to it, in the form of fire, light, and brilliance. It could be seen. Wherever God's glory is, there God is.

> The glory of the Lord settled on Mount Sinai, and the cloud covered it six days; and on the seventh day he called to Moses out of the midst of the cloud. Now the appearance of the glory of the Lord was like a devouring fire on the top of the mountain in the sight of the people of Israel (Ex. 24:16-17).

But the vision of the glory of God was not to be confined to Israel. In its magnificent vision of the redemptive acts of God, the Book of Isaiah describes it like this:

A voice cries:
"In the wilderness prepare the way of the Lord,
   make straight in the desert a highway for our God.
Every valley shall be lifted up,
   and every mountain and hill be made low;
the uneven places shall become level,
   and the rough places a plain.
And the *glory* of the Lord shall be revealed,
   and all flesh shall see it together,
for the mouth of the Lord has spoken"
   (Isa. 40:3-5, italics mine).

The wonder of God's glory is sharply contrasted with man's flesh in Isaiah 40:6-7. It would appear that, to the Old Testament, glory is "God-stuff" as flesh is "man-stuff."

As such, then, glory and holiness are intimately related. Both refer to the very being of God. God is the holy God. He fills the earth with his glory. When Ezekiel viewed God's departure from the Temple, he saw the glory depart (Ezek. 10:18). Later, when God returned to his house, the glory returned (43:2-5).

God is both living and personal. His essential being is described as glory or holiness. But this still does not fill out the Old Testament portrait of the being of God.

The Names of God

We have already considered in this chapter the name of God as partial evidence of Israel's understanding of God as a person. In doing this, we briefly considered the meaning of that name (Yahweh) for the light that it shed on their understanding of God's personhood. However, even though this is the personal name of the God of Israel, there were other titles by which the ancient Hebrews addressed their God. Each of these shed some light on their understanding of God's essential nature.

However, before we consider the Old Testament names for God, we must first give attention to Israel's concept of a "name." In our society, a name is usually little more than a title by which we address someone. It usually identifies the family from which we come. It also usually identifies whether we are male or female, although some names do not even give this help. Aside from these things, names tell us little more about a person. This has not always been true. In the ancient Near East in general, and in ancient Israel in particular, names were considered to reveal something of the nature or character of the person. Giving a name was a very serious business and was taken quite seriously. The whole study of names within the Old Testament is quite fascinating. It is equally as fascinating in the New. Thus, the name Jesus means Savior. He changed Simon's name to Cephas, an Aramaic word meaning "rock." (The Greek word is *petros,* from which we get Peter.) In the Old Testament, when God changed Jacob's nature, he also changed his name from Jacob (meaning "supplanter/ trickster," or "deceiver") to Israel (meaning "he who strives with God," or "God strives").

If the names of people were significant, surely the names of God are more so. We have already noted that the personal name of Israel's God was Yahweh. Its meaning appears to have focused upon his existence and his creative power. He was the God who really lived. This personal name occurs between five and six thousand times in the Old Testament. This alone should show that he was and is the basic subject of the Old Testament.

The Hebrews were a Semitic people and their language was a Semitic language. In common with most Semitic peoples, they also used the title *El* for God. It was the most common Semitic designation for God, although it only occurs in the Old Testament about two hundred twenty-five times. Its root meaning was apparently "power," or "strength." Its focus was upon the power of God to act in the world.

As far as Israel was concerned, the most significant usage of *El* was in combination with other words, giving a more specific description of the nature of their God. Thus Exodus recorded:

> And God said to Moses, "I am Yahweh. I appeared to Abraham, to Isaac, and to Jacob as El Shaddai (God Almighty), but by my name Yahweh I did not make myself known to them (Ex. 6:2-3, author's translation).

This particular title focused attention upon the sovereign power of Israel's God. All things were possible with him.

On the other hand, when Abraham paid his tithes to Melchizedek, he was introduced as the priest of El Elyon (God

Most High, Gen. 14:18, author's translation). In the ancient Near East, most nations worshiped a number of different gods. At the same time, there was usually a chief god who was identified as their high god. The Genesis author was pointing out that the God of Melchizedek was "Most High," thus higher than the high gods of any other nation. He was exalted over all gods.

God was identified by Abraham in his worship at Beersheba as El Olam (God of the Dim Unknown, or, "Everlasting God," Gen. 21:33). Here the title called attention to the fact that God went as far back and as far forward as they could comprehend. He was not subject to the limitations of time. Abraham might pass off the scene; God would not.

There are at least three other titles of this kind which are of lesser significance. God was identified as El Roi ("God of seeing") in Genesis 16:13. This pointed to the fact that nothing was hidden from him. He was also identified as El Bethel (God of the House of God, or "God of Bethel") and as "El-Elohe-Israel" (God, the God of Israel, Gen. 31:13; 33:20). This calls attention to his identification with Israel and their early sanctuary.

From the very common title of God, Israel developed another title *Elohim*. This is a plural form which became the most common Old Testament designation for God apart from his personal name. It occurs over two thousand times. Apparently this title in Israel's Semitic neighbors merely summed up all of the gods which they had. It is sometimes used this way in Israel, summing up all of the gods of all the nations. But more generally, Israel used it with a singular verb, indicating that they understood it as referring to the one God. Its focus was upon the fact that God summed up all of the attributes of all the gods of all nations. It has also been interpreted as being a "plural of majesty." It may possibly also serve as the first glimmerings in the Old Testament that there was a manyness to God. If so, this would be the first tentative root of the later development of the concept of the Trinity. (We shall return to this in the next chapter.)

There were two other names which were used of the God of Israel in the Old Testament which we must consider. The first of these is Baal. Although commonly used of the many

fertility gods of Canaan and of the chief god of the Phoeni-
cians, the God of Israel was occasionally called by this title.
Thus Hosea said,

> "And in that day," says Yahweh, you will call me,
> 'My man' (or 'My husband'), and no longer will you
>   call me, 'My Baal' " (Hos. 2:16, author's translation).

The word *Baal* means Lord, or Master. Hosea was looking
to the new day when Israel's relation to God would be that of
a loving bride instead of a slave or servant. The other term,
similar in meaning, which Israel used for God was *Adhon*.
This is the word commonly translated as Lord, and referred
to Israel's relation to God as that of obedient servants. This
was what they were always to be. At the same time, calling
God "Lord" showed that there was a clear recognition of his
power and authority over them.

Each of these names, taken alone, portray something of
the nature of God as Israel understood it. Taken together,
they portray a sovereign God, one who actually lived as a
person, and one who ruled over all of life. For Israel, this
was all wrapped up in their understanding of the God who
had revealed himself to them. He was the God who is. Other
gods simply did not exist. Their God did. Men could learn
about other gods. Men met the God of Israel. It was that simple. God was the primary fact of life for them. He still is.

It is this basic understanding of God which pervades the
New Testament. Each of the apostles was a Hebrew. Each
of them came to Jesus with this understanding of God. It
was upon this that they built the New Testament faith. We
can do no more. We dare do no less.

3
The God Who Acts

Anyone with a good set of tools can take an automobile apart. But you would have difficulty taking those parts and putting a car together unless you had a very good idea of what an automobile was and how it operated. It is far easier to discuss the various characteristics of God than to understand him as a whole. We need to be very clear about the fact that few, if any, Old Testament people would have discussed, or even thought about, the various aspects of God's character. They just did not "take him apart." They met him. In short, they experienced him in life. But they seldom, if ever, seem to have tried to analyze his nature.

At the same time, even though we know and accept this, it is really impossible for us to come to grips with their understanding of God unless we at least try to sort out and describe his various characteristics in their experience of him.

As we have noted previously, the Hebrews came to their understanding of God through his revelatory acts. They experienced him in their lives and from these experiences came their understanding of his nature. We will continue in this chapter to try to answer the question: What did they learn about God from his actions?

Acts of Love

It has long been popular to say that the New Testament is the book of love and the Old Testament is the book of law.

Like many such trite sayings, this is just not true. God is the same in both Testaments. The basic understanding of God in the Old Testament is his loving nature. Granted, there was a difference in Israel's understanding of his love and that we find in the New Testament. But his loving nature is still central.

There are two basic terms used in the Old Testament to describe God's love. In order to grasp a full understanding of God's love as revealed there, we must give careful attention to both of these terms and to the difference between them.

Love in God's Free Choice. The first of the two words describing God's love is *'ahabh* (sometimes transliterated as *'ahav*). This term is frequently used to describe human relationships and is used less often to describe God's love.

In its secular usage, *'ahabh* is normally used to describe the love or affection of a superior for an inferior, such as that of a king for his subjects. In the few occasions where the reverse is true, the context seems to describe a humble, dutiful love. It is never used to describe the love of a wife for her husband, nor of the love of a child for a parent. It was used once to describe the love of a woman for a man, where "Saul's daughter Michal loved David" (1 Sam. 18:20). It was also used once of the love of a woman for a woman, where Ruth loved Naomi (Ruth 4:15).

In its religious usage, it is almost equally used of God loving man and of man loving God, or loving God's name. In trying to understand its meaning as applied to God's love, perhaps the best place to begin is by noticing its contrast to hate. Thus God said,

"I have loved you," says the Lord. But you say, "How hast thou loved us?" "Is not Esau Jacob's brother?" says the Lord. "Yet I have loved Jacob but I have hated Esau; I have laid waste his hill country and left his heritage to jackals of the desert" (Mal. 1:2-3; cf. Rom. 9:13).

First of all, note that hate does not seem to mean what we usually mean by hate. It apparently refers to God's rejection of Esau as reflected in Genesis. This is clearly the way Paul understood it. Since love is its opposite, it would apparently refer to God's choosing to accept Jacob. A further pursuit of this contrast in ideas appears to demonstrate the

accuracy of this conclusion. *'Ahabh* consistently refers to
the idea of choosing, even in its nonreligious usages. Thus
God's love for Israel is described in terms of his choice of
Israel. Their deliverance from Egypt, as well as their deliverance from exile can be understood as the result of God's
free choice of them. (Norman Snaith in his delightful little
book, *Distinctive Ideas of the Old Testament,* suggests that
the best translation of this Hebrew word is "election-
love.")

This love springs from God's own nature, having no bearing on the lovability of its object. It is totally free, absolutely unmerited, and unrestricted in its selectivity. It was
this Hebrew idea which served as the basis for the New
Testament concept of unconditional, unmerited grace.

Such unconditional love flowed again and again in God's
acts of loving choice. There was no basis in God's love of
Israel for any pride on their part.

It was not because you were more in number than any
other people that the Lord set his love upon you and chose
you, for you were the fewest of all peoples; but it is because
the Lord loves you . . . that the Lord has brought you out
with a mighty hand (Deut. 7:7-8).

Furthermore, God's loving choices were presented as
mysterious and, in human terms, unpredictable. They
rested in his very nature. As such, they were clearly beyond
the powers of human comprehension. Thus it was so surprising to Hosea when at the conclusion of his experience
with his unfaithful wife, God said:

Go again, love a woman who is beloved of a paramour and
is an adulteress; even as the Lord loves the people of Israel,
though they turn to other gods and love cakes of raisins
(Hos. 3:1).

The depth of God's love for unfaithful Israel was clearly set
forth by the prophet.

Therefore, behold, I will allure her,
    and bring her into the wilderness,
    and speak tenderly to her (Hos. 2:14).

In acts which sprang from God's redemptive love, he was
going to begin again with Israel, starting over in the wil-

derness. But this was his choice, not their deserving. It was his grace, not their merit.

It almost seems as if the entire message of the New Testament gets its basis from this concept of God's unmerited love. God acts in deliberate choice to do good for those whom he will. No one deserves such love. In Christ, all are offered it.

Love in God's Steadfast Loyalty. The second basic term used in the Old Testament to describe God's acts of love is *hesed* (sometimes transliterated as *chesed*). This is one of the more difficult words in the Old Testament to translate into English. There is no single term which really begins to approximate its depth of meaning. It has been translated as loving-kindness, mercy, loyal love, steadfast love, faithfulness, and covenant-love.

Its root meaning seems to reflect the idea of eagerness, coupled with steadfastness. It appears to have later developed the ideas of mercy and loving-kindness. Within the Old Testament, it appears never to have been used outside of the context of the covenant between God and Israel. In its earliest usage within the Old Testament, it was used to describe the attitude of faithfulness and loyalty which existed (or should have existed) between the parties to a covenant. The basic eagerness of the root seems to have described the attitudes which brought the parties to the covenant. At the same time, the attitudes of mercy and loyalty described the motives which held on to a faithless party to a covenant. Steadfastness described the ultimate commitment to the covenant. There was always an emphasis of a determined and stubborn faithfulness by God to his covenant commitment.

The consistent use of this term in connection with the covenant clearly demonstrates that its choice was neither accidental nor indiscriminate. The mercy which it does describe is totally bound up with the idea of a firm commitment between the covenant parties. It reflects the behavior expected of parties in a covenant and includes their loyalty to such bonds. Thus God says,

Go, and proclaim these words toward the north,
    and say,
"Return, apostate Israel," says the Lord,
"I will not look on you in anger,
    because I am steadfastly merciful," says the Lord,

"I will not be angry forever" (Jer. 3:12, author's translation).

On the other hand, the psalmist knew that this aspect of God's character was so reliable that he could announce with joy,

> Surely goodness and steadfast mercy shall pursue me
> all the days of my life,
> and, that being so, I shall dwell in the house of
> the Lord
> to length of days (Ps. 23:6, author's translation).

Furthermore, from the depths of sin and guilt, acknowledging his own unfaithfulness to God, we hear him lean upon the steadfast loyalty of God. Crying out,

> Have mercy on me, O God,
> according to thy steadfast love [hesed];
> according to thy abundant mercy
> blot out my transgressions (Ps. 51:1).

When God mercifully forgave, he cried out in joyous confidence,

> Many are the pangs of the wicked;
> but steadfast love [hesed] surrounds him
> who trusts in the Lord (Ps. 32:10).

Ultimately, Israel's future hope was based upon the steadfast love and mercy of God. Thus the Book of Isaiah proclaimed:

Ho, every one who thirsts,
  come to the waters;
and he who has no money,
  come, buy and eat!
Come, buy wine and milk
  without money and without price.
Why do you spend your money for that which is not bread,
  and your labor for that which does not satisfy?
Hearken diligently to me, and eat what is good,
  and delight yourselves in fatness.
Incline your ear, and come to me;
  hear, that your soul may live;
and I will make with you an everlasting covenant,
  my steadfast, sure love [hesed]
  for David (Isa. 55:1-3).

It was this aspect of God's love which gave Israel hope. God would be loyal, steadfast, and merciful to those whom he has chosen. But it was also this aspect of God's love which gave rise to a problem in understanding. It was a problem for the prophets. It is a problem for many people today. How can we understand God's righteousness in the light of his steadfast love? God's righteous demands must be obeyed. Yet his steadfast love would not let Israel go. How can God be both righteous in his dealings with Israel and steadfastly loyal at the same time? It is at this point that we must turn our attention to the Old Testament understanding of the righteousness of God.

Acts of Righteousness

The root picture behind the word meaning "to be righteous" originally was "to be straight," "to be firm." You could depend upon that which was straight or firm. Then it came to mean conforming to that which was straight. From this it can easily be seen how the idea that one who was righteous was one who conformed to the proper standards or "lines" of behavior.

Righteousness is applied within the Old Testament to inanimate objects, such as weights or measuring cups. Thus the Hebrews were warned:

You shall not have in your bag two kinds of weights, a large and a small. You shall not have in your house two kinds of measures, a large and a small. A full and righteous weight you shall have; a full and righteous measure you shall have; that your days may be prolonged in the land which the Lord your God gives you. For all who do such things, all who act dishonestly, are an abomination to the Lord your God (Deut. 25:13-16, author's translation).

Business dealings between people became totally impossible if weights and measures were not standard.

The term is also applied to less concrete things, such as the "paths of righteousness," into which the psalmist knows God will lead him (Ps. 23:3). Furthermore, the term is also regularly connected with the Hebrew word for judgment, referring to a decision handed down by a judge. In this context, it becomes obvious that righteousness can refer either to justice or to legal obligation.

For the ancient Hebrew, righteousness came to mean the demands of God's law, as well as the commands which God gave to his people from time to time. It involved matters governing the relationship between people, the rituals of worship, and the relationship between anyone and God.

Ultimately, therefore, righteousness came to mean the standard which God established in the world. He set up his rules, expectations, and demands. They were based upon his nature, not upon some capricious whim. As such, they were firm, straight, and immovable. People learn what righteousness is through the revelation of God. This comes through the written Word and through those who are the mouthpieces of his will.

More important for our purposes here, since righteousness was the standard established by God, whatever he did was righteous. He himself was the basis upon which his standards were established. Since he was the living God, ever active, his actions were always righteous. His very nature was righteousness. Contrary to the gods of the other nations who were capricious and whimsical, the God of Israel was dependable and consistent with his own nature.

Thus his acts set the standard which governed the acts of Israel. Furthermore, his acts set the standards by which all men and nations were to be measured.

Therefore, righteousness was always dynamic and active. It was never an abstract moral principle, but a concrete demonstration of standards set forth by actions. It was precisely upon this base that Jesus built when he said,

You will know them by their fruits. Are grapes gathered from thorns, or figs from thistles? So, every sound tree bears good fruit, but the bad tree bears evil fruit. . . . Thus you will know them by their fruits (Matt. 7:16-20).

If this was true of man, it was certainly true of God. He, by his very nature, is righteous. His actions always revealed what was right. They still do. Man is not the judge of righteousness. God is. Whatever his dealings with humanity, they are always just and right.

Thus there was no conflict between God's righteousness and his steadfast love. Both were outward demonstrations of his inner nature. In fact, righteousness at times became synonymous with salvation and deliverance. In the great victory song of Deborah, she described God's deliverance of Israel and inserted this declaration:

> To the sound of musicians at the watering places,
> there they repeat the righteousness of the Lord,
> the righteousness of his peasantry in Israel.
> (Judg. 5:11, author's translation).

And the great singer of Israel's deliverance from exile proclaimed:

> I bring near my righteousness,
> it is not far off,
> and my salvation will not tarry;
> I will put salvation in Zion
> for Israel, my glory (Isa. 46:13, author's translation).

We have earlier seen that God has revealed his nature in the natural world which surrounds us. The psalmist adds to this:

> The heavens proclaim his righteousness;
> and all the peoples behold his glory (Ps. 97:6).

The nature of God which is so revealed is righteousness. Whatever God does is righteous. Whatever he wills is righteous. Both spring from his very nature which is both consistent and dependable. The Old Testament has clearly said that God's very nature is love. It just as clearly claims that his very nature is righteous. These are in no way incompatible. They complement each other.

When God acts in love, it is his righteousness acting as well. When he acts in judgment, that is also his righteousness. When he acts in salvation and deliverance, that is also his righteousness.

Because his acts are righteous, he expects the same from his people.

> I hate, I despise your feasts,
> and I take no delight in your solemn assemblies.
> Even though you offer me your burnt offerings and
>   cereal offerings,
> I will not accept them,
> and the peace offerings of your fatted beasts
> I will not look upon.

> Take away from me the noise of your songs;
>   to the melody of your harps I will not listen.
> But let justice roll down like waters,
>   and righteousness like an ever-flowing stream
> (Amos 5:21-24).

Hosea, the Old Testament book of God's all-conquering love, concludes with these words:

> Whoever is wise, let him understand these things;
>   whoever is discerning, let him know them;
> for the ways of the Lord are right,
>   and the righteous walk in them,
>   but transgressors stumble in them
> (Hos. 14:9, author's translation).

Righteousness, then, is the way of God. Righteous people live his way. God's righteousness is clearly seen by what he does. The same should be true of his people.

Based upon this concept of God's righteousness being seen in his acts, Paul's description of God's gift through Jesus Christ takes on new meaning.

> Since all have sinned and fall short of the glory of God, they are justified by his grace as a gift, through the redemption which is in Christ Jesus, whom God put forward as an expiation by his blood, to be received by faith. This was to show God's righteousness . . . to prove at the present time that he himself is righteous (Rom. 3:23-26).

Furthermore, Paul admonished the saints to "be imitators of God" (Eph. 5:1). Whatever God does, his people are supposed to copy.

In the end, when Paul came to the conclusion of his life and ministry, he rested his future hope in the righteousness of God.

> For I am already on the point of being sacrificed; the time of my departure has come. I have fought the good fight, I have finished the race, I have kept the faith. Henceforth there is laid up for me the crown of righteousness, which the Lord, the righteous judge, will award to me on that Day, and not only to me but also to all who have loved his appearing (2 Tim. 4:6-8).

That he based his hope upon God's righteousness is both extremely significant and deeply instructive.

Acts of Judgment

It is quite common for some biblical interpreters to dwell upon those passages and ideas which conform to previously adopted ideas. Thus those who do not wish to believe in the wrath or judgment of God find it convenient either to ignore these ideas, water them down, or try to explain them away. The rationale for such actions lies in the belief that such ideas as wrath and judgment are incompatible with the concept of a loving God.

As a matter of fact, it is quite difficult to eliminate wrath from the New Testament. It is impossible in the Old. When you actually read the Old Testament instead of just thinking about it, the concepts of wrath and judgment are seen in so many books, from so many periods, and in so many different types of literature that it becomes quite obvious that they are a mainstream in the many acts of God.

One might not be surprised to hear these words from Nahum:

Who can stand before his indignation?
Who can endure the heat of his anger?
His wrath is poured out like fire,
and the rocks are broken asunder by him (Nah. 1:6).

To hear similar words from Jeremiah attracts our attention a bit more.

But the Lord is the true God;
he is the living God and the everlasting King.
At his wrath the earth quakes,
and the nations cannot endure his indignation
(Jer. 10:10).

And to hear the same ideas in the midst of one of the most redemption-conscious portions of the Old Testament should become completely convincing.

Because of the iniquity of his covetousness I was angry,
I smote him, I hid my face and was angry (Isa. 57:17).

Yet, even with the multiplicity of such evidence, many still try to explain away God's wrath and judgment. From the earliest days, Jews, Christians, and pagans have tried to say that such descriptions are foreign to the love of God as revealed in the Old Testament and in Christ. Such attitudes and actions on the part of God are usually described as merely being a condescension to the limited understanding of God's people.

Such dodges are really unnecessary. They are certainly false to the message of the Old Testament in particular and of the Bible in general. If the Hebrew prophets had wished to describe God's passions, or the absence of them, in other ways, they could surely have done so. We must assume that God's Spirit could have led them to use other terms and ideas if he had so desired. The very multiplicity of such words from so many different sources must be taken with seriousness. The usage is so common as to have become far more than just a mere figure of speech. It is certainly more than a simple concession either to human language or to human limitations.

But then, how are we to understand God's acts of judgment in the light of his acts of love? Can the two be reconciled? This is precisely the point. The Jewish people had experienced God's love and his wrath and had discovered that they were both holy. Both came from God. Whatever came from God was good.

Our culture makes us recoil from such descriptions of God. No passion has been so thoroughly condemned in modern society as that of anger. It has been pictured as a sinister, malignant passion, an evil force which under all circumstances must be repressed. This attitude is wrong. Anger by itself is not evil. But its consequences may become so.

Since the Old Testament does not really separate God's acts of judgment from his wrath, we cannot consider one without the other. But since the prophets seem to see God's judgment as springing from his wrath or anger, we must turn our attention to that concept first.

The Wrath of God. There are numerous words used in the Old Testament to describe God's wrath. They are generally the same words which we use to describe wrath and do not ever seem to possess a force significantly different from their meaning when used to describe human passions.

However, we must note that the Old Testament pointedly condemns either irrational anger or the loss of self-control on the part of man. Edom was denounced because he

>   . . . cast off all pity,
> and his anger tore perpetually,
> and he kept his wrath forever (Amos 1:11).

The Book of Proverbs tells us in numerous places that anger produces strife.

With this attitude toward wrath, it appears quite unlikely that the very prophets whose major message was the righteousness of God should describe him as having a moral defect. Our problem appears to have been that we have tried to understand God's anger psychologically. Let us approach it theologically, instead.

The Old Testament never viewed God's anger as something which could not be accounted for. The divine anger was never an irrational, spontaneous outburst, but a reaction to the conduct of people. As such, it was predictable. So clearly defined were its causes that warnings could be issued to those things which brought it forth. God's anger was never a blind, explosive force, but voluntary and purposeful. It was always motivated by his concern for right and wrong.

To us, anger usually denotes recklessness, some spite, and some iniquity. But as applied to God, it is more in the category of what we call righteous indignation. It was aroused by mean, shameful, and rebellious acts on the part of God's people. Because God is a righteous Judge, righteous indignation is a part of him.

>   God is a righteous judge,
> and a God who has indignation every day (Ps. 7:11).

A judge is impartial to people. He is never impartial to evil.

This brings us to the heart of the matter. It is precisely God's love and concern which are both prerequisite to and the source of his anger. Because he cares for his people, his anger may be kindled against them. The prophets were terrified of the wrath of God. But this never caused them to be shaken in their trust of and commitment to God.

Indifference to evil is an evil which most of us condone. Furthermore, most of us are guilty of it. We sit on the sidelines of life, remaining neutral, impartial, and seldom moved by wrongs done to other people. Indifference to evil may ultimately be more serious than evil itself. It is apparently more universal, and certainly more contagious and more dangerous. The prophets discovered this indifference on the part of God's people. Thus their awareness of the intense anger of God became even greater.

The Old Testament was also aware that the divine anger was related to the divine patience and forebearance.

> The Lord is merciful and gracious,
>   slow to anger and abounding in steadfast love.
> He will not always chide,
>   nor will he keep his anger for ever.
> He does not deal with us according to our sins,
>   nor requite us according to our iniquities.
>
> . . . .
>
> As a father pities his children,
>   so the Lord pities those who fear him.
> For he knows our frame;
>   he remembers that we are dust (Ps. 103:8-14).

God is patient, long-suffering, and slow to anger. But he is never indifferent. He cares what we do. Thus divine forgiveness is never indulgence, complacency, or indifference.

Furthermore, the wrath of God seldom appears to be God's last word. There is always a contingency to it. The actions of people provoke it. The actions of people may revoke it. Thus Jeremiah proclaimed:

> Now therefore amend your ways and your doings, and obey the voice of the Lord your God, and the Lord will turn from the evil which he has pronounced against you (Jer. 26:13, author's translation).

This was precisely the problem of Jonah. He knew the nature of God's wrath and its contingency. So when God spared Nineveh,

> He prayed to the Lord and said, "I pray thee, Lord, is not this what I said when I was yet in my country? That is why I made haste to flee to Tarshish; for I knew that thou art a gracious God and merciful, slow to anger, and abounding in steadfast love, and moved from evil" (Jonah 4:2, author's translation).

The prophets were well aware that God did not delight in anger. It may have been necessary. But it never pleased him. Then what did please him?

I am the Lord who practice steadfast love, justice, and righteousness in the earth; for in these things I delight, says the Lord (Jer. 9:24).

Or again,

Behold, I will gather them from all the countries to which I drove them in my anger and my wrath and in great indignation; I will bring them back to this place, and I will make them dwell in safety.
I will rejoice in doing them good, and I will plant them in this land in faithfulness, with all my heart and all my soul (Jer. 32:37,41).

Among the nations which were Israel's neighbors there was a conception that the gods were filled with malice and spite. But this was never true within the Old Testament. Anger was never conceived as being either the natural disposition of God or his habit. His anger passed. His love went on forever (Ex. 20:5-6). Again and again, the prophets proclaimed that God had loved his people with an everlasting love.

Who is a God like thee, pardoning iniquity
    and passing over transgression
    for the remnant of his inheritance?
He does not retain his anger for ever
    because he delights in steadfast love (Mic. 7:18).

Anger seems only to have been used of God in describing his acts, never as an adjective describing his nature. The secret behind his anger was his love. Anger was always the product of this love. His wrath was never considered to be the opposite of love but the outgrowth of it toward disobedience. God's anger certainly produced destruction and distress. But among his people it never produced despair. Calamity and judgment were accepted because they came from God. Even these were evidence of his love.

So the Old Testament saw the anger and wrath of God as a tragic necessity. It was tragic because it was not what God desired for his people. It was necessary because of their stubborn rebelliousness. The divine anger was always viewed as bringing calamity to man and grief to God. It was never arbitrary, but was aroused by man's sin.

The Judgment of God. God's wrath toward sin issued in

judgment upon the sinners. It is to this divine judgment that we must now turn our attention.

The Hebrew word for judgment is used in two different ways in the Old Testament. We must carefully distinguish between them. The first of these usages refers to legal matters. It may describe a law or statute. "Now these are the judgments which you shall set before them" (Ex. 21:1, author's translation). It is also used to describe the decision or sentence rendered by a judge (Ezra 7:25-26). Neither of these usages is particularly significant at this point in our consideration.

The second use of this Hebrew term sprang from this latter concept. This applies to God's actions in punishing his people for their sins. It is obviously related to the decision of the sovereign Judge. But its immediate focus was always upon the actual events which God used in punishing sin. Yet, within this use, there were two basic concepts. It was used to describe God's acts in the immediate present and in the near future. But it was also used to describe his acts of judgment in the end of time and at the dawn of the great new era of the future. This latter usage we will ignore until we consider Israel's hope for the future.

The major emphasis of the Old Testament understanding of God's judgment was always within history, in Israel's immediate present or in their near future. As such, God's judgment always sprang from his wrath. Far too frequently, we consider God's judgment as being primarily punishment for sin. Now it was punishment, but this was not its primary emphasis. Rather, its basic emphasis appears to have been not so much upon punishment as upon redemption. Thus Isaiah proclaimed: "Zion shall be redeemed through judgment" (Isa. 1:27, author's translation). To further underscore this, Amos described a whole series of God's judgments which had not accomplished his purpose of causing Israel to return to God.

"I gave you cleanness of teeth in all your cities,
    and lack of bread in all your places,
yet you did not return to me,"
    says the Lord.
"And I also withheld the rain from you
    when there were yet three months to the harvest;
. . . .

yet you did not return to me,"
says the Lord.
"I smote you with blight and mildew;
   I laid waste your gardens and your vineyards;
. . . .
yet you did not return to me,"
says the Lord.
"I sent among you a pestilence after the manner of Egypt;
. . . .
yet you did not return to me,"
says the Lord.
"I overthrew some of you,
   as when God overthrew Sodom and Gomorrah,
. . . .
yet you did not return to me,"
says the Lord (Amos 4:6-11, italics mine).

Amos clearly saw these temporal judgments as having had
the primary purpose of bringing Israel back into a right relationship with God. This was so obvious to the prophets
that they could not comprehend why Israel did not so respond. Thus Isaiah questioned his people.

Why will you still be smitten,
   that you continue to rebel?
. . . .

Your country lies desolate,
   your cities are burned with fire;
in your very presence
   aliens devour your land;
   it is desolate, as overthrown by aliens (Isa. 1:5-7).

The evangelizing, redemptive purpose of God's judgments was always seen as being fundamental in the mind
and heart of God. When Judah complained because of oppression by her enemies, the Lord responded,

"Why do you complain against me?
You have all rebelled against me,"
   says the Lord.
"In vain have I smitten your children,
   they took no correction;
. . . .

"Behold, I will bring you to judgment
   for saying, 'I have not sinned' " (Jer. 2:29-35)

The punishment was real. But the purpose was redemptive.
Furthermore, the judgment of God was historical. It
could involve natural calamity, such as drought or locusts.
It could also involve enemies, such as Assyria or Babylon.
Isaiah announced the punishment which would come on his
people by proclaiming:

> Ah, Assyria, the rod of my anger,
>   the staff of my fury!
> Against a godless nation I send him,
>   and against the people of my wrath I command him,
> to take spoil and seize plunder,
>   and to tread them down like the mire of the
>   streets (Isa. 10:5-6).

In addition, the prophets clearly saw the judgment of God
as inescapable.

> Why would you have the day of the Lord?
> It is darkness, and not light;
> as if a man fled from a lion,
>   and a bear met him;
> or went into the house and leaned with his hand
>   against the wall
> and a serpent bit him (Amos 5:18-19).

> Therefore I have begun to smite you,
>   making you desolate because of your sins.
> You shall eat, but not be satisfied,
>   and there shall be hunger in your inward parts;
> you shall put away, but not save,
>   and what you save I will give to the sword.
> You shall sow, but not reap;
>   you shall tread olives, but not anoint yourselves
>   with oil;
> you shall tread grapes, but not drink wine
>   (Mic. 6:13-15).

The violation of God's righteous commands demanded punishment. But the power of his love would not let Israel go.
As he punished, he also sought to draw her back. Judgment, though sure, was aimed at redemption. His acts of
judgment in history were intended to restore the relationship which Israel had destroyed with her sin.

It was upon this foundation that Paul declared that "God
has not destined us for wrath, but to obtain salvation
through our Lord Jesus Christ" (1 Thess. 5:9). God's ulti-

mate purpose is for "all men to be saved and to come to the knowledge of the truth" (1 Tim. 2:4).

In summary, God's judgment is real. But it springs from God's love. While demanded by his righteousness, in history, it is always intended to be redemptive.

Acts of Sovereign Power

In a very real sense, all of God's acts are acts of power. But there are some of his acts which focus primarily upon his sovereign power, rather than upon his love, righteousness, or judgment. The Old Testament saints were absolutely sure of the sovereign power of the God of Israel. Nothing was beyond his abilities. This is still so.

Sovereign in Deliverance. The Old Testament is filled with the records of God's acts of power which reveal him as sovereign in acts of deliverance. The books of the Former Prophets and those of the Chronicler bear abundant witness to this. But the prime record of his deliverance is found in Exodus, which records the divine deliverance of a group of slaves from Egypt.

No other nation in the ancient world ever wrote so candidly of their own history. Other nations looked back for their founding to some grand, golden age of the past. Israel looked back to the powerful acts of a sovereign God who freed them from Egyptian slavery, delivered them from Egyptian arms, and led them through a hostile wilderness in safety. Throughout the entire episode, they show up as doubting, grumbling, complaining, and rebelling.

Because of the order of the books of the Bible, we usually turn to creation (Gen. 1—2) for the first evidence of God's power. But a careful reading of the Old Testament shows that Israel's major focus on God's power came through the Exodus experience. Outside of Genesis, Job, Isaiah, and a few psalms, little is said of God's creative power. In almost every book, there are constant references to his power in deliverance.

They sang about this power in their worship.

> I will call to mind the deeds of the Lord;
>   yea, I will remember thy wonders of old.
> . . . .
>
> Thou didst with thy arm redeem thy people,
>   the sons of Jacob and Joseph.

. . . .

Thy way was through the sea,
   thy path through the great waters;
   yet thy footprints were unseen.
Thou didst lead thy people like a flock
   by the hand of Moses and Aaron (Ps. 77:11-20)

While they sang of his power, they also acknowledged their
own sin and their sinful heritage.

Both we and our fathers have sinned;
. . . .

Our fathers, when they were in Egypt,
   did not consider thy wonderful works;
   they did not remember the abundance of thy steadfast
      love,
   but rebelled against the Most High at the Red Sea.
Yet he saved them for his name's sake,
   that he might make known his mighty power.
. . . .

So he saved them from the hand of the foe,
   and delivered them from the power of the enemy.
. . . .

Then they believed his words,
   they sang his praise (Ps. 106:6-12).

The prophets made constant reference to his sovereign
power as evidenced by this great act of deliverance. Hosea
pointed to this when he said,

When Israel was a child, I loved him,
   and out of Egypt I called my son (Hos. 11:1).

Amos underscored the emphasis,

Also I brought you up out of the land of Egypt,
   and led you forty years in the wilderness (Amos 2:10).

The point of this emphasis was to underline the divine
purpose behind these mighty acts of deliverance. They
were never merely to show off God's power. Rather, there
was a twofold purpose in his acts of deliverance. First, it
was to demonstrate to Egypt the sovereignty of God.

And the Egyptians shall know that I am the Lord, when I
stretch forth my hand upon Egypt and bring out the people
of Israel from among them (Ex. 7:5).

The second purpose behind God's mighty acts of deliverance was to demonstrate to Israel that God was sovereign. Even before the final act of the great drama of redemption, Moses and his people were admonished that God was delivering them, so

that you may tell in the hearing of your son and of your son's son how I have made sport of the Egyptians and what signs I have done among them; that you may know that I am the Lord (Ex. 10:2).

The gods of Egypt were powerless before the sovereign God of Israel. Even when Assyria defeated Israel and Babylon defeated Judah, it was not their gods who had been victorious but the sovereign God of the Hebrews who used those foreign nations to punish his own people. Ultimately, God delivered Israel from exile.

Comfort, comfort my people,
    says your God.
Speak tenderly to Jerusalem,
    and cry to her
that her warfare is ended,
    that her iniquity is pardoned,
that she has received from the Lord's hand
    double for all her sins.

Behold, the Lord God comes with might,
    and his arm rules for him;
behold, his reward is with him,
    and his recompense before him.
He will feed his flock like a shepherd,
    he will gather the lambs in his arms,
he will carry them in his bosom,
    and gently lead those that are with young
        (Isa. 40:1-2,10-11).

It is obvious what a major part the Old Testament faith in God's acts of deliverance played in the developing New Testament concept of redemption. The God who had brought Israel out of Egypt, brought his Son forth from the grave and his people forth from sin. God's supreme act in the New Testament was *the* act of deliverance at Calvary. As Israel looked back to the deliverance of the Exodus as the basis for all their future hopes in God, so the New Testament looked to it to describe both what God had done for us in Christ and what he will yet do in the final act of deliverance.

Sovereign in Creation. In beginning to discuss the Old Testament's teachings about God's acts of power in creation, there are several things which need to be clearly understood. Israel did not live in a vacuum and her faith did not develop in a vacuum. She was a part of the ancient world. Every ancient nation had a series of stories or fragments of stories telling about the creation of the world. The Hebrew writers were clearly aware of many, if not all, of these. They make frequent reference to them. It would be most surprising if they did not. But referring to them does not necessarily mean that the biblical writers believed in them.

As an illustration of what I mean, consider the visit of the apostle Paul to Athens. There is nothing in the least which would indicate that he believed in any of the idols worshiped at the many altars there. Yet, he began his major sermon there by referring to the altar inscribed "To an unknown god" (Acts 17:16 ff.). He used their idolatry as a basis for beginning his sermon of God as Creator and Redeemer. Furthermore, as he developed his sermon, he quoted from their ancient writers (Acts 17:28). He used those ancient references to other gods and reapplied them to God, the Father of our Lord Jesus.

In essence, the Old Testament writers did something like this. They apparently used some such ancient references to say to the people of their world that the God of Israel was the Creator. Much has been made of the similarities between some of these ancient accounts. It would be surprising if there were no similarities. It is the differences which show us precisely what these ancient preachers were saying about the God of Israel.

Because they had known him as Redeemer, in the Exodus experience, they became concerned about him as Creator. Let us learn from them at this point. Their primary witness was always to God's acts of power in redemption. It was only after this primary witness had been fully considered that they really gave much attention to God's acts of creative power. Genesis 1 to 11 sets the stage for the story of redemption which began with God's call of Abraham (Gen. 12:1-3). A renewed emphasis on God's creative power did not arise until centuries after their deliverance from Egypt.

I know of no one who has been led to a saving faith in

Jesus by a discussion of creation. Men are led to salvation by being told of God's redemptive acts. Once they have come to know him as Savior, then they are ready to try to understand him as Creator.

The Genesis writer said many things about God's creative acts. But his focus was upon two things. First of all, he focused his attention upon God as the Author of creation. In the first creation account, Genesis 1:1 to 2:4a, the name of God occurs thirty-four times. In the second account, Genesis 2:4b-25, the name, "the Lord God," occurs eleven times. There was to be no question left in anyone's mind but that, whatever happened, God did it.

The second emphasis of the Genesis writer rests upon the fact that man is the highest point of God's creation. He was made in God's image and given possession and dominion over the world. This was not for exploitation but for use as a divine stewardship.

So God created man in his own image, in the image of God he created him; male and female he created them. And God blessed them, and God said to them, "Be fruitful and multiply, and fill the earth and subdue it; and have dominion over the fish of the sea and over the birds of the air and over every living thing that moves upon the earth" (Gen. 1:27-28).

Here we are introduced to the two main characters in the divine study of redemption: God and man. But the creation accounts have still more to say about God's sovereign power.

We are told that God created merely by the spoken word. Other ancient stories have all sorts of fanciful developments as to how their gods brought the world into being. The Old Testament accounts tell of God speaking, with the power of his word bringing things to pass.

We are also told that there was an orderliness to God's creative acts. There was a deliberate plan that was carried out step by step. Creation was not something that happened by accident, nor by a series of accidents. It was the fruit of the deliberate will and purpose of God. Furthermore, the world was so established that it operated in an orderly or a lawful way.

Beyond this, we are plainly told that creation was good.

Many ancient peoples and some modern ones seem to think that the world is in itself evil. Not so! The Genesis writer plainly states that "God saw everything that he had made, and behold, it was very good" (Gen. 1:31).

God was totally sovereign in his creation. No one else was needed. Nothing got out of his control. There was no conflict from which the world sprang as some sort of celestial garbage heap. He did it alone and it happened just as he planned. Whatever else might be said, these things were both basic and central.

Furthermore, the world is still under his control. The Books of Job (38:1 to 41:34), Isaiah (40:12-26; 42:5; 45:18), and Psalms surely demonstrate this part of Israel's faith. The God who acted to create the world still controls it.

> For thus says the Lord,
> who created the heavens
>   (he is God!),
> who formed the earth and made it
>   (he established it;
> he did not create it a chaos,
>   he formed it to be inhabited!):
> "I am the Lord, there is no other" (Isa. 45:18).

His acts of creative power demonstrate his absolute sovereignty.

Sovereign in Miracle. The Hebrews were totally sure that the God who demonstrated his power in acts of deliverance and creation also showed his power in what we call miracles. It is imperative here that we seek to understand miracles in the Old Testament's own terminology, lest we go astray.

Our terms for miracle are usually intended to refer to some kind of supernatural event. However, we are not really very precise in so using it. We would certainly speak of Jesus' healing the sick or raising the dead as miracles. But we also speak of the "miracle of birth." Now there is nothing more normal than birth. All of us entered the world that way. When we speak of miracle in this sense, we are referring to an act which may demonstrate God's power and love, but it certainly is not supernatural. Because of this lack of precision in our own terminology, we must try to understand these acts of God in the Old Testament's own terms. This will be both clearer and more accurate. There are three key words which must be considered.

The most common word used to describe a miracle in the Old Testament is "sign." It may be used to describe something or some event. Thus Moses was given the signs of the rod which turned into a serpent and of his hand which became leprous. " 'If they will not believe you,' God said, 'or heed the first sign, they may believe the latter sign' " (Ex. 4:8). The rainbow in the heavens was a sign to Noah (Gen. 9:13). These serve to illustrate that a sign may be either natural or supernatural. The major focus of this term rests in the fact that a sign points to a meaning beyond itself. It is the truth behind it that is important. It is quite easy to become so concerned with the sign itself that we ignore the truth to which it points. About one third of the times this term is used in the Old Testament apply to the plagues of Egypt. In almost every instance the sign pointed to God's sovereignty over the gods of Egypt. Too often we miss this fact in reading of these great events.

The second most common term in the Old Testament's vocabulary of miracles is usually translated as "wonder" or "marvel." This always refers to an extraordinary event, though not necessarily a supernatural one. Thus the song of Moses refers to God's deliverance of the Israelites at the sea.

Who is like thee, O Lord, among the gods?
  Who is like thee, majestic in holiness,
  terrible in glorious deeds, doing wonders? (Ex. 15:11).

Now the Bible tells us that the waters were parted "by a strong east wind" which blew all night (Ex. 14:21). There is nothing more normal than an east wind. What it accomplished was abnormal, extraordinary.

This term is perhaps nearer to our idea of miracle than any in the Old Testament. It is always extraordinary and is always a demonstration of God's amazing power. Yet it is never done just to demonstrate the divine power but to accomplish his will and purposes.

The third major term for miracle is used almost as frequently as the second, but there is little consistency in its translation. It is translated as "sign," "wonder," and even as "miracle." The term itself refers to an extraordinary

event which strikes the heart of the perceiver with awe.
About half of its occurrences are in connection with the
plagues of Egypt.

The term usually refers to some form of tragic calamity,
but can refer to an event which is good. Either way, the very
nature of the event reaches into the inner recesses of the
human mind, producing both awe and terror at the power of
the God who performed it.

As far as the vocabulary itself is concerned then, an Old
Testament miracle aroused awe in the mind of the be-
holder. It could be either a natural, an abnormal, or a supernatural event. Whatever the actual nature of the event, it
was always performed by God to accomplish his purposes.
Furthermore, it regularly pointed to a meaning beyond itself. The meaning was the ultimate significance of the
event.

God never manifested his power for its own sake. His miracles were witnesses to his presence, his care, his power,
and his sovereignty. At this point, perhaps we should note
that there appears to be three things present in any event
which the Old Testament describes with its terminology of
miracle. First, there is always the matter of time and place.
Whether the event was ordinary, supernatural, or anywhere in between, it happened at the right time and the
right place. It would have done no good for Israel if the wind
which parted the sea had blown three days earlier or later.
Neither would it have been of any value if it had happened
five miles further along in either direction on the coast.
Furthermore, the matter of time and place were frequently
the result of a specific prediction. These things happened
both when and where they were predicted to happen.

The second basic feature of Old Testament miracles
seems to involve a competent interpreter. There had to be
someone there who could say with authority, "This is the
hand of God." Neither Israel nor Egypt might have known
that the east wind was sent by God unless there had been a
Moses present to tell them so. There are many events in the
Old Testament where an outside observer might have said,
"What a strange set of circumstances." But it was the man
of God who could point out that this was what God had done.

The third basic feature which always appears to be present in an Old Testament miracle story is the matter of its

meaning. It always points to a greater truth than the event itself. To the Israelites coming out of Egypt, the deliverance at the sea was of tremendous significance. It was a matter of life and death. But once the actual event was over, it would have merely been an interesting story of one of God's great deeds in their past. Instead, it served as the basis not only of praise to God, but of hope in God.

> He rebuked the Red Sea, and it became dry;
>   and he led them through the deep as through a desert.
> So he saved them from the hand of the foe,
>   and delivered them from the power of the enemy.
> And the waters covered their adversaries;
>   not one of them was left.
> Then they believed his words;
>   they sang his praise.
>
> . . . .
>
> Save us, O Lord our God,
>   and gather us from among the nations,
> that we may give thanks to thy holy name
>   and glory in thy praise.
> Blessed be the Lord, the God of Israel,
>   from everlasting to everlasting!
> And let all the people say, "Amen!"
>   Praise the Lord! (Ps. 106:9-12,47-48).

To the Hebrews, then, it was not merely enough to know that God had acted in creating their world. They also knew that he was sovereign over it now. He could and did act in the world in which they lived. He could use both natural and supernatural forces. The entire universe was subject to his will and power. It still is!

Each of these categories of God's acts of power had a clear impact upon the New Testament. The vocabulary and the concepts of God's acts of deliverance served as the basis for the New Testament concept of God's ultimate deliverance in Christ Jesus. Matthew focused attention upon this by relating Israel's deliverance from Egypt to Jesus being brought from there to Nazareth (Matt. 2:13 ff.). Further, when Jesus sought to describe his mission and ministry on the last night before his crucifixion, he did so in terms of the Passover and the covenant, both of which came from God's greatest act of deliverance in the Old Testament.

While the New Testament does not give a great deal of attention to God's acts of creation, they do serve as a basis for two key ideas. Paul pointed back to God's creation of man when he said, "If any one is in Christ, he is a new creation" (2 Cor. 5:17). Furthermore, John looked forward to an entirely new creation.

Then I saw a new heaven and a new earth; for the first heaven and the first earth had passed away. . . .
And he who sat upon the throne said, "Behold, I make all things new" (Rev. 21:1,5).

Lastly, the concepts of miracle are thoroughly foundational to the New Testament understanding of God's miraculous acts. Jesus himself never performed a miracle just to demonstrate his power. There was always a meaning behind it. In fact, the temptations as described in the Gospels show Jesus absolutely refusing to perform miracles just for themselves (Matt. 4:1-10; Luke 4:1-13). In addition, one of the more common expressions used to describe Jesus' miraculous acts of power is "sign."

Acts Through Mediation

Frequently, the Old Testament speaks of God's acts as being performed or carried out by some mediating force or some go-between. In a very real sense, these may not technically be acts of God but acts of the mediator. Yet, at the same time, they are regularly described as being God's acts. Few, if any, of these mediating ideas reached their full fruition within the Old Testament. They all developed more fully in the postcanonical Jewish literature and in the New Testament. Yet, since they are clearly rooted in the Old Testament, we must consider them. They cannot be ignored.

First among these is the creative word, or the "word of the Lord." There are several ideas which must be drawn together here. Among these is the basic Hebrew understanding of "word." To the Hebrew, a word once spoken had a power all of its own. It became a concrete force in the world. There is an old Jewish story of a man and his son who were approached by an enemy. When the enemy began to curse them, the father threw his son to the ground and laid on top of him to protect him from the words of the enemy. If such were true of the words of men, how much more true would it be of the word of God? His words, once spoken, seem to possess a power all of their own to accomplish his will.

Further, the creation account of Genesis 1:1 to 2:4a clearly reflects the power of God's spoken word. When God speaks, things happen, his word has a creative force.

Beyond this, there was the idea among the prophets of "the word of the Lord." Over and over they repeat the expression, "the word of the Lord came to me." Now there is no clear evidence that they ever thought of "the word of the Lord" having a separate existence or identity. But neither is there any evidence that they did not. We must at least raise the question, since the Gospel of John plainly begins by saying,

In the beginning was the Word, and the Word was with God, and the Word was God. He was in the beginning with God; all things were made through him, and without him was not anything made that was made (John 1:1-3).

John clearly connected the personal existence of God's Word with his creative acts.

In addition, the Book of Isaiah also clearly describes God's word as having a creative power. It may even describe it as having a creative identity and personality.

For as the rain and the snow come down from heaven,
    and return not thither but water the earth,
making it bring forth and sprout,
    giving seed to the sower and bread to the eater,
so shall my word be that goes forth from my mouth;
    it shall not return to me empty,
but it shall accomplish that which I purpose,
    and prosper in the thing for which I sent it (Isa. 55:10-11).

It would certainly be false to claim that God's creative word was considered by the Old Testament to be a person. But the roots for such a development appear to be plainly there. God's word is portrayed as accomplishing God's purposes. It does seem to have a power of its own. John clearly built upon the idea in his magnificent portrayal of Christ, as being coexistent with God, as well as identical with him.

The second mediating force to which the Old Testament refers is the Spirit of God. The two words commonly used for "spirit" have as their root ideas "wind" or "breath." The words can be so translated wherever they occur. Only the context can help us determine if more is meant. In Genesis 1:2, it appears to me that far more than "breath" or "wind" was intended when the writer said, "The Spirit of God was hovering over the face of the waters" (author's translation). Yet in Genesis 2:7, probably nothing more than "breath" was intended when it said, "The Lord God . . . breathed into his nostrils the breath of life." But even though its earliest use seems to reflect more than breath, there is certainly no indication of anything like personality. At the same time, the Spirit of God is associated with God in creation in the Book of Job (Job 34:13-14).

In addition, there are a number of sources which associated the Spirit of God with prophetic inspiration. Thus Samuel told Saul after he had anointed him king, "The spirit of the Lord will come mightily upon you, and you shall prophesy" (1 Sam. 10:6). Ezekiel told of falling before God when he was called to be a prophet.

And he said to me, "Son of man, stand upon your feet, and I will speak with you." And when he spoke to me, the Spirit entered into me and set me upon my feet; and I heard him speaking to me (Ezek. 2:1-2).

The prophet Isaiah described the Messiah as being filled with the Spirit of the Lord.

There shall come forth a shoot from the stump of Jesse,
    and a branch shall grow out of his roots.
And the Spirit of the Lord shall rest upon him,
    the spirit of wisdom and understanding,
    the spirit of counsel and might,
    the spirit of knowledge and the fear of the Lord.
And his delight shall be in the fear of the Lord (Isa. 11:1-3).

Furthermore, when Jesus actually began his ministry, he turned to a similar word from the Book of Isaiah to describe his own ministry.

The Spirit of the Lord God is upon me,
    because the Lord has anointed me
to bring good tidings to the afflicted,
    he has sent me to bind up the brokenhearted,
to proclaim liberty to the captives,
    and the opening of the prison to those who are
        bound;
to proclaim the year of the Lord's favor
    (Isa. 61:1-2a; Luke 4:16-19).

In addition, it also appears that some Old Testament writers seem to conceive of the Spirit of God as being either parallel to or identical with the mind and will of God. Thus the wisdom writer exclaims,

> Give heed to my reproof;
> behold, I will pour out my spirit to you,
> I will make my words known to you.
> (Prov. 1:23, author's translation).

And Isaiah clearly identified the Spirit with the purpose and will of God (Isa. 30:1).

But even beyond this, the Spirit of God appears to be presented as some kind of a life principle which can be given, withheld, or withdrawn.

> When thou hidest thy face, they are dismayed;
> when thou takest away their breath, they die
> and return to their dust.
> When thou sendest forth thy Spirit, they are created;
> and thou renewest the face of the ground
> (Psa. 104:29-30).

The Spirit also comes to reflect the presence of God among his people.

> Like cattle that go down into the valley,
> the Spirit of the Lord gave them rest.
> So thou didst lead thy people,
> to make for thyself a glorious name (Isa. 63:14).

It also seems to reflect his presence within the heart of the individual.

> Create in me a clean heart, O God,
> and put a new and right spirit within me.
> Cast me not away from thy presence,
> and take not thy holy Spirit from me (Ps. 51:10-11).

Now there is no question but that the Old Testament in its overall message does not understand the Holy Spirit in the same exalted way that he is understood in the New. On the other hand, to say that there were no glimpses of him as being representative of and perhaps identical to the power, presence, and purpose of the living God in the world of men would also be quite false. The Spirit of God in the Old Testament does mediate the presence and purpose of God to men.

3   The third mediating force or concept within the Old Testament is wisdom. Originally, wisdom was a practical shrewdness and an understanding related to the conduct of daily life. But in Job (particularly Job 28), some psalms, and in Proverbs 1 to 9, there is a growing change in understanding and emphasis. In Proverbs 1 to 9 wisdom takes on a growing personification. Here wisdom cries aloud in the streets. Her advice, though offered, is rejected. Her teachings, if heeded, lead to loyalty to God and to an abundant, bountiful life.

In postcanonical Jewish literature, there is no question about the personification of wisdom. There she becomes fully personal, associated in the task of leading men to God and to live a godly life.

4   The fourth mediator which the Old Testament presents is the "angel of the Lord." Now the Old Testament clearly distinguishes the "angel of the Lord" from all other angelic beings. There is something very distinctive here.

The angel of the Lord is first mentioned in Genesis 16, in the story of Hagar. Hagar, driven from home by Sarah, was found by the angel of the Lord in the wilderness. After a lengthy conversation, she concludes by addressing him as the Lord, saying, "Thou art a God of seeing" (Gen. 16:13).

He is perhaps more clearly seen however, in the call of Moses. There, "the angel of the Lord appeared to him in a flame of fire out of the midst of a bush" (Ex. 3:2). But when Moses turned aside to see this, it was God who spoke to him from the bush! (Ex. 3:4).

It would appear that the relationship between the angel of the Lord and God himself is even more clearly set forth in a later encounter with Moses. There God said,

> Behold, I send an angel before you, to guard you on the way and to bring you to the place which I have prepared. Give heed to him and hearken to his voice, do not rebel against him, for he will not pardon your transgression; for my name is in him.
> But if you hearken attentively to his voice and do all that I say, then I will be an enemy to your enemies and an adversary to your adversaries (Ex. 23:20-22).

Remembering that the Hebrew concept of name involves both character and nature, the angel of the Lord is presented as partaking of the divine nature. Further, he does what only God can do, pardon sin. Whatever else we may say of this being, he is very closely identified with the God of Israel. In a very real way he is an extension of God himself.

Now there have been attempts made to try to identify one or more of these mediators (or mediating acts or powers) with either the Son or with the Holy Spirit as presented in the New Testament. All such attempts have met with doubtful success. It does not appear to be at all possible to draw a direct line of connection. But there does seem to be some connection between the approach made to these extensions of God in the Old Testament and to the concept of Father, Son, and Holy Spirit as seen in the New.

It has long been suggested by some that the biblical doctrine of the Trinity was wholly a New Testament development or a post-New Testament development, just as others have tried to see it clearly taught in the Old Testament. I think that the truth lies somewhere between these two extremes. The question which we must ask and answer is: Are there any bases in the Old Testament which served as roots for the New Testament Trinitarian revelation?

It would appear that the answer is unequivocally clear. There are several distinct roots upon which the New Testament revelation of a Triune God grew. Just as we have seen the Old Testament did not spring up in a vacuum, so we must recognize that the New did not do so either.

First of all, the Old Testament clearly teaches that God is one, a unity. Thus the basic cry of the Old Testament was and is, "Hear, O Israel: the Lord our God, the Lord is one" (Deut. 6:4, author's translation). At the same time, there is a growing awareness of the divine transcendence. He just does not fit into human categories. The Old Testament is intensely aware of the fact that "I am God and not man" (Hos. 11:9). God was just beyond man's ultimate comprehension.

Historically, the names of God were not an expression of his plurality or his "manyness." On the other hand, there was couched in them an awareness of his diversity, both in character and activities. There was a many-sidedness to God.

The plural forms used in the creation accounts have been lightly dismissed as a plural of majesty or a holdover from ancient polytheistic accounts. Yet, when God fully sought to reproduce his image, he made a community of love, not just one being. (We shall consider this further in chapter 5.)

It would appear that the Genesis writer was projecting the image of God as being fully seen in a relationship of love. One person cannot have a relationship with himself.

Each of the mediators, or mediating acts or powers which we have just considered seem to be a further development in the direction of plurality. At the very least, they project the many-sideness of God. He revealed himself in several different ways.

Thus it would appear to me to be utterly false to say that there were no glimmers of Trinitarian concepts in the Old Testament. On the other hand, we must clearly recognize that, without the New Testament, there would certainly never have developed any doctrine of the Trinity. We might have developed a doctrine of God's plurality. The Trinity is clearly the flower of this Old Testament root. But it is the flower. Only the root was present at the beginning.

But when this is all said, we must come back to the fact that whatever Israel knew of God, it knew of him from his acts. His very nature was discovered by the things they experienced with him. God was neither discovered nor thought up. He was met. They experienced his love and his righteousness. Springing from these, they experienced his anger and his judgment. But they experienced these things because he loved them and demanded righteousness. Through it all they experienced his power. In every area of life, in every avenue of experience, God was there. He was the inescapable presence in every moment of life, as close as breath itself.

> Whither shall I go from thy Spirit?
>   Or whither shall I flee from thy presence?
> If I ascend to heaven, thou art there!
>   If I make my bed in Sheol, thou art there!
> If I take the wings of the morning
>   and dwell in the uttermost parts of the sea,
> even there thy hand shall lead me,
>   and thy right hand shall hold me (Ps. 139:7-10).

Thus, above all else, Israel knew God as one who acted. Theirs was no worship of an "unmoved Mover" of the Greeks. For Israel, God was seen and known by what he did. This is also true for the followers of Jesus Christ. When God sought how best to reveal himself, he gave us a Life to see, a Redeemer who saves, and a Lord who leads.

4
The God Who Chooses

Although we have sought to be both fair with the evidence and faithful with the biblical emphases, if you had asked an ancient Israelite, "What is God like?" he would probably not have answered with what we have said in the preceding chapters. It is certainly true that Israel believed that God was living, personal, and holy. It is also true that they believed that God revealed himself through his acts. Through such he showed himself to be loving, righteous, and powerful, mediating his presence and blessings to them in a variety of ways.

But there was something far more central to Israel's understanding of God and their relation to him. He was the God of choice and covenant. They believed that God had sought them out, choosing them for himself.

For you are a people holy to the Lord your God; the Lord your God has chosen you to be a people for his own possession, out of all the peoples that are on the face of the earth (Deut. 7:6).

Through that act of gracious choice, God then established his covenant with Israel, confirming the relationship which was to exist between them.

And Moses summoned all Israel, and said to them, "Hear, O Israel. . . . The Lord our God made a covenant with us in Horeb. Not with our fathers did the Lord make this covenant, but with us, who are all of us here alive this day (Deut. 5:1-3).

100

Although the Old Testament was sure that God was the God of the whole earth, it was also sure that he was the God of Israel. He had chosen them, delivered them, and established his covenant with them. So Israel constantly directed their attention to the fact that they were the people of God's free choice. Although some interpreters believe that the central emphasis of the Old Testament was upon God's covenant with Israel, it appears to me that the central emphasis was God's choice or election of Israel. Because he had chosen and delivered them, the covenant became significant. Without the divine choice and deliverance there would never have been a covenant at all.

Regardless of which idea is the central emphasis, it is true that the two ideas are opposite sides of the same coin. There would have been no covenant without God's choice. On the other hand, the covenant stands as the supreme evidence of his free choice of Israel.

This brings us to consider God's choice of Israel. This idea has normally been considered under the title of the biblical doctrine of election. However, this sounds so theological as to be somewhat threatening. Therefore we shall use "God's choice of Israel." Israel was completely convinced that God's supreme act on their behalf was choosing them to be his people.

Let us clearly recognize from the very outset, however, that this very conviction was to be a source of great problems for them. They regularly considered God's choice of them to be a guarantee of privilege. They forgot that it carried added responsibility. It was their failure to remember this which constantly forced the prophets to call them back to the proper understanding of God's choice.

I. God's Choice of Israel

The idea of a god choosing a people was nothing new in the ancient Near East. Peoples other than Israel had national gods. Moab, for example, had Chemosh. Like Israel's God, Chemosh gave guidance for his people's military campaigns. The Moabites were also described as "sons of Chemosh" (Num. 21:29, author's translation), just as Israel was described as "sons of the Lord your God" (Deut. 14:1). Thus it might appear at the outset that Israel's understanding of their relationship with God was little different from their understanding of any other nation's relationship with its god.

But there was a difference. The difference between the two lay in their belief in God's free act of redemptive choice. It becomes quite obvious with only a brief glance that Israel was bound to their god in a different way from that in which Moab and Chemosh were bound. In fact, the gods of other nations depended upon the continued well-being of their nation for their own existence. If Moab ceased to be, Chemosh would die. With no one to worship him, he would simply pass out of existence. The bond between god and nation in those other countries was purely naturalistic.

Israel's bond with their God was totally different. There was never any question of God ceasing to exist if Israel did. Israel was dependent upon God. But God was never dependent upon Israel. Other gods were dependent upon their people for the sacrifices which fed them. Not so was the God of Israel.

> If I were hungry, I would not tell you;
>   for the world and all that is in it is mine (Ps. 50:12).

> For every beast of the forest is mine,
>   the cattle on a thousand hills (Ps. 50:10).

Rather, it was not God's need of Israel but his choice of Israel that always lay at the heart of their relation. From Israel's standpoint, it was always God's choice which was central.

> When Israel was a child, I loved him,
>   and out of Egypt I called my son (Hos. 11:1).

> It was not because you were more in number than any
> other people that the Lord set his love upon you and
> chose you, for you were the fewest of all peoples; but
> it is because the Lord loves you (Deut. 7:7-8a).

In this divine act of redemptive choice, we find the very foundation of Israel's faith. There are many words used to describe this act of divine choice. But three are basic to our study at this point. They are all verbs, words of action.

The first of these is the verb "to choose." It refers to a free act of grace, God's choice of whomsoever he would for the purpose of using or blessing them. Israel was described as "my chosen" by God (Isa. 45:4). He picked them out from all the nations of the earth to be his own possession (Deut. 7:6).

Behold, to the Lord your God belong heaven and the heaven of heavens, the earth with all that is in it; yet the Lord set his heart in love upon your fathers and chose their descendants after them, you above all peoples, as at this day (Deut. 10:14-15).

Because of his special choice of Israel, God exercised special care over them, saying,

> for I give water in the wilderness,
> rivers in the desert,
> to give drink to my chosen people (Isa. 43:20b).

So characteristic is the use of this verb to describe God's relation with Israel, that they ultimately came to call themselves "the chosen people." Furthermore, it was precisely this term which was picked up in 1 Peter to describe the Christian community as the new people of God. There we are described as "a chosen race" (1 Pet. 2:9). Israel's choice by God was always fundamentally understood as sheer grace. It was both unearned and undeserved. It still is.

The second key term in the biblical vocabulary of God's free choice of Israel is the verb "to know." As was pointed out in chapter 1, "knowledge" in the Old Testament was something learned by intimate experience. The verb "to know" meant to have that kind of intimate experience. Thus we are told that "Adam knew Eve his wife, and she conceived and bore Cain" (Gen. 4:1). There the word was used to describe the most intimate knowledge a man and a woman can have of each other, that of the sexual relation. Now, while this verb does not usually refer to sex, it does always appear to refer to personal, intimate, experiential knowledge which one person may have of another.

It was from this basis that God spoke through Amos to Israel, saying,

> You only have I known
> of all the families of the earth;
> therefore I will punish you
> for all your iniquities (Amos 3:2).

In the preceding chapters, Amos had made abundantly clear that God was aware of other nations. What was being

said here was that his "knowing" of Israel was on a different level from that of the other nations. Furthermore, this
was a continuing experience shared by God and his people.
Thus he said,

> I know Ephraim,
> and Israel is not hid from me (Hos. 5:3).

For some reason which springs only from the nature of
God, he chose to enter into Israel's experiences and to allow
them to experience him in a unique way. It was upon this
foundation that Jesus later built when he said, "I am the
good shepherd; I know my own and my own know me, as the
Father knows me and I know the Father" (John 10:14-15a).
There is an intimate relationship between Jesus and his
followers of the same kind as that which exists between the
Son and the Father.

But, to return to the Old Testament, this experiential
relation which was shared between God and Israel laid a
special obligation upon Israel. Since they had been highly
privileged, they were expected to be faithful servants.
Therefore, a failure at this point was especially tragic.
Furthermore, failure called for sure and certain punishment.

The third major term used in the context of God's free
choice of Israel is translated "to get," "to acquire," or "to
buy." It was from this word that the concept of God's purchase of Israel arose.

> Do you thus requite the Lord,
>   O people foolish and unwise?
> Is not he your father, who purchased you
>   who formed you and set you up?
>   (Deut. 32:6, author's translation).

> Remember thy congregation, which thou has gotten
>   [purchased] of old,
>   which thou hast redeemed to be the tribe of thy
>   heritage! (Ps. 74:2).

Further, God's unique relationship with Israel was considered to be a basis for fear on the part of others.

> Now are the chiefs of Edom dismayed;
>   the leaders of Moab, trembling seizes them;
>   all the inhabitants of Canaan have melted away.
> Terror and dread fall upon them;

> because of the greatness of thy arm,
>   they are as still as a stone,
> till thy people, O Lord, pass by,
>   till the people pass by whom thou hast purchased
>   (Ex. 15:15-16).

It should be noted that there was never any indication that God's purchase of Israel involved a price he had to pay to anyone else. It was simply a price that had to be paid. The emphasis was upon the result: by this he got Israel. They belonged to him in a special way.

From a survey of this basic vocabulary and its use, we see why Israel was convinced that God had chosen them. This choice was reflected in his knowing them, and in his purchase or acquiring of them. The divine relation to Israel was never natural but the result of God's moral choice. Israel's continued existence was never seen as being necessary for his own being. Although the people seem to have sometimes felt that their continued existence was necessary for the maintenance of God's honor, this was not so. This was one of the more profound lessons which the prophets sought to teach Israel. The people prided themselves that they were the Chosen People. Therefore they expected God to give them victory, protect their interests, and exalt them among all nations. The prophets announced that it was the other way around. Because they had been chosen, their responsibility for obedient service was greater. Furthermore, because they failed to render this the judgment upon them would be more sure. They had been chosen not because of their lovability but because of God's love. It was sheer grace, unmerited favor. They were expected to be filled with wonder at God's choice, rather than lifted up with conceit.

In addition to the basic terminology of God's choice, there were two pictorial images of this choice which appeared frequently in the words of the prophets. These are fatherhood and marriage. Thus Israel was described both as God's child, his firstborn, and as his bride. Sometimes both images are used in the same passage. Thus Hosea cried,

> Plead with your mother, plead—
>   for she is not my wife,
>   and I am not her husband—
> that she put away her harlotry from her face
>   and her adultery from between her breasts (Hos. 2:2).

But he also wept,

> When Israel was a child, I loved him,
>   and out of Egypt I called my son.
> The more I called them,
>   the more they went from me;
> they kept sacrificing to the Baals,
>   and burning incense to idols.
> Yet it was I who taught Ephraim to walk,
>   I took them up in my arms;
> but they did not know that I healed them (Hos. 11:1-3).

And when Isaiah denounced the sins of Judah, he did so with the words,

> Hear, O heavens, and give ear, O earth;
>   for the Lord has spoken:
> "Sons have I reared and brought up,
>   but they have rebelled against me.
> The ox knows its owner,
>   and the ass its master's crib;
> but Israel does not know,
>   my people does not understand" (Isa. 1:2-3).

Jeremiah, on the other hand, drew with pathos upon the image of Israel as a bride.

> I remember the devotion of your youth,
>   your love as a bride,
> how you followed me in the wilderness,
>   in a land not sown (Jer. 2:2).

It might be claimed that these figures were drawn from the naturalistic religions of the peoples surrounding Israel, and there may have been some relationship. But Israel held to these ideas with a unique difference. This was their emphasis upon God's free choice. God was related to Israel not because he had to be but because he had chosen to be. Furthermore, Israel had to decide whether or not to respond. God had called them out of Egypt, but they did not have to come. He had led them in the wilderness, but they did not have to follow.

Lest we push the image of sonship too far and see the relationship as naturalistic, Ezekiel sought to make another dimension clear. He portrayed Israel's sonship as that of adoption (Ezek. 16:1-7). But he also pointed out that this was followed by the betrothal and marriage (Ezek. 16:8-14).

Since they had been doubly chosen, their final rejection of God's choice was even more abhorrent.

It is obvious what an impact these images had on the New Testament. Paul made several references to the adoption of Christians into God's family. And the Revelation proclaimed its vision of the final consummation by saying,

And I saw the holy city, new Jerusalem, coming down out of heaven from God, prepared as a bride adorned for her husband (Rev. 21:2).

The Old Testament clearly interweaves two traditions of God's choice of Israel. One of these goes back to his choice of them in the Exodus. The other goes back to God's choice of Abraham, Isaac, and Jacob, the patriarchs. Although they both reflect the same divine initiative, there are slightly different emphases.

The tradition of patriarchal election turned their attention to the overarching purpose of God. It focused upon the long processes of history which God used to effect his will and his choice. The tradition of choice in the Exodus experience, on the other hand, called attention to a great, cataclysmic event where God broke into history to make Israel his own.

In their subsequent history, the two traditions had radically different results in Israel's self-image. Reliance on being the "sons of Abraham" became a very real danger. It was a source of great pride and had to be attacked even by John the Baptist.

Do not presume to say to yourselves, "We have Abraham as our father"; for I tell you, God is able from these stones to raise up children to Abraham (Matt. 3:9).

On the other hand, the memory of the deliverance from Egypt was both humbling and encouraging. The God who had made something worthwhile from a group of helpless slaves could do it again. The Egypt tradition reminded Israel that they had been chosen from sheer grace. With a proper understanding, the patriarchal tradition reminded Israel that they had been chosen for service,

I will make of you a great nation, and I will bless you, and make your name great, *so that you will be a blessing* (Gen. 12:2, italics mine).

Both tendencies are still with us. When we who are followers of Jesus Christ remember what we were when Jesus saved us, we are humbled and encouraged. We are humbled by his amazing love. We are encouraged by the hope that he who saved us can surely keep us. On the other hand, when we turn our attention too much upon our new relationship with God, there is a real tendency to become proud of what we are. How sad that we have not learned the lesson that God's redemptive choice is sheer grace, unmerited favor.

There were two subsidiary but related ideas which arose from Israel's understanding of God's choice. The first was that his choice of them was primarily that they should be used in service. We cannot ignore the fact that his choice carried with it glory and honor. But the purpose seems always to have been that Israel should respond to him with obedient loyalty. The covenant, which we shall consider in greater detail later in this chapter, was not a bargain between God and Israel. It was based upon what God had already accomplished. Israel was already free from Egypt when she came to Sinai. The covenant was offered to Israel following her response to God's grace.

Further, it laid no obligation upon God. He had already taken his obligations up before the covenant was given. God freely assumed a relation to Israel, chose her, delivered her. In response, she was to serve and obey him.

Now therefore, if you will obey my voice and keep my covenant, you shall be my own possession among all peoples; for all the earth is mine, and you shall be to me a kingdom of priests and a holy nation (Ex. 19:5-6).

As an outgrowth of the service which Israel owed to God, there was a growing awareness that she had an obligation to the nations. This was most clearly seen in the call of Jeremiah. To him God said,

> See, I have set you this day over nations and over
>   kingdoms,
> to pluck up and to break down,
> to destroy and to overthrow,
> to build and to plant (Jer. 1:10).

This awareness of a mission to the nations grew even more strong during the Exile and beyond. If God is the only God, then it became Israel's task to share him with the nations. So Israel's choice by God came to focus upon the fact that they were the mediators of his revelation to all men. If they had not treasured God's revelation, there would have been no record upon which the New Testament might build. But in serving God and in ministering to the nations, Israel reflected the nature and character of the God who had chosen her.

II. God's Choice of Individuals

In general, books considering God's choice of Israel frequently ignore his choice of individuals or merely give it a brief treatment. It is far too important for that. The divine choice of individuals to render obedient service is very fundamental to the Old Testament. It has become quite common in evangelical circles to speak of God's "call." God's call is his choosing an individual to serve him.

There are really two basic kinds of individuals whom God is seen to choose within the Old Testament. The first, and perhaps least important, involved those who were called to some form of service other than being a prophet. There were many of these.

The patriarchal narratives obviously focus upon the choice of Abraham, Isaac, and Jacob.

Now the Lord said to Abram (Abraham), "Go from your country and your kindred and your father's house to the land that I will show you. And I will make of you a great nation, and I will bless you, and make your name great, so that you will be a blessing. I will bless those who bless you, and him who curses you I will curse; and by you shall all the families of the earth be blessed" (Gen. 12:1-3, author's translation).

Abraham was being called to obedient service. He was to relocate his family without knowing where he was going. In so doing, he would be blessed. But he would also become a blessing to all others of the human race. Both things happened.

Although we are not given the same amount of detail in the call of Isaac and of Jacob, it is obvious that the later Old Testament materials certainly accepted the idea that all three were united in the repeated call. Throughout the rest of the Old Testament, the beginnings of Israel as a people were consistently referred back to these three patriarchs. It is easy to dismiss the patriarchal call as really being national, since the nation of Israel was descended from these men. On the other hand, the biblical narratives focus upon them as individuals with personal differences. Abraham was the towering figure of faith. Isaac was quiet and retiring. Jacob was the schemer and confidence man. But all were used by God in fulfilling his divine purpose. In spite of the weaknesses which they had, they were called, they obeyed, and God's blessings both rested upon them and flowed through them to others.

There is also a major tradition in the Old Testament concerning the divine choice of David as king.

The Lord said to Samuel, "How long will you grieve over Saul, seeing I have rejected him from being king over Israel? Fill your horn with oil, and go; I will send you to Jesse the Bethlehemite, for I have provided for myself a king among his sons."

Then Samuel took the horn of oil, and anointed him in the midst of his brothers; and the Spirit of the Lord came mightily upon David from that day forward (1 Sam. 16:1, 13).

Later, God's call to David was reaffirmed and enlarged.

Thus says the Lord of hosts, I took you from the pasture, from following the sheep, that you should be prince over my people Israel; and I have been with you wherever you went, and have cut off all your enemies from before you; and I will make for you a great name, like the name of the great ones of the earth. . . . Moreover the Lord declares to you that the Lord will make you a house. . . . And your house and your kingdom shall be made sure forever before me; your throne shall be established forever (2 Sam. 7:8-16).

Again, here was an individual chosen by God from an unlikely heritage to fulfill a great purpose. Certainly God blessed him, and others through him. But his call did not give any special privilege above others called to serve. Later, when David sinned with Bathsheba, he was called to account and faced judgment because he had abused his responsibility (2 Sam. 11—12). Again, some have tried to deny this as an individual call, saying that it focused upon his entire family, not upon him. Actually, the reverse was true.

It first focused upon him and then was enlarged to include his house and lineage.

We could enlarge this list almost indefinitely. God chose kings, priests, judges, and others. They came from all walks of life and included both men and women. All of them were leaders upon whom the Spirit of the Lord had obviously placed his gifts. They were each empowered with whatever abilities were necessary to accomplish the divine purposes. They were all chosen for service, to serve God through serving his people.

If one of these called individuals abandoned his responsibilities, such as King Saul did, God did not immediately abandon him. Rather, God sought to bring him back. But in every instance, each one appears to have been free in his decision to obey or not.

The major focus of individual election in the Old Testament rested in the call to be a prophet, a spokesman for God. Each described the experience of being called in his own way. Isaiah said, "I saw the Lord sitting upon a throne, high and lifted up" (Isa. 6:1). Jeremiah simply recorded, "Now the word of the Lord came to me" (Jer. 1:4). Ezekiel was more graphic, painting a picture of the Lord coming to him in a storm. He summed up,

Such was the appearance of the likeness of the glory of the Lord. And when I saw it, I fell upon my face, and I heard the voice of one speaking. And he said to me, "Son of man, stand upon your feet, and I will speak with you" (Ezek. 1:28b to 2:1).

Amos, on the other hand, was more prosaic, reporting,

I am no prophet, nor a prophet's son; but I am a herdsman, and a dresser of sycamore trees, and the Lord took me from following the flock, and the Lord said to me, "Go, prophesy to my people Israel" (Amos 7:14-15).

Each of God's prophets was going about his own affairs when God broke in upon them. Moses was "keeping the flock of his father-in-law, Jethro," when God broke in upon him (Ex. 3:1). Isaiah was worshiping in the Temple (Isa. 6:1). Ezekiel was a captive of Babylon, in exile near the river Chebar (Ezek. 1:1-3). Hosea was at home, experiencing the heartache of a broken home and an unfaithful wife (Hos. 1—3).

In spite of their individual differences, there was a common strain running through their experiences. So much so, in fact, that their calls appear to be recorded with a common outline, giving the same basic type of information about each. It is almost as if these things needed to be present to establish the prophet's credentials for speaking God's words.

First of all, to each of those whose call is recorded came the sense of God's presence. The call was always initiated by God. Although we at times speak of some of the prophets as volunteers, yet we must clearly understand that the initiative always rested with God. Regardless of what each of these persons was doing, God broke in upon his consciousness.

God always came with a message. The message involved a number of different things, but it always wound up with an absolute revelation of the fact that the prophet had been chosen to do God's work on earth. Thus God said to Moses,

I have seen the affliction of my people who are in Egypt, and have heard their cry because of their taskmasters; I know their sufferings, and I have come down to deliver them out of the hand of the Egyptians, and to bring them up out of that land to a good and broad land, a land flowing with milk and honey. . . . Come, I will send you to Pharaoh that you may bring forth my people, the sons of Israel, out of Egypt (Ex. 3:7-10).

Jeremiah not only felt this sense of chosenness, he also was aware of a sense of predestination to his task. More than anyone else in the Old Testament, he was aware of his place in the ultimate purposes of God.

Now the Word of the Lord came to me, saying,
"Before I formed you in the womb I knew you,
  and before you were born I consecrated you;
  I appointed you a prophet to the nations" (Jer. 1:4-5).

Occasionally a prophet might appear to be a volunteer, such as Isaiah, who said to God, "Here am I! Send me" (Isa. 6:8). But the initiative had already rested with God. He came to Isaiah first.

The prophets' calls also included a revelation of God's ultimate purpose for their lives. Furthermore, there was a commission to a specific task within that purpose. Each of them were different but all of them were similar. Moses was to go back to Egypt and lead Israel out of their bondage to Pharaoh and his people. Amos was to go to the Northern Kingdom. Isaiah was to stay and preach to the Southern Kingdom. Jeremiah had a mission both to Judah and to all the neighboring nations. Ezekiel had a mission to the exiles in Babylon.

When confronted with those awesome tasks, the prophets responded in various ways. Moses first tried to change the subject. Finally, he sought to avoid the call altogether (Ex. 3:11; 4:13). Isaiah, faced with a ministry to a people who would not respond, cried, "How long, O Lord?" (Isa. 6:11). Jeremiah pled his youthful inadequacy, responding, "Ah, Lord God! Behold, I do not know how to speak, for I am only a youth" (Jer. 1:6).

God's ultimate word to each of these men was addressed to their specific situation. Moses was rebuked. Isaiah was cleansed and empowered. Jeremiah was gently encouraged. But God met each of their individual needs.

Although the prophetic calls shared this common form, each had its own uniqueness. Each individual brought his own personality to the confrontation with God. Each of them were unique individuals, facing their own particular historical crisis. Not one of them was a carbon copy of any other. Through them all, God spoke his word to specific historical situations. He used the men as they were, offering his power, moving them by his purpose, but accomplishing his will.

So God not only called the nation of Israel to do his will, he also called individuals within that nation to serve him as well. This sense of divine call underlay much of the New Testament. No one raised any question as to whether or not God acted in that way. When the Holy Spirit led the church at Antioch to send forth missionaries, no one questioned the fact (Acts 13:1-3). There was also a real sense of awareness that the entire Christian community had been chosen by God. Thus Paul called Christians "God's chosen ones" (Col. 3:12). And the First Epistle of Peter described them (and us) as "a chosen race" (1 Pet. 2:9). Thus this sense of a special call to a special service permeated the entire New Testament.

II. God's Choice of Non-Israelites

One feature of God's free choice which is frequently overlooked is the fact that the Old Testament regularly described him as choosing people or nations other than Israel or Israelites. Other nations could be and were chosen for a service which seems to have carried no measure of privilege. It could be described as a choice without a covenant.

Nations other than Israel could be called from the ends of the earth to accomplish the will of God. Thus Isaiah viewed Assyria,

> Ah, Assyria, the rod of my anger,
>   the staff of my fury!
> Against a godless nation I send him,
>   and against the people of my wrath I command him,
> to take spoil and seize plunder,
>   and to tread them down like the mire of the
>   streets (Isa. 10:5-6).

Jeremiah had a similar view of the tribes of the north and of Babylon.

> Because you have not obeyed my words, behold, I will send for all the tribes of the north, says the Lord, and for Nebuchadrezzar the king of Babylon, my servant, and I will bring them against this land and its inhabitants, and against all these nations round about (Jer. 25:8-9).

It is important that we note that even though Isaiah viewed God as using Assyria to punish Judah, he was also aware that Assyria had no idea of this. He says of Assyria,

> But he does not so intend,
>   and his mind does not so think;
> but it is in his mind to destroy,
>   and to cut off nations not a few (Isa. 10:7).

The very fact that God could use Assyria to fulfill his purposes, even when they were unaware of it, was considered to be a testimony to the greatness of his power and to the reality of his sovereign wisdom. Thus God can integrate into his purpose and will that which by its own nature is utterly alien to his will.

When such a nation was used by God, it gave no basis for boasting.

When the Lord has finished all his work on Mount Zion
and on Jerusalem he will punish the arrogant boasting of
the king of Assyria and his haughty pride.
Shall the axe vaunt itself over him who hews with it,
    or the saw magnify itself against him who wields it?
As if a rod should wield him who lifts it,
    or as if a staff should lift him who is not wood!
    (Isa. 10:12,15).

These nations and peoples were merely instruments in the
hand of God. They could be used and cast aside as it pleased
him. Let us clearly understand that this has nothing to do
with God's love or their spiritual condition. It is merely
another evidence of his sovereignty.

Furthermore, we must never be guilty of merely suppos-
ing that this idea was simply based upon some view of history that made God responsible for everything that happened. God specifically chose these nations to do his will.
But there was no implication that they were either submis-
sive or obedient to that will in any conscious sense. Furthermore, this kind of divine choice had no embodiment of
an understanding of God's nature nor even of a knowledge
of him. It is also clear that there was no summons here to
missionary activity.

The point is that these nations could and did perform acts
which were morally reprehensible but which God could use
without their collaboration. This view of God's choice of foreign nations is found not only in the prophets, but in the
historical books and in Deuteronomy. Paul clearly reflects
this idea that God can use all things to accomplish his will
(Rom. 8:28).

The Old Testament was also sure that God could use non-
Hebrew individuals as well as nations. But here there ap-
pears to have been a greater variety of choices reflected.
There were some chosen by God to a service which was also
accompanied by some degree of honor. Thus Cyrus, king of
Persia, overthrew Babylon and issued an edict, declaring,

Thus says Cyrus king of Persia, "The Lord, the God of
heaven, has given me all the kingdoms of the earth, and he
has charged me to build him a house at Jerusalem, which is
in Judah. Whoever is among you of all his people, may the
Lord his God be with him. Let him go up" (2 Chron. 36:23).

It should be noted that this was his policy toward all of the peoples who had been held captive in Babylon.

But God said of Cyrus,

He is my shepherd,
and he shall fulfil all my purpose (Isa. 44:28).

Thus says the Lord to his anointed, to Cyrus,
   whose right hand I have grasped,
to subdue nations before him
   and ungird the loins of kings,
to open doors before him
   that gates may not be closed
"I will go before you
   and level the mountains

. . . .

For the sake of my servant Jacob,
   and Israel my chosen,
I call you by your name,
   I surname you, though you do not know me" (Isa. 45:1-4).

It is obvious that in no way was Cyrus really acting in conscious submission to the will of God. He had not experienced God in the sense that Isaiah or David had. But at the same time his will and purposes were in harmony with God's will and purposes.

There were other ancient individuals who were used by God without any such commonality of purpose. Their actions were simply used to effect God's will. The point which the biblical writers were making was that God was absolutely sovereign.

There is none beside me;
I am the Lord, and there is no other (Isa. 45:6).

IV. God's Gift of the Covenant

As we pointed out earlier, the concepts of covenant and choice are significantly related. Neither can really be understood apart from the other. However, if God had not chosen Israel, there would have been no covenant. At the same time, it is quite doubtful if we would ever completely understand God's choice of Israel apart from the covenant. It is that to which we must now direct our attention.

There is no question but that the idea of the covenant between God and Israel is a central feature for understanding the relationship which existed between God and Israel. The covenant was not the redemptive act which brought Israel into being but was the outward expression and public confirmation of such an act. God's redemptive act in its most obvious expression was the deliverance from Egypt. This event was always considered the fundamental fact of Old Testament faith and religion. However, it is certainly evident that the experience of God's free choice of Israel in the Exodus was given a formal expression and confirmation in the covenant. Thus the fullest expression of God's redemptive act can be found in the covenant.

Although the covenant appears to be subsidiary to the divine election, it cannot be dismissed lightly. It belongs to the earliest sources of the Old Testament and may be traced throughout the entire tradition. From beginning to end, the Old Testament authors were deeply concerned with the covenants between Israel and God.

Before taking a closer look at the Old Testament concept of the covenant itself, we should first examine the typical covenants of the ancient Near East. There were two basic types of covenants in Israel's world. The first of these has been classified as the "parity treaty" or "parity covenant." This kind of covenant was between persons who were essentially equals in social or political status. This was the kind of agreement into which Jacob and Laban entered.

Then Laban answered and said to Jacob, ". . . Come now, let us make a covenant, you and I; and let it be a witness between you and me" (Gen. 31:43-44).

It was also the kind of covenant by which David and Jonathan had pledged their love for each other (1 Sam. 20:8). By such agreements, peace was secured between the two parties and each was committed to the other, if not in love, at least in friendship. The entire thing was sealed and witnessed in the presence of God.

The parity covenant was negotiated between these equals. It could be, and often was, stated and restated until both parties were satisfied with its terms.

However, the basic covenant concept in the Old Testament was not between equals but between God and Israel. For a long time, interpreters considered it either to be a modification of the parity treaty or a form which was unique to Israel. We now know that this idea was incorrect. In recent years, due to the results of archaeology, there has been a significant amount of study done with governmental documents of the nations of western Asia dating to the second millenium BC. Among these documents were a number of treaties which were different from the more common parity covenants. These have generally been called "suzerainty treaties." They were made between a suzerain or "great king" and his vassal. The suzerain or "great king" differed from an ordinary king in that he ruled over many kingdoms. The Assyrians, for example, called their king by this title.

Then the Rabshakeh stood and called out in a loud voice in the language of Judah, "Hear the word of the great king, the king of Assyria!" (2 Kings 18:28).

The people of Israel used this title for the Assyrian king. Thus Hosea said,

> When Ephraim saw his sickness,
> and Judah his wound,
> then Ephraim went to Assyria,
> and sent to the great king (Hos. 5:13).

Furthermore, this suzerain was sometimes called the "king of kings and lord of lords." This title indicated his authority over other rulers in the region. He was not merely a ruler among equals, but possessed an authority over them. It is important to realize that this was precisely the role assumed by the God of Israel. He is the Lord of hosts. It is also noteworthy that the victorious Son of God is called "King of kings and Lord of lords" (1 Tim. 6:15; Rev. 19:16).

The covenant which was made between the suzerain and his vassal was a promise or a bond which was made binding by an oath between the two parties. It was an agreement into which each of them entered, although there were no legal means of enforcement. There was no court to which any appeal could be made if either party violated the terms.

A detailed study of these suzerainty treaties shows that there were seven common features which can be identified in most of them. Not every covenant had all of these. Neither were they always in the same order, although the order was usually fairly consistent.

The typical suzerainty treaty began with the identification of the great king. He was the one who gave the treaty.

Thus it might say, "I am the great king, XYZ, king of kings and lord of lords." This immediately reminds us of the beginning of the covenant statement in Exodus,

And God spoke all these words, saying, "I am the Lord your God" (Ex. 20:1-2).

The same kind of expression is found in the covenant renewal ceremony under Joshua: "Thus says the Lord, the God of Israel" (Josh. 24:2).

#2 The second feature of the suzerainty treaty was usually a detailed presentation of the historical background, describing the relation which had existed between the suzerain and the vassal. This usually placed a special emphasis upon the benevolent actions of the suzerain. This was never a mere stereotype, but was told as a historical recitation. Its purpose appears to have been an attempt to bind the vassal to the suzerain by bonds of affection. This, too, is paralleled in the Old Testament covenant statement: "who brought you out of the land of Egypt, out of the house of bondage" (Ex. 20:2). Joshua's covenant renewal ceremony recounted God's leadership and deliverance from the time of Abraham to his own time (Josh. 24:2-13).

#3 A third feature of the typical suzerainty treaty was a prohibition against the vassal's entering into any foreign alliances. His only treaty commitment was to be with the great king. Note how this shows up in the Old Testament. In the fundamental document in Exodus, Israel was told: "You shall have no other gods before me" (Ex. 20:3). In Joshua's covenant renewal statement, Israel was told to "put away the gods which your fathers served beyond the River, and in Egypt" (Josh. 24:14).

#4 The fourth feature of the suzerainty covenant was the statement of the basic stipulations and obligations of the covenant. It was made up of a list of the vassal's obligations to the great king. This is precisely in line with the covenant which Moses brought to Israel.

You shall not make for yourself a graven image. . . .
You shall not take the name of the Lord your God in vain. . . .
Remember the sabbath day, to keep it holy. . . .
Honor your father and mother, . . .
You shall not kill.
You shall not commit adultery.

You shall not steal.
You shall not bear false witness against your neighbor.
You shall not covet (Ex. 20:4-17).

These were the duties and obligations which Israel had to
God. They were owed to him because of what he had done for
them.

#5   A fifth feature of the suzerainty treaty was the stipula-
tion of where the treaty document was to be deposited and
when it was to be publicly read. Usually, it was kept in the
sanctuary of the vassal and was to be read publicly at stated
intervals. In Israel, they were commanded to put the two
tablets of the covenant into the ark, which was to be kept in
the holy of holies (Ex. 25:21; 1 Kings 8:9). Furthermore, it
was read publicly on frequent occasions. Moses held such a
renewal ceremony following Aaron's sin with the golden
calf, and later when Israel reached the plains of Moab (Ex.
34; Deut. 5). Joshua had such a renewal ceremony when he
came to the end of his life (Josh. 24). In addition, it appears
that such ceremonies were at least held each time a new
king was enthroned and perhaps more frequently.

#6   A sixth feature of the normal suzerainty covenant in-
volved the matter of witnesses. The gods of the great king
and of his vassal were called upon to serve as witnesses to
the treaty. This was usually followed with a call to the
mountains and the rivers, the heavens and the earth, and
the winds and the clouds to be witnesses. As would be expected, in Israel's covenant, such witnesses are missing.
However, it should be noted that in Joshua's renewal ceremony, the people were identified as witnesses.

Then Joshua said to the people, "You are witnesses
against yourselves that you have chosen the Lord, to serve
him." And they said, "We are witnesses" (Josh. 24:22).

In addition, when the prophets thundered their denuncia-
tions against Israel for violating the covenant, they consistently called upon the heavens and the earth to bear witness
against Israel.

Hear, O heavens, and give ear, O earth;
for the Lord has spoken
. . . .

"but Israel does not know,
my people does not understand" (Isa. 1:2-3).

Hear what the Lord says:
  Arise, plead your case before the mountains,
  and let the hills hear your voice.
Hear, you mountains, the controversy of the Lord,
  and you enduring foundations of the earth;
for the Lord has a controversy with his people,
  and he will contend with Israel (Mic. 6:1-2).

The seventh and concluding feature of the suzerainty treaty was a list of blessings and curses. These were to fall upon the vassal, depending upon whether or not he kept the terms of the treaty or violated them. These were the only sanctions found within the treaty. Although none of these are directly tied in with the covenant statement in Exodus 20, there are several lists of them in covenant contexts within the Old Testament (Ex. 23:20-33; Lev. 26; Deut. 27—28).

The study of these ancient documents also showed that when one of the parties died, either the suzerain or the vassal, the covenant had to be renewed. Now, while this was not directly true in Israel, it might further explain the numerous times of covenant renewal. This might also explain the contrast between "us" and "our fathers" in the renewal ceremony in Moab.

And Moses summoned all Israel, and said to them, "Hear, O Israel, the statutes and the ordinances which I speak in your hearing this day, and you shall learn them and be careful to do them. The Lord our God made a covenant with us in Horeb. Not with our fathers did the Lord make this covenant, but with us, who are all of us here alive this day (Deut. 5:1-3).

In summary, the evidence is overwhelming that the basic document and statement of the Israelite faith was given a framework which was borrowed from the world in which they lived. It was clearly adapted and filled with new meaning. But the framework itself is both recognizable and identifiable. It is precisely this which makes it so important. Certain forms communicate certain things, before you ever read the contents. When you get an official-looking envelope and the label identifies it as "Form 1040," you do not even need to open it to know that the letter has to do with your income tax. When your car has been parked overlong on a city street and you see an official looking slip tucked under the windshield wiper, you do not even need to read it to know that you owe a fine to the city. The form itself communicates. So it was with the form in which Israel's covenant was placed. Before any word was read, it was clearly recognizable as identifying God as the great King of Israel. They were to be his obedient servants. The form alone communicated this. The form, then, laid the foundation for their understanding both the content and the claim of God's covenant.

With this as background, let us now turn our attention to the basic meaning of the covenant for Israel. Its foundation rested in the kingship of God. He was the supreme ruler of their nation. Thus, when they later asked for a human king to rule over them, it was seen as a rejection of God.

Then all the elders of Israel gathered together and came to Samuel at Ramah, and said to him, "Behold, you are old and your sons do not walk in your ways; now appoint for us a king to govern us like all the nations." But the thing displeased Samuel. . . . And Samuel prayed to the Lord. And the Lord said to Samuel, "Hearken to the voice of the people in all that they say to you; for they have not rejected you, but they have rejected me from being king over them" (1 Sam. 8:4-7).

It was the covenant which had clearly established the king-servant relationship between God and Israel.

The basic term for covenant in the Old Testament appears to originally have meant "bond" or "fetter." When persons were committed to a covenant, they were considered to have been bound together. In a very real sense, it came to reflect an artificial brotherhood, or an adopted family relationship. This, too, is precisely what is described as existing between Israel and God. The covenant sealed the fact that they had been chosen by God as his sons, or as his bride. We have already pointed this out in our consideration of God's choice of Israel.

Furthermore, the covenant relationship implied a common aim and purpose for the parties to it. In a very real sense, entering into a covenant was equivalent to making peace. The ancient suzerainty treaty was frequently the final act in drawing conflict to a close. While this idea of ending conflict may not have been true in Israel, at the same time, the covenant was frequently connected with the idea of peace. Thus, when Ezekiel looked forward to Israel's restoration after the Exile, he described it in such terms.

I will make with them a covenant of peace and banish wild beasts from the land, so that they may dwell securely in the wilderness and sleep in the woods. And I will make them and the places round about my hill a blessing; and I will send down the showers in their season; they shall be showers of blessing (Ezek. 34:25-26).

I will make a covenant of peace with them; it shall be an everlasting covenant with them; and I will bless them and multiply them, and will set up my sanctuary in the midst of them for evermore. My dwelling place shall be with them; and I will be their God, and they shall be my people (Ezek. 37:26-28).

Making a covenant in the Old Testament was described by the phrase, "to cut a covenant." This may have referred to methods of writing in the ancient Near East, one of which was to inscribe figures in soft clay, while another was to chisel them in stone. Either way, the letters were literally cut into the writing material. On the other hand, covenants were frequently sealed by cutting an animal in half (Gen. 15). The image behind this was the threat that violating the terms of the covenant would result in being treated as the sacrificial victim had been.

Covenants were frequently sealed with a handshake or a kiss (1 Sam. 10:1; 2 Kings 10:15). They were also sealed with a gift (1 Sam. 18:3-4). Covenants of a more serious nature were often sealed with a communion meal (Gen. 26:27-31; 2 Sam. 3:17-21). Although there was no meal directly associated with the giving of the covenant in Exodus, throughout Israel's history the Passover meal was considered to be the major covenant celebration. It is also obvious that Jesus picked up this idea and used it when he instituted the Lord's Supper as the confirmation of his new covenant (Matt. 26:26-28; Mark 14:22-25; 1 Cor. 11:23-26).

It must also be reiterated that the covenant between God and Israel can in no way be considered or evaluated in terms of a treaty between persons on an essential equal footing. There was never any thought of a bargain or of a negotiated agreement. At Sinai, it is quite evident that the initiative was entirely God's. The covenant was offered to Israel on God's terms. They could accept it or reject it. They could not alter it. This may help us to draw a line between the divine

choice of Israel and the covenant with Israel. God chose Israel, and the people had nothing to do with that. The covenant was the expression of his will for the chosen people.
They could reject that. His will was first known in his
choice. It was enlarged and spelled out in his covenant. In
the Exodus, God demonstrated his choice of Israel. At Sinai,
he laid his claims upon their obedient service.

Furthermore, this linking of choice with covenant implied that there was no sense in which the covenant was bi-
lateral. It laid no obligations upon God. He had already
taken up his obligations in his choice of Israel. What the
covenant did was lay obligations upon Israel in obedient
response to the divine act of gracious choice.

The essential fact is that the covenant was unconditional.
It offered no right of termination. Since it rested upon God's
act of choice which sprang from his very nature, he would
always remain loyal to his choice. On the other hand, God
would in no way compel Israel to remain in the covenant.
Such compulsion would destroy its very nature. But the Old
Testament makes it very clear that Israel, once committed
to the covenant, had no right to withdraw from the covenant. The prophets consistently indicated that if Israel
brought the covenant to an end, it was not because she had
the right to do so. Any withdrawal from it was considered as
a dishonorable repudiation. Such actions were described as
treachery and infidelity. They were always morally reprehensible.

Israel could withdraw. God would not. But if Israel did
withdraw, it was always in sinful rebellion. Thus Isaiah
described them,

> Sons I have reared and brought up,
>   but they have rebelled against me.
> . . . .
> Ah, sinful nation,
>   a people laden with iniquity,
> offspring of evildoers,
>   sons who deal corruptly!
> They have forsaken the Lord,
>   they have despised the Holy One of Israel,
>   they are utterly estranged (Isa. 1:2-4).

Hosea and other prophets drew upon the image of adultery
to describe Israel's violation of the covenant. Jeremiah
summed it up,

> Surely, as a faithless wife leaves her husband,
> so have you been faithless to me
> O, house of Israel,
> says the Lord (Jer. 3:20).

Israel's rejection of the covenant was itself rejected by the prophets.

The covenant traditions of the Old Testament place a major emphasis upon the formal covenant at Sinai. At the same time, there was a less formal expression of the covenant with the patriarchs. They both fit well into the whole Old Testament concept of divine choice and divine covenant. Whenever God chose to act in grace, he sealed that choice with a covenant which laid obligations upon his people. The obligations were always for their own good, though they did not always see them that way at the time.

Finally, in the ultimate understanding of the covenant, we are brought face to face with the loyalty of God as contrasted with the failure of Israel. The entire history of Israel demonstrated that Israel failed to keep the covenant over and over again. When Israel rejected the covenant, it was considered treachery and infidelity.

Furthermore, we have noted that even if Israel rejected the covenant, God would not reject his chosen ones. He would not fail Israel, even if Israel failed him. This is precisely what he did. In his grace, he did not cast them off but pursued them, seeking to renew his claim upon their loyalty.

Hosea proclaimed this most effectively.

> Therefore I will hedge up her way with thorns;
> and I will build a wall against her,
> so that she cannot find her paths.
> She shall pursue her lovers,
> but not overtake them;
> and she shall seek them,
> but shall not find them.
> Then she shall say, "I will go
> and return to my first husband,
> for it was better with me then than now."
> . . . .
>
> Therefore, behold, I will allure her,
> and bring her into the wilderness,
> and speak tenderly to her.
> . . . .

> And there she shall answer as in the days of her
>   youth,
>   as at the time when she came out of the land of
>   Egypt.
> And in that day, says the Lord,
>   you will call me, "My husband"
>   (Hos. 2:6-7,14-16).

He described God as taking Israel back into the wilderness where he would again woo and win her love, initiating a new betrothal and marriage.

Thus the prophets portrayed God's judgment of Israel as being redemptive in purpose. He was constantly seeking to win her back to his love and to the fruits of his blessings within the covenant. So the story of Israel became a story of sin and salvation, of judgment and redemption, and of rebellion and restoration. God was ever able to bless and to save. He was ever willing to do so if and when Israel would return to his loving will in obedience.

It was out of this that there grew the hope of a new covenant. Hosea first stated it (Hos. 2:18-23). But Jeremiah fully developed it with his magnificent vision of God's future.

Behold, the days are coming, says the Lord, when I will make a new covenant with the house of Israel and the house of Judah, not like the covenant which I made with their fathers when I took them by the hand to bring them out of the land of Egypt, my covenant which they broke, though I was their husband, says the Lord. But this is the covenant which I will make with the house of Israel after those days, says the Lord: I will put my law within them, and I will write it upon their hearts; and I will be their God, and they shall be my people. And no longer shall each man teach his neighbor and each his brother, saying, "Know the Lord," for they shall all know me, from the least of them to the greatest, says the Lord; for I will forgive their iniquity, and I will remember their sin no more (Jer. 31:31-34).

This idea will be dealt with more fully in chapter 8, when we consider Israel's hope for the future.

However, we must note that the covenant was expected to be man's response to God's free choice. When the response failed, Israel put herself outside of the covenant. But she could not put herself outside of God's free choice. That still stood.

Increasingly, the prophets realized that Israel's capacity to respond to the claims of God's gracious acts would be possible only if God did something to her heart, to her very nature. It was that for which they longed and that to which they looked with eager expectation. So God said through Ezekiel,

A new heart will I give you, and a new spirit I will put within you; and I will take out of your flesh the heart of stone and give you a heart of flesh. And I will put my spirit within you, and cause you to walk in my statutes and be careful to observe my ordinances (Ezek. 36:26-27).

Only by God's new act of grace could the covenant be renewed and its claims be met. Through all of this, one conviction remained sure. God's covenant with Israel would never be broken on his side.

One last word needs to be said about the covenant. Since we have the advantage of viewing it from this side of the cross and know the ultimate fulfillment of the New Covenant concept in Jesus, we must note that there were certain limitations to the old covenant which had to be removed before it could ultimately be fulfilled. It, too, was a step in God's developing revelation.

It was not with individuals, but with the nation. This became a real issue in the preaching of Jeremiah and Ezekiel. The response of a group can never command the inner response of an individual. Furthermore, the old covenant was primarily with those having legal rights. Thus it really did not command the response of children, wives, slaves, and foreigners. They were merely carried along with the group.

Finally, the covenant itself presented only a limited understanding of God. He was met primarily as King and Lawgiver. Through its background, he was also seen as Redeemer. But he was not seen in the covenant in the full revelation of his person. This remained for Jesus Christ to reveal.

So the old covenant was limited. It failed. But it pointed beyond itself to the God of elective choice who ultimately called all people to himself through Jesus Christ. Further, it prepared us to better understand what Jesus did and is doing.

5
Man as God's Creature

INTRO

To this point, we have given our attention to the Old Testament understanding of God. He was the supreme fact of life for Israel. But we must remember that there were two main characters upon the stage of the experience of these ancient men. They were God and man. Genesis 1 points out the place of God in his universe as sovereign Lord. Genesis 2 describes the creation of man and the dominion he was given over his world. All the rest of the Bible gives its attention to these two central figures and the relationships between them. To fully grasp the roots which the Old Testament has for understanding the New Testament, we must now turn our consideration to this second actor on the stage of the divine drama of redemption.

We have noted that God was primarily understood by the Hebrews in relation to his actions in their world and lives. We should also note that their understanding of mankind, of themselves, was primarily framed by their relation with God. So if we are really going to grasp something of their self-awareness, we must do so by directing our attention to "man as God's creature."

I. Man as an Individual

The problem of the nature of man is just about as old as man himself. It has been raised from the earliest times.

When I look at thy heavens, the work of thy fingers,
  the moon and the stars which thou hast established;
what is man that thou art mindful of him,
  and the son of man that thou dost care for him?
Yet thou has made him little less than God,
  and dost crown him with glory and honor.
Thou has given him dominion over the works of thy hands;
  thou hast put all things under his feet (Ps. 8:3-6).

The Hebrews were always aware of man's significance and insignificance. In considering their own existence, they focused their attention upon two major aspects of his existence, his individuality and his corporateness. He was always an individual, standing in the presence of God. But at the same time, he never stood alone. He was always part of a larger group, a family, a clan, a tribe, or the nation itself. We must become familiar with both of these dimensions of his self-understanding.

   Man as a Creation of God. Human nature was always in the forefront of the Hebrew's self-consciousness. He knew himself to be something far less than God. A good summary of this aspect of his thinking can be found by considering the basic words by which he described himself. These portray both his finitude, his creatureliness, and his relationship to God.

   Foundational to this aspect of his existence was the term "dust." We are told,

   the Lord God formed man of dust from the ground,
   and breathed into his nostrils the breath of life;
   and man became a living being (Gen. 2:7).

Following Adam's rebellion in the Garden of Eden, God concluded his pronouncement of judgment by saying,

     In the sweat of your face
       you shall eat bread
     till you return to the ground,
       for out of it you were taken;
     you are dust,
       and to dust you shall return (Gen. 3:19).

There was no basis for pride or self-exaltation here. It is quite humbling to be described as dust. Dust is something you tread on, shake off your feet, and sweep away.

The proper understanding of this idea is most fruitful for grasping the Old Testament concept of human life. That man was made by God out of "dust from the ground" and had life breathed into him was a basic affirmation of the Old Testament. Whatever else he might become, whatever else he might achieve, man was still dust.

Man was never thought of as a noble spirit temporarily imprisoned in the evil matter of the body. That idea, in fact, became one of the heresies which the New Testament Christians had to combat. In his natural state as God had created him, man was a unified creation, having life in the same manner as all of God's living creatures. The material world was man's natural habitat. Whatever else may be added to both the Old Testament and the New Testament conceptions of life, this can never be subtracted.

Yet, even though man was dust, he was more than mere dust. He was the special creation of the living God. God had breathed something into him.

The Hebrews also described man as "flesh." This had a much wider meaning than animal flesh. Flesh can be an outer manifestation of the inner being. It clearly refers to the entire human being.

> Therefore my heart is happy,
>   and my glory rejoices;
> yea, my flesh dwells securely
>   (Ps. 16:9, author's translation).

Furthermore, to be of "one flesh" by either kinship or by marriage is to have the whole being related to another (Gen. 37:27; 2:24).

For the Old Testament, man was of the earth. He was flesh and dust. Yet, he was more than this, much more. For he was also a soul, a living soul. Unfortunately, a number of poor translations in years gone by have given us some misconceptions concerning the meaning of this idea. When we are told that God "breathed into his nostrils the breath of life; and man became a living being" (Gen. 2:7), the Hebrew term is *nephesh hayah*. Some interpreters have sought to use this to differentiate between man and animals. But this cannot be done. For when Genesis tells us that God made "living creatures" (Gen. 1:20-21,24), the term there is also *nephesh hayah*. What, then, does this term describe?

First, the *nephesh* cannot be separated from the body. Man is animated dust, indwelt by a *nephesh*. There is reason to believe that its original meaning was "throat" or "neck." (It was never used with this meaning in the Old Testament, but it does have that use in other Semitic languages.) By Old Testament times, the word had had a slight shift in meaning. When applied to man, it appears to have three related meanings. It was the basic life principle. Closely akin to breath, it was that which was absolutely necessary for life to exist. It was associated both with breath and with blood. In the absence of either, life was not possible. It was also occasionally used almost like a pronoun, referring to the person as a whole.

The most common usage of *nephesh* when applied to a person referred to the totality of his being. Desire and excitement originated in the *nephesh*. It apparently referred to the inner life of a person, but there was always some kind of outward manifestation. It is imperative that we note that the *nephesh* did not go on with some kind of separate existence after death. In fact, there is at least one reference where a corpse was called a *nephesh* (Num. 5:2). Intimately related to life itself, the *nephesh* of a person normally existed only as long as the person lived. It was certainly a step in the revelation of the concept of the soul of man. But in no way can it itself really be described as a human soul. Unfortunately, we have no English word which adequately translates this Hebrew term. Therefore, more often than not, translators use either "breath," or "soul." Neither is at all adequate.

It is worth noting that the Hebrews had no word for body. When they wished to speak of a person's body, they used either the word for flesh or they used *nephesh*. When they used this latter term, they seemed to reflect the idea that the *nephesh* was an inner aspect of the body. A person's physical existence apparently was the outer manifestation of his *nephesh*.

The last term we shall use to help us understand man's creatureliness is the word for spirit. In its background, this word also apparently originally meant "wind," or "breath." There was no difference in the form of the word when it was used of God's Spirit or when it was used of man's spirit.

Frequently it was used in such a way as to make man's spirit be understood as a gift of God which was not really permanent within a man (Num. 11:17,25-26; 1 Sam. 11:6; 16:14). In this sense it referred to some kind of divine power which indwelt a person. Yet, there is also a sense in which the spirit of a person was always present as long as there was life. In this sense it is clearly man's spirit and not God's Spirit.

Again, we must note that the Hebrews never viewed the spirit of man as the ancient Greeks did. In the Old Testament, the spirit may be a permanent part of man. But the Hebrews never understood the spirit of a man to have an existence apart from the body. Rather, it appeared to refer to the higher and nobler aspects of man's consciousness. For the Hebrew, neither spirit, *nephesh*, nor human flesh existed apart from one another. It took all three together to have a real person.

We might say that the spirit was the upper or higher part of the *nephesh*. The *nephesh* was always the lower, more earthy side of man's spiritual being. Both spirit and *nephesh* were the inner aspect of the flesh of a person. Flesh was the outer side of a person's spiritual nature.

It is very significant to note the impact this whole concept had on the development of God's revelation. Given this kind of understanding of human existence, no Hebrew could ever have believed that Jesus was alive after his crucifixion if there had not been a bodily resurrection. From their standpoint, it was necessary for flesh, *nephesh*, and spirit to be reunited for there to be any meaningful life. Furthermore, the same is true for the New Testament hope of an individual bodily resurrection. This, too, was necessary for the hope to have any real meaning to the Hebrews of Jesus' day. The Greeks could have believed in a "spiritual" existence and been satisfied. Not so the Hebrews. Thus it was that God provided precisely the evidence which was needed to offer the early Jewish Christians a basis for both faith and hope. Such is the divine power and wisdom.

Man, then, was God's creature. He was not equal with God, since he had been made by God. Yet at the same time, neither was he just a higher animal. He was related to the animals by his flesh and his *nephesh*. But his spirit made him different. Although he was made of the earth, by his spirit he was intended for fellowship with God.

B. ***Man's Self-Understanding.*** The Hebrews had a larger view of man, however, than simply as God's creature. We can begin to understand some of this larger self-understanding by examining the way in which they described the various parts of the body. It is obvious that a man is more than the mere sum of the parts of the body. At the same time, a study of this kind of self-analysis is a great help in aiding our understanding of what the Hebrews really thought about themselves.

To the ancient Hebrews, the heart was not connected with the emotions (as we use it) but with the will, mind, and purpose. Directly connected with the intellectual side of man, the heart was the center of willing and reasoning. The Hebrew had no word for brain, calling it simply, "marrow of the head." Neither did they have a word for the human will. Here they frequently used "heart" to refer to the purpose of a man. Thus, they said, "Pharaoh's heart was hardened," to indicate that his purpose was solidly set (Ex. 7:13). And when the inhabitants of Shechem had a set purpose to follow Abimelech, we are told: "And their hearts inclined to follow Abimelech" (Judg. 9:3). Furthermore, when Jonathan's armor-bearer wished to express a common purpose with his master, he said simply, "Behold, I am with you, as is your heart, so is mine" (1 Sam. 14:7, author's translation).

The more common usage of the heart, however, was simply to describe the mind. A very common expression, "call to heart," simply meant to remember, to call to mind. In addition, when Solomon responded to God's offer of a gift, he prayed,

Give thy servant therefore an understanding heart to govern thy people, that I may discern between good and evil; for who is able to govern this, thy great people? (1 Kings 3:9, author's translation).

Further, the psalmist prayed,

Let the words of my mouth
and the meditation of my heart
be acceptable in thy sight,
O Lord, my rock and my redeemer (Ps. 19:14).

The heart was the place of judgment, thought, and meditation. Heart was also used to describe what we mean by
conscience. Thus Job appealed to a clear conscience as
proof of his innocence.

> I hold fast my righteousness,
>   and will not let it go;
> my heart does not reproach me
>   for any of my days (Job 27:6).

And when David was hit by a guilty conscience, we are told,
"And afterward David's heart smote him, because he had
cut off Saul's skirt" (1 Sam. 24:5). The Psalms described a
man's desire for a clear conscience by saying,

> Create in me a clean heart, O God,
>   and put a new and right spirit within me (Ps. 51:10).

Jeremiah also denied the validity of the old saying, "Let
your conscience be your guide," by bluntly proclaiming,

> The heart is deceitful above all things,
>   and desperately corrupt;
> who can understand it? (Jer. 17:9).

Thus the heart was not so much where a person felt, it was
where he thought, determined his life's purposes, and
knew guilt or innocence. This is of major significance, for it
places a new emphasis upon the evangelism of the New
Testament. Paul wrote,

> If you confess with your lips that Jesus is Lord and be-
> lieve in your heart that God raised him from the dead, you
> will be saved. For man believes with his heart and so is jus-
> tified, and he confesses with his lips and so is saved (Rom.
> 10:9-10).

His basis for salvation was the commitment of the mind,
the will, or the purpose to the Lord Jesus. Salvation is not
dependent upon a response of the emotion but of the will.
This does not mean that there may not be any emotion to it.
But it does mean that the fundamental commitment to
Christ must come from the will. This is the emphasis of the
last invitation which the Bible contains.

> The Spirit and the Bride say, "Come." And let him who
> hears say, "Come." And let him who is thirsty come, let him

who *desires* [wills, purposes] take the water of life without price (Rev. 22:17, italics mine).

The second major term which aids understanding of the Hebrews' self-awareness is "blood." Obviously, in most instances blood refers literally to the fluid which flows in the human body. However, the word also seems to be symbolic of death, particularly of violent death. When the prophets speak of the land being "filled with blood," they are using this meaning.

For our purposes, the most significant meaning of blood is set forth in the expression, "the life is the blood."

You shall not eat flesh with its life, that is, its blood (Gen. 9:4).

For the life of the flesh is in the blood; and I have given it for you upon the altar to make atonement for your souls; for it is the blood that makes atonement, by reason of the life (Lev. 17:11).

Only be sure that you do not eat the blood; for the blood is the life, and you shall not eat the life with the flesh (Deut. 12:23).

The basis for these statements was probably the practical observation that whenever a person or an animal lost its blood; it quit living. However, the theological significance is far greater. The context of these and other passages seem to indicate very clearly that this emphasis was clearly descriptive of the life which ended when the blood was released. Thus a murderer was said to have blood upon his hands or upon his head. It was not really the blood which was there but the guilt of having taken a life. "To conceal blood" was to hide the fact that a life had been taken. To murder a man, or to take his life by any unjust means was "to sin against innocent blood."

Now, if blood became synonymous with life, and it appears that it did, then the sacredness of blood would appear to rest in the fact that only God can give life. Man can take it away, but he cannot give it. Therefore, the blood was especially sacred, for it was the symbol of what God alone could give—life!

The significance of this for its New Testament development is quite obvious: the blood of Jesus. Thus, Paul said,

Since, therefore, we are now justified by his blood, much more shall we be saved by him from the wrath of God. For if while we were enemies we were reconciled to God by the death of his Son, much more, now that we are reconciled, shall we be saved by his life (Rom. 5:9-10).

Here he was drawing a conclusion based upon the Old Testament concept that the life is in the blood. For Paul, when Jesus gave his blood for our sins, he had given his life.

The third term of major significance for our understanding of the Hebrews' self-awareness is "bowels." This was the seat of the emotions. This is paralleled by our contemporary expression of a "gut-feeling." Used in a similar way were the words for "kidneys" or "loins." Thus Job said, after his great passage of hope and confidence, "My kidneys faint within me" (Job 19:27, author's translation). Furthermore, we are all familiar with the expression, "bowels of compassion," as used in the King James Version of the Bible (1 John 3:17).

In addition, there are other terms describing parts of the body which give further insights into their self-understanding. Thus the "right hand" became symbolic for authority. The "arm" became a synonym for power. The "foot" was often used in the sense of one person subjugating another. In all of these (as well as in others) man was always seen as limited. He was bound by limitations of space and time. He might be more than a body, but without a body, he was nothing. The Hebrew emphasis upon the concrete is never more plainly seen than in his understanding of his own nature.

Co   **Death as the End of Life.** In numerous ways, the Old Testament view of death is quite different from that of modern people. At death, the unity of man was broken up. When flesh, *nephesh*, and spirit were separated, man ceased to exist. Men were never allowed to forget their mortality. Man was certainly akin to God. But he was also akin to the animals in that he dies. The Genesis writer clearly pointed out that the illusion of a natural or inherent immortality was the serpent's lie. It was the serpent who said to Eve, "You will not die" (Gen. 3:4). Rather, death was the common denominator for all men. "The wise man dies just like the fool!" (Eccl. 2:16).

The Old Testament had no general concept of life after death. When death came, all was over. Although there were some glimmers of the possibility of life after death, they never became the mainstream of Old Testament thought. (We shall consider this in detail in chapter 8 in the section on "Individual Destiny.") We must remember that the whole question was still very much in dispute in New Testament times. The Sadducees, who did not believe in a resurrection, sought to entrap Jesus in such an argument (Matt. 22:23-33). Furthermore, when Paul was put on trial in Jerusalem, the mention of the resurrection of the dead put the entire Sanhedrin into conflict.

A dissension arose between the Pharisees and the Sadducees; and the assembly was divided. For the Sadducees say that there is no resurrection, nor angel, nor spirit; but the Pharisees acknowledge them all. . . . And when the dissension became violent, the tribune, afraid that Paul would be torn in pieces by them, commanded the soldiers to go down and take him by force from among them and bring him into the barracks (Acts 23:7-10).

But even in the mainstream of Old Testament thought, death was never regarded as mere nonexistence. Death was seen as a very weak form of life. The Hebrews spoke of "shades" or "shadows" who lived in the abode of the dead. But theirs was not a true existence, such as life on earth. On the other hand, they were related to those who had gone before in the same way that a person's shadow is related to his actual body. This was apparently a step in the developing idea of some kind of life beyond the grave. The most common Old Testament expression for death was being "gathered to his fathers." This was an apparent reference to joining their shades in this shadow world of existence.

The abode of the dead was known as Sheol. This at times seems to be little more than a synonym for the grave. At other times, it comes to be understood as the place where the shades lived. It was there that people's shadows went after death. At the very best, it was a foul region of virtual annihilation. Once a person entered Sheol, the gates were locked tight and no one could return to the "land of the living." Furthermore, in Sheol there could be no fellowship with God, the Giver of life. Thus the psalmist mourned,

> For in death there is no remembrance of thee;
> in Sheol who can give thee praise? (Ps. 6:5).

But not only is Sheol the abode of the dead, "drawing near to Sheol" refers to the approach of death, or at least of the threat of death. It becomes clear from a study of the many psalms which speak of Sheol that the fear of death arose not so much from the fear of extinction but from the fear of an ultimate separation from God.

At best, Sheol was but a pale reflection of the world of life and light. The very darkness of Sheol reflected the absence of any real presence of God. At worst, Sheol became the land of silent forgetfulness, from which all light was banned and any relationship with God was halted.

In a very real sense, to the Hebrew death was both the end of life and the weakest form of life. Because of this, any kind of weakness in life could be described as a form of death. To be alive, really alive, implied the possession of one's powers in their fullness. Anything less than this was something less than full life. The basic Hebrew view then came to be that to have sickness or disability in body was to already have begun experiencing the disintegrating power of death. This probably explains the reason behind the fact that infirmity of body brought about the same kind of ritual uncleanness as death did.

In addition, to be or become sick or infirm was to be brought to the very gates of Sheol. But the opposite was also true. To enjoy good health was to be allowed to walk with God in the fullness of life.

Although the Genesis writer plainly connected death with man's sinful rebellion, this became a major belief in later Old Testament times. Any form of death, illness or otherwise, came to be understood as a direct consequence of man's sin. (To this we shall return in chapter 6, in the section on "The Consequences of Sin.")

The Hebrew attitudes toward death were generally very little different from those which we find common today.

There was an attitude of complete indifference. As evidence of this, consider the conniving and the struggle between Jacob and Esau while their father Isaac was about to die (Gen. 27). Death was faced as a normal reality of life. It could neither be avoided nor escaped. The affairs of life were far more important than the impending death of a loved one.

On the other hand, when death faced an individual, he was not so indifferent or fatalistic in his attitude. The psalmists reflect a growing terror at the coming of death. There are several instances recorded where a person about to die took extreme measures to ward off the onslaught of death. In this case, consider the plight of Hezekiah or of Naaman the leper (Isa. 38:1-8; 2 Kings 5:1-14). There was a definite and growing opposition to death.

But at the same time, there were those whose lives had become so distasteful that they longed for death. Job is a case in point.

> After this Job opened his mouth and cursed the day
> of his birth. And Job said:
> "Let the day perish wherein I was born."
> "Why did I not die at birth,
> come forth from the womb and expire?"
> "Why is light given to him that is in misery,
> and life to the bitter in soul,
> who long for death, but it comes not,
> and dig for it more than for hid treasures;
> who rejoice exceedingly,
> and are glad, when they find the grave?"
> (Job 3:1-3,11,20-22).

Jeremiah on several occasions also appears to have longed for death.

In general, however, the Old Testament attitude toward death was that of common sense. They did not spend much time in what we would call philosophical reflection. Death was a fact of life. It was unavoidable. It came unsought, but it was not to be denied when it came. Man's mortality was not generally protested. The world was good. God was good. Since death was a part of the world experience, it would have been both impious and ungrateful to have treated death as otherwise. Thus Job expressed the traditional attitude when he said,

Naked I came from my mother's womb, and naked shall I return; the Lord gave, and the Lord has taken away; blessed be the name of the Lord (Job 1:21).

Shall we receive good at the hand of God, and shall we not receive evil? (Job 2:10).

Near the end of the Old Testament era, Israel began to raise questions about whether or not there was not something more or better beyond. They began to raise some questions which the traditional attitudes could not answer. But we must wait to discuss their answer until we get to the whole concept of their hope for the future.

Man as a Part of a Community

In contemporary society, we have placed great emphasis upon man as an individual. We praise individuality and seem to place a premium upon establishing our own identity. This was not so in ancient Israel. They placed a major emphasis upon being a part of a larger group, whether that group was a family, a clan, a tribe, or the nation. The larger group appears to have had a solidarity of which the individual was a distinct but interrelated part. No person was an island, but what he was impinged upon all other members of his group, even as what they were impinged upon him. In a very real sense, the individual was often thought to be the extension of his group.

Foundational to this is the concept of corporate responsibility for sin. The private sin of a person was never thought of as his own private affair. When Israel was told to destroy everything in Jericho, "Achan the son of Carmi, son of Zabdi, son of Zerah, of the tribe of Judah, took some of the devoted things" (Josh. 7:1). Although only one man sinned, we are told that "the people of Israel broke faith" (Josh. 7:1). This was later underscored when Joshua was told,

Israel has sinned; they have transgressed my covenant which I commanded them; they have taken some of the devoted things; they have stolen, and lied, and put them among their own stuff. Therefore the people of Israel cannot stand before their enemies (Josh. 7:11-12).

Ultimately, when it was discovered that Achan was guilty, it was not considered sufficient to destroy Achan, but his family and all of his possessions were destroyed as well (Josh. 7:24-25). Achan's sin brought punishment to all of Israel and his guilt rested upon his whole family.

The same thing could be pointed out about Jeroboam, the son of Nebat, the first king of the Northern Kingdom of Israel. We are told frequently that he sinned and that "he made Israel to sin." By this it was apparently meant not merely that he set a bad example for the nation through his sin, but that his sin brought corporate guilt upon the entire nation. Furthermore, we also see in this example that a person was not only related corporately to his contemporaries, but that he was united both with those generations which had gone before and those which would come after.

This sense of corporateness has a very specific relation to the development of the New Testament. Thus Jesus wraps all believers in his own personality, so that we receive the benefit of his death and resurrection. Further, one of Paul's favorite images of the church is the "body of Christ." By this he clearly seems to indicate that we are all part of one another. While the finger is not the hand and the eye is not the foot, no part of the body can get along without all the rest.

> For the body does not consist of one member but of many. As it is, there are many parts, yet one body.
> If one member suffers, all suffer together; if one member is honored, all rejoice together. Now you are the body of Christ and individually members of it (1 Cor. 12:14,20, 26-27).

Now all of this is not to deny that a person is also an individual. But we need to recognize that the Old Testament clearly teaches our interrelatedness and the New Testament picks this up and further emphasizes it. This sense of corporateness was so central, in fact, that the people constantly explained the catastrophes which came upon them by blaming the sins of their fathers. It remained for both Jeremiah and Ezekiel to attack this idea, laying an emphasis upon individual responsibility as well.

> In those days they shall no longer say:
> "The fathers have eaten sour grapes,
>   and the children's teeth are set on edge."
> But every one shall die for his own sin; each man who

eats sour grapes, his teeth shall be set on edge
   (Jer. 31:29-30).

The word of the Lord came to me again: "What do you
mean by repeating this proverb concerning the land of Israel, 'The fathers have eaten sour grapes, and the children's teeth are set on edge'? As I live, says the Lord God,
this proverb shall no more be used by you in Israel. Behold,
all souls are mine; the soul of the father as well as the soul
of the son is mine: the soul that sins shall die" (Ezek.
18:1-4).

At the same time, however, even though these prophets
underscored personal responsibility for sin, they also continued to emphasize the corporateness of the nation. Man
then, was both individual and corporate. Always belonging
to a group, he was also personally responsible for his own
sin. He could not blame someone else.

To the absolute contrary, modern society has developed
its psychology and sociology. At one time, we wish to assert
our individuality, claiming, "What I do won't hurt anyone
else." Yet, whenever we get into trouble, we wish to blame
our heritage, our childhood, or our society. We do not wish
to accept responsibility for our acts. How tragic. We desper-
ately need to hear this word from the Old Testament. I am a
part of a corporate body. There is no way I can escape this.
But at the same time, I am responsible for my own sin. I cannot escape that either.

III. The Image of God

Of extreme significance in any consideration of the Old
Testament's view of man as God's creature is the image of
God. This is a term which has frequently been ignored by
interpreters and even more frequently treated with a su-
perficiality which belies its importance. The concept is certainly of more importance than the number of passages in
which it occurs might indicate. It underlies a great deal of
the Old Testament thought about man and was also picked
up and used in the New Testament.

The key passage for our consideration is found in the first
chapter of the Bible.

Then God said, "Let us make man in our image, after our
likeness; and let them have dominion over the fish of the

sea, and over the birds of the air, and over the cattle, and over all the earth, and over every creeping thing that creeps upon the earth." So God created man in his own image, in the image of God he created him; male and female he created them. And God blessed them, and God said to them, "Be fruitful and multiply, and fill the earth and subdue it; and have dominion over the fish of the sea and over the birds of the air, and over every living thing that moves upon the earth" (Gen. 1:26-28).

It is both easy and simple to state that man was created in God's image. It is quite another thing to clearly understand what was meant by that expression.

It has been suggested that the Hebrews conceived of God as having some kind of form long after he outgrew the ancient anthropomorphisms of an earlier age. God is spirit, but he was never conceived of as being formless spirit. It would appear that he differs at this point from man, not in the absence of form but in the "stuff" of his being. The Old Testament is clear about the fact that God exhibits his form in glory (Ex. 16:7,10; 24:17; 33:18,22; and others). In the light of this we may conclude that man was created in a bodily form on the divine pattern.

There are those who would disagree most emphatically. They begin by describing the Old Testament anthropomorphisms as mere accommodations to human speech, in no way to be taken literally. They would say that God was understood as pure spirit, able to assume a form when necessary without having any. If this is true, then it becomes very difficult to assume that the image of God refers to any kind of form at all. Rather, it would apply only to spiritual and intangible characteristics.

It appears to me that the truth lies somewhere between these extremes. The identical words used to describe the relation between God and man in Genesis 1 were also used to describe the relationship between Adam and Seth just four chapters later.

When Adam had lived a hundred and thirty years, he became the father of a son in his own likeness, after his image, and named him Seth (Gen. 5:3).

It is quite obvious here that the writer was using the terms "image" and "likeness" to refer to a physical resemblance.

A son does resemble his father. To deny any kind of form, then, seems too strong a position to take. On the other hand, God is spirit. He is certainly far more than form. It would appear that merely to limit the image of God to a resemblance in form is to be far too limiting. The image of God in man is far more than mere form.

In God's plan before man's creation was the idea of dominion, authority. In his first command to man after his creation, authority and dominion were given. Mankind was told to reproduce, to subdue the earth, and to have an authority over all the living creatures of the earth. Just as God had supreme authority over his creation, so man was given a limited authority and power over the world and its creatures. This would certainly seem to indicate that "the image of God" included this authority.

Furthermore, within the Genesis narrative we note that the distinction between man and the other orders of animal life was not so much a matter of physical form as of a spiritual nature. It was this that he shared with God over against the lower creation. Like the animals, he had a physical body which was vitalized by breath and blood. Yet, it is certainly not a complete statement of the biblical view of man to say that he is simply an animated body. In his spiritual nature he was made for God's fellowship and obedient service. With no other creature did God fellowship! Yet he walked and talked with man in the cool of the evening. Furthermore, no command of God was laid upon the animals as it was upon man. And to none of the animals was moral freedom attributed. Thus we can also say that a part of the image of God appears to be the spiritual nature of man.

It is characteristic of the thought of the Old Testament that man may understand and do the will of God. He is expected to walk in the way which God designates. He was not just God's creature. He was created for God's service. The psalmist sings,

> Yet thou hast made him little less than God,
>   and dost crown him with glory and honor (Ps. 8:5).

If angels are thought of as having been created to serve God in heaven, man is thought of as having been created to serve God on earth. God's command was laid upon him in the moment of creation. The command was not something harsh or irksome that subjected man to harsh domination by his Creator. It was also recognized that obedience to God was not just man's duty. It was also his privilege. Further, obedience to God brought blessing.

It was this obedience which made fellowship possible with God. But that fellowship with God was broken by man's disobedience. The ultimate calamity which befell man in the narrative of his sin in the Garden of Eden was that he was thrust forth from the presence of God and no longer enjoyed the free intercourse with his maker. In the beginning, however, there was fellowship.

Following the breach of this fellowship, the story of the Old Testament and the history of mankind points up the fact that man has an incurable religiosity. From all ages and under all conditions, man has sought for God. There is something in the image of God that makes it impossible for man to find a complete life apart from God. It just may be that man's search for God is also a part of the image of God.

Be that as it may, image is almost certainly to be seen in the statement, "male and female he created them" (Gen. 1:27). This is not to imply that there is a male-female relationship within the Godhead. This is very pointedly denied throughout all of the Old Testament. Rather, it appears that the image of God is most clearly seen in a loving relationship, in a community of love. Perhaps nowhere else is God's image seen so clearly as in the loving, self-giving relationship of two people who are committed to one another.

The idea of the image of God does not occur anywhere else in the Old Testament outside of Genesis. It is only restated one time here.

Whoever sheds the blood of man, by man shall his blood be shed; for God made man in his own image (Gen. 9:6).

In this blunt passage on judgment, mankind was warned that justice and judgment would be visited upon anyone who destroyed the image of God in another. Is it possible that this also warns us against destroying the image of God in ourselves?

Even though the actual term, "the image of God" does not show up elsewhere in the Old Testament, its implications show up over and over again. It may be and almost certainly is in the idea of man's spirit, the upper, higher dimension of his *nephesh*. God is spirit and man has spirit. Man's physical being, as we have seen earlier in this chapter, is an outward expression of his inward being. His inner being is an expression of God's image.

Certainly, the New Testament picks up the concept of the image of God and carries it further. Thus Paul described Jesus as being "the image of the invisible God" (Col. 1:15). He goes immediately from this and relates it to authority, fellowship, and obedience. Further, when God sought to reestablish the image which man had marred with his sin, he placed the redeemed man in a new community of love, the church. It is in this new community of love that the image of God is most clearly seen. Being new creatures in Christ, the divine image has been recreated in us (2 Cor. 5:17).

If any man would see the perfect image of God, we must point him to Jesus. If he would see the image of God in ordinary human lives, we should point him to the church. The image of God in the world today should be best seen, not in the individual Christian, but in the Christian who is in a loving relationship with his fellows. How tragic that we so frequently mar that renewed image with our same old pride and pettiness.

Man's Relationship with God

Man, then, is God's creature. Each of us is an individual, yet we are all part of one another. We cannot, we dare not isolate ourselves from one another. Furthermore, we were all made in the image of God. We were intended for fellowship with him and for service of him. We were intended to live in a loving relationship with one another. We were also given a spiritual nature, so that our hearts would be restless until they found rest in God.

It is our spiritual kinship with God which is at the bottom of all man's religiousness. It is, sadly, this spiritual kinship which exalts our pride, making us seek to be equal with God. This is the basis of our sin, as we shall see in the following chapter.

Yet the Old Testament never lost sight of the fact that man is other than God. He has been made but little lower than God, but he is always lower than God (Ps. 8:5). On the other hand, the Old Testament is equally clear that man should not be thought of as totally different from God. Any such idea could hardly be accepted by any believer in the incarnation.

Man's body is clearly inhabited by something more than breath. He also has a spirit—a personality which both differentiates him from the animals and identifies him with God. God is also thought of in terms of spirit. As such, he is able to communicate his Spirit to man. This is a major element in the Old Testament thought of both God and man.

Man also has the commands of God laid upon him. He is expected to obey them in serving God. But the commands are always for man's own best interests. They are designed so that obeying them brings blessing upon man.

Finally, man may in some measure be lifted into the very personality of God. He can be inspired, hear the word of God, speak with God, and proclaim God's word to other men. He can be filled with God's spirit to serve at the altar, exercise political leadership, or share wisdom with those who follow after.

When all else is said, man is God's special creation. As such, he has a special relation with his Creator. But man can destroy that relationship. Man was created to be little lower than God. This is his best. But at his worst, man becomes little better than a demon. It is this side of his nature to which we must now turn.

6
Man
in Rebellion

INTRO Most children's fairy tales end with the refrain, "and they lived happily ever after." It would certainly seem that the Old Testament story of man should have ended that way. Man was God's creature, the capstone of creation. Made in the image of God, he was intended for fellowship with his Creator. Made little lower than God, he was the object of the loyal love of his sovereign Lord.

But the Old Testament is no fairy tale. Adam and his children did not live happily ever after. The story had a tragic ending. Man's life with God was marred, the relationship was spoiled, and man became little higher than the demonic. The Old Testament is quite clear about what God's intent for man was. But it is equally clear that all did not go well. This brings us face to face with man's sinful rebellion against his creator. If we are going to understand the rest of the Old Testament message, we must grasp its understanding of sin, for man was a sinner. He still is. And the Old Testament has a great deal to say about this fact of human existence.

I. The Concepts of Sin

In the thought of the Old Testament, man had been given moral freedom. He could freely make his own choices, establishing his own patterns of life. Therefore, he could

148

use his freedom to resist the will of God. This he did. It was sin that came between man and God, destroying the intimate fellowship of the Garden days. Its ultimate consequence was to bring calamity upon man.

As we consider the Old Testament teachings about sin, it becomes obvious that a large number of the specific sins which are mentioned were ritual offenses, violations of the worship codes. But this was not the whole concept of sin in the Old Testament. In fact, outside of those sections which deal with Levitical or priestly concerns, it was really not very significant. We must not ignore the fact that while much of the law codes were concerned with ritual, the Old Testament has a deep and genuine concern with moral sin.

Furthermore, all acts of ritual cleansing for which provision was made were to be accompanied both by penitence and by restitution where it was possible. The law itself never encouraged the easy thought that sin was a light matter. It was never the intention of the law that sin could be dealt with merely by a formal act which was no more than a formal act.

It is also quite likely that those who, in Israel's later history, so magnified ritual offenses had a deeper truth in mind. If ritual sins were to be taken so seriously, then the more grievous sins were to be held with the deepest horror.

At the outset, sin was recognized as being man's own spontaneous act of disobedience to God. Even when man listens to the seductive voices which lure him away from God, his act of disobedience is always his own. The fundamental character of sin as portrayed in the Old Testament is seen to be that it drives a wedge between a man and his Maker, separating him from God. Before God thrust Adam forth from the Garden, Adam had first hidden from God (Gen. 3:8,23). Once sin had entered the arena of human experience, man became aware of a barrier between him and God which was of his own making, not God's.

Furthermore, all sin is basically against God. God's reaction to sin was not merely to punish it. In a very real sense, it is the sinner who punishes himself and those around him. However, the Old Testament clearly recognized that God was not merely a spectator in this world. Active on the plane of human history, God did not simply make a moral universe which would discipline a sinner. Rather, he himself was active in the discipline of the sinner. This is certainly evidence both of God's wrath and of his righteousness. But it is also evidence of his love. God's love drove him to discipline man for his own good and to seek to awaken in him a sense of folly. Even in those cases where it appears that there was no hope of reform, God's judgment seems to be for the purpose of awakening within others a sense of the utter foolishness of sin. It is far more characteristic of the Old Testament to regard the punishment for sin as disciplinary rather than penal, and as redemptive rather than destructive. However, all such thoughts were present to some extent.

There appear to be four basic categories or types of sin which the Old Testament describes. The ancient Hebrew might not have categorized his sin in these precise ways. At the same time, the kinds of sin which he described well fit into these categories.

First, there are those acts which simply describe deviation from the right way. The focus here was upon the external act. Thus, when God announced to Samuel the fall of the house of Eli, he said,

> I am about to punish his house forever, for the iniquity which he knew, because his sons were blaspheming God, and he did not restrain them (1 Sam. 3:13).

Saul's confession to David is set in the same kind of terms.

> I have done wrong; return, my son David, for I will no more do you harm, because my life was precious in your eyes this day; behold, I have played the fool, and have erred exceedingly (1 Sam. 26:21).

The same kind of sin was denounced by Isaiah, as he said,

> These also reel with wine
>   and stagger with strong drink;
> the priest and the prophet reel with strong drink,
>   they are confused with wine,
>   they stagger with strong drink;
> they err in vision,
>   they stumble in giving judgment (Isa. 28:7).

In each of these cases, the major emphasis appears to have

been upon the outward act, which fell short of God's demands and expectations.

 The second basic category of sin which the Old Testament describes emphasizes the guilt which the sinner bears. The focus here is upon the consequence which the act brings upon the head of the one who has committed it. It carries to the sinner the awareness that he is guilty. There is no question of pleading innocence; the sinner knows full well that he is guilty and makes no bones about it. Such was the cry of Pharaoh to Moses:

> I have sinned this time; the Lord is in the right, and I and my people are in the wrong (Ex. 9:27).

When Abimelech of Gerar upbraided Isaac for claiming that his wife was merely his sister, he said,

> What is this you have done to us? One of the people might easily have lain with your wife, and you would have brought guilt upon us (Gen. 26:10).

Thus there was a general concern with the burden of guilt which had to be borne by one who had sinned.

A third class of sin described by the Old Testament directs our attention upon rebellion. Here the focus was upon the motive for the sinful act. In these instances, the sinner had consciously, willfully, and treacherously violated the commands and betrayed the loyalty of one to whom he was responsible. That this is the intent can be clearly seen from a secular use of such an idea. When Jehoram was king of Judah, "Edom revolted from the rule of Judah, and set up a king of their own" (2 Kings 8:20). Its religious emphasis is set forth in the law codes,

> When a man or woman commits any of the sins that men commit by breaking faith with the Lord, and that person is guilty, he shall confess his sin which he has committed; and he shall make full restitution for his wrong, adding a fifth to it, and giving it to him to whom he did the wrong (Num. 5:6-7).

The fourth kind of sin of which the Old Testament speaks is that where the act is simply wrong. There is an inherent evil to such actions about which no one could debate. Thus, when Samuel told Israel of their evil in asking for a king and rejecting God, he said,

> You shall know and see that your wickedness is great, which you have done in the sight of the Lord, in asking for yourselves a king (1 Sam. 12:17).

The author of Proverbs set forth this concept and its consequences in quite blunt words, "He who sows injustice will reap calamity" (Prov. 22:8). Also, the judgment against an adulteress is set forth in similar terms:

> They shall bring out the young woman to the door of her father's house, and the men of her city shall stone her to death with stones, because she has wrought folly in Israel by playing the harlot in her father's house; so you shall purge the evil from the midst of you (Deut. 22:21).

Simply put, sin in the Old Testament was one and all of these things. Sin always fell short of the right thing, was always a departure from the right way. It always produced guilt on the part of the sinner. He stood condemned before his Judge. It was always a rebellion against a rightful authority. No one else could really be blamed for the sinner's sin but himself. And finally, sin was inherently wrong. It was not merely a matter of violating some capricious rule, it was a matter of doing evil.

Although this kind of analysis is quite accurate and true to the message of the Old Testament, it leaves something to be desired. It is frequently done both by expositors and exegetes. At the same time, it might be considered as forcing a modern approach upon an ancient system of thought. Perhaps we can gain a better insight by making a study of the basic vocabulary of sin which the Old Testament uses.

II. The Kinds of Sin

It has been suggested that the people who speak any language develop numerous words to describe those things with which they are most familiar and have only a few words to describe things of lesser familiarity. Thus Arabic has numerous words to describe various kinds of sand while possessing very few words for snow. Among the Eskimo people, however, the reverse is true. The Hebrews had more words to describe sin than almost any other idea

in their language. This probably says that they were very
conscious of sin in their lives. The Old Testament would
certainly lend itself to that view. In studying Israel's vocabulary of sin, we shall limit our consideration to five major
words and their synonyms. These were key words in describing the Old Testament sin consciousness. The list
could be significantly enlarged, but would not add much
more to our ultimate understanding.

Sin as Missing the Mark. The basic Hebrew word for sin
comes originally from the idea of throwing, slinging, or
shooting at a target. It is the word *chata'*, and means simply
"to miss the mark." In describing the army of the tribe of
Benjamin, the word was used in its original sense.

> Among all these were seven hundred picked men who
> were left-handed; every one could sling a stone at a hair,
> and not miss (Judg. 20:16).

The ancient meaning of this word provides the basic clue
as to its meaning when used in reference to sin. The word is
usually translated simply *sin*. Its emphasis always rested
on the fact that a person had missed his goal in living up to
the things expected of him. The word itself carries no indication as to the reason for missing. It could be intentional
or it could be accidental. Only the context can help us determine the reason for missing. In many passages there is
absolutely no way to make this kind of decision. But the
central fact was always clear. For whatever reason, the sinner had missed the goal. His life was less than what God
had expected it to be. The term was used with equal force in
the legal sense or the moral sense. It can mean failing to
live up to a stated law or failure to live up to a moral obligation.

When Saul was threatening David, Jonathan rebuked
him, saying,

> Let not the king sin against his servant David; because he
> has not sinned against you, and because his deeds have
> been of good service to you; for he took his life in his hand
> and he slew the Philistine, and the Lord wrought a great
> victory for all Israel. You saw it, and rejoiced; why then will
> you sin against innocent blood by killing David without
> cause? (1 Sam. 19:4-5).

Jonathan did not deny that the king, his father, had the authority to kill David. But to do so without cause was to miss the mark.

This is the commonest of all Old Testament words for sin. The word itself never seemed to define the motive for sin. Rather, it simply pointed to the basic fact that sin was failure. It certainly laid the foundation for the statement of the apostle Paul that there was no basic difference between Jew and Gentile as they stood before God, "since all have sinned, and fall short of the glory of God" (Rom. 3:23).

This basic word for sin is sometimes used as a synonym for *rasha'*, which is translated as "to be wicked," or "to be guilty." Here is a term which appears to be more legal in character, carrying the idea that not only has a person missed the mark but he also has been found guilty for missing it. This also implies that the motive for missing was intentional. The wicked or guilty person stands condemned before the court of God's justice. Paralleling the two ideas, the psalmist proclaimed:

> Blessed is the man
> who walks not in the counsel of the wicked
> nor stands in the way of sinners (Ps. 1:1).

His advice was simple. Do not stand in the company of those who have missed the mark. Further, do not listen to the advice of those who stand condemned for having missed it. The reason for this is boldly set forth by Isaiah:

> "There is no peace," says the Lord,
> "for the wicked" (Isa. 48:22).

It was underscored by Ezekiel. God spoke through him, saying,

> Behold, all souls are mine; the soul of the father as well as the soul of the son is mine: the soul that sins shall die (Ezek. 18:4).

The end result of missing the mark was death. It was upon this that Paul built when he wrote, "The wages of sin is death" (Rom. 6:23). Missing the mark, whether accidental or intentional, was fatal. It still is.

B. **Sin as Going Astray.** The second major Old Testament word for sin is the word *shagah.* Its root picture simply

meant "to wander off," "to go astray." It portrayed the idea
of a sheep wandering away from the flock. It is a word
which has given translators a great deal of difficulty, having been translated as "erring," "sinning through error,"
"sinning unwittingly," or "going astray."

In searching through the passages where it is used, it
appears to have two basic emphases. It is quite frequently
used with a sense of sinning in ignorance, rather than in
rebellion or in negligence. Thus the ritual law stated:

> If any one sins unwittingly in any of the things which the
> Lord has commanded not to be done, and does any one of
> them, . . . then let him offer for the sin which he has com-
> mitted a young bull without blemish to the Lord for a sin
> offering.
> If the whole congregation of Israel commits a sin unwit-
> tingly and the thing is hidden from the eyes of the assem-
> bly, and they do any one of the things which the Lord has
> commanded not to be done and are guilty; when the sin
> which they have committed becomes known, the assembly
> shall offer a young bull for a sin offering and bring it before
> the tent of meeting (Lev. 4:2-3,13-14).

Ezekiel further emphasized this, by admonishing:

> You shall do the same on the seventh day of the month for
> any one who has sinned through error or ignorance; so
> shall you make atonement for the temple (Ezek. 45:20).

The psalmist, praising the Word of God, pointed out that it
kept him from this kind of sin.

> Before I was afflicted I went astray [erred];
>   but now I keep thy word.
> It is good for me that I was afflicted,
>   that I might learn thy statutes.
> The law of thy mouth is better to me
>   than thousands of gold and silver pieces
>   (Ps. 119:67,71-72).

The major emphasis of the word, then, clearly appears to
point to a creaturely going astray.

At the same time, there is another emphasis which is not
quite so obvious, but is none the less real. There is a deeper
emphasis which implies a right intention on the part of the
one who went astray. He intended to do right but failed.

This points up both the tragedy of human failure as well as the demonic side of sin. No other word for sin in the Old Testament carries quite this emphasis.

The word thus describes a person who was struggling to live up to God's demands and expectations, but he failed. He failed either because his human nature or his circumstances denied him the possibility of success. There was something demonic in his world which forced him to miss. But, since God made both him and his world, this kind of sinner turned on God and blamed him. Thus Job cried out in agony

> In his hand is the life of every living thing
>> and the breath of all mankind.
> The deceived and the deceiver are his (Job 12:10,16).

Even when Job appeared ready to confess some sin, yet he still blamed God.

And even if it be true that I have erred,
> my error remains with myself.
Know then that God has put me in the wrong,
> and closed his net about me (Job 19:4,6).

In this case the sinner was aware of his sin, but was even more aware that he had been deceived and misled. He had surely failed, but there was something outside himself which drove him to the failure. This word pointed to that overpowering force which drove men to sin. It focused upon the helplessness of one who was being swept onward to destruction. It described the tragic sense of futility which overcame the person who wanted to do good but failed.

It is precisely upon this sense of sin that Paul built when he wrote with a sense of agonized futility,

> I am carnal, sold under sin. I do not understand my own actions. For I do not do what I want, but I do the very thing I hate. . . . So then it is no longer I that do it, but sin which dwells within me. For I know that nothing good dwells within me, that is, in my flesh. I can will what is right, but I cannot do it. For I do not do the good I want, but the evil I do not want is what I do (Rom. 7:14-19).

This is a most graphic description of the situation in which each of us has found ourself. We intend to do good, but fail. How tragic is that failure.

Sin as Rebellion With the third key word for sin in the Old
Testament, we come to a very active, dynamic concept. The
word *pasha'* means "to rebel" and is usually so translated
in its verbal forms. However, when used as a noun, the
translators frequently use "transgression." It would appear to be far more accurate and to be more consistent to
use "rebellion," for it is this sense which the Hebrew word
really carries.

This meaning of the word is quite clear from its secular
usages. It was regularly used to describe the intentional
revolt of a vassal against his master. As such it destroyed a
covenant or peaceful relationship. Thus, in describing the
revolt of the northern tribes against David's grandson,
Rehoboam, it was said, "So Israel has been in rebellion
against the house of David to this day" (1 Kings 12:19). It
was also used to describe the revolt of Edom against Judah
(2 Kings 8:20).

In its religious use, the word described rebellion against
God, rather than the rejection of commands or violation of
law. Sin, then, was considered to be rebellion against the
will and authority of God. It is for this reason that I feel that
"transgression" is a very weak and perhaps misleading
translation.

It is the prophets who really bring this word to the front of
Israel's sin-consciousness. Amos shouted in a sarcastic
invitation to the Northern Kingdom.

Come to Bethel, and rebel;
> to Gilgal, and multiply rebellion (Amos 4:4, author's
> translation).

Amos was describing the idolatrous worship and the unjust behavior of Israel as being an open defiance of their
God. He pointed to the haughty pride of the people who asserted themselves over their God. Their acts of rebellion
were described in a long list of arrogant injustices.

> For I know how many are your rebellions,
> and how great are your sins (Amos 5:12, author's
> translation).

Here were a people who had missed the mark because they
had intentionally rejected the will of their God.

Hosea also used the term in warning his people of the
consequences of rebellion. His very last word to Israel was:

> Whoever is wise, let him understand these things,
>   whoever is discerning, let him know them;
> for the ways of the Lord are right,
>   and the upright walk in them,
>   but rebels stumble in them
>   (Hos. 14:9, author's translation).

Further, in denouncing the open apostasy of Judah, Isaiah of Jerusalem thundered,

> Hear, O heavens, and give ear, O earth;
>   for the Lord has spoken:
> "Sons have I reared and brought up,
>   but they have rebelled against me" (Isa. 1:2).

He further announced God's judgment upon them.

> But rebels and sinners shall be destroyed together,
>   and those who forsake the Lord shall be consumed
>   (Isa. 1:28).

The section of the Book of Isaiah which deals with God's great redemption also makes frequent reference to the rebellion of God's people. In giving the basis for Israel's exile, God said,

> Behold, for your iniquities you were sold,
>   and for your rebellions your mother was put away
>   (Isa. 50:1, author's translation).

And in the great prediction of a future deliverance, God spoke through the prophet, saying,

> But he was wounded for our rebellions,
>   he was bruised for our iniquities;
> upon him was the chastisement which made us whole,
>   and with his stripes we are healed.
> By oppression and judgment he was taken away;
>   and as for his generation, who considered
> that he was cut off out of the land of the living,
>   stricken for the rebellion of my people?
>   (Isa. 53:5,8, author's translation).

This rebellion did not always refer to an "armed insurrection." Rather, it more often than not implied simply that the sinner had exalted himself above God. His arrogant pride had led him into rebellion. It was this which happened to Adam and Eve in the Garden (Gen. 3). It was this which led the prodigal son astray in Jesus' parable (Luke 15:11-24). But it was the same kind of arrogant pride that kept the elder brother out in the darkness in the same parable (Luke 15:25-32). It was also precisely this kind of sinner whom Paul described when he wrote,

> They were filled with all manner of wickedness, evil, covetousness, malice. Full of envy, murder, strife, deceit, malignity, they are gossips, slanderers, haters of God, insolent, haughty, boastful, inventors of evil, disobedient to parents, foolish, faithless, heartless, ruthless. Though they know God's decree that those who do such things deserve to die, they not only do them but approve those who practice them (Rom. 1:29-32).

Rebellion is the creature's open rejection of the authority of the Creator. It is the human attempt to exalt oneself above God.

Sin as Turning Away. There are two words which the Old Testament used to describe sin as turning aside. Somewhat related in idea to the concept of rebellion, these words do not seem to carry quite the same emphasis upon arrogance or pride. These words carry more the idea of defection or apostasy. The idea is not so much that of turning aside in rejection of God as in defection, or betrayal of him. There appears to be more of an underlying note of treachery here.

The more common of these two words is derived from *shubh.* This is the same word which is also used to describe "turning to God," or "repentance." The prophets clearly describe the fact that men can turn to God, denying the claims of others, just as they have turned away from God to others, denying his claims on them. The second word is *sarar.* Less frequently used, this appears to carry the identical connotations of the first. There is absolutely no consistency among translators in rendering these words into English. They have been translated as "apostasy," "backsliding," "faithlessness," "rebellion," as well as other similar but less frequently used expressions.

Thus Hosea used forms of *shubh* to describe Israel's sin.

> My people are bent on turning away from me;
>> so they are appointed to the yoke,
>> and none shall remove it (Hos. 11:7).

But he used similar forms to invite Israel back to God.

> Return, O Israel, to the Lord your God,
> for you have stumbled because of your iniquity.
> Take with you words
> and return to the Lord (Hos. 14:1-2).

This was followed by God's promise of acceptance, using the same root:

> I will heal their faithlessness [turning away];
> I will love them freely,
> for my anger has turned from them (Hos. 14:4).

Jeremiah also pointed to this dimension of Israel's sin. It is he who so clearly showed that the two terms are parallel in meaning, also.

Your wickedness [*sarar*] will chasten you,
and your apostasy [*shubh*] will reprove you (Jer. 2:19).

Jeremiah also showed the double sense of the concept in a beautiful play on words, when he invited,

Return, O turning sons,
I will heal your turnings (Jer. 3:22, author's translation).

He again emphasized this double meaning, proclaiming:

> Why then has this people turned away
> in perpetual turnings?
> They hold fast to deceit,
> they refuse to return (Jer. 8:5, author's translation).

And when he confessed his people's sin, begging God to act in deliverance, he again emphasized the betrayal of his people.

> Though our iniquities testify against us,
> act, O Lord, for thy name's sake;
> for our backslidings are many,
> we have sinned against thee (Jer. 14:7).

The people of Judah had missed the mark because they had treacherously turned away from God.

Jeremiah also used *sarar* in describing his people's sin, saying,

But this people has a stubborn and treacherous heart;
they have betrayed and gone away (Jer. 5:23, author's translation).

He was aware that they were stubbornly set on going their own way and doing their own thing. The psalmist also made this emphasis,

> that they should set their hope in God,
> and not forget the works of God,
>   but keep his commandments;
> and that they should not be like their fathers,
>   a stubborn and rebellious [sarar] generation,
> a generation whose heart was not steadfast,
>   whose spirit was not faithful to God (Ps. 78:7-8).

It is quite likely that this idea of "doing your own thing" may underlie one of the most profound contrasts in the New Testament. Peter described Judas's treachery by saying, "Judas turned aside, to go to his own place" (Acts 1:25). On the other hand, to the others, Jesus had said, "I go to prepare a place for you" (John 14:2). The height of sin is turning aside from the place which the Lord has prepared for us to prepare our own place. It always leads to treachery and betrayal. But not only is such an act the height of sin, it is also the height of folly. The person who loudly proclaims of his life, "I did it my way," is both a traitor and a fool.

E.   ***Sin as Guilt.*** The fifth basic description of sin in the Old Testament emphasized the guilt of the sinner. It was a legal term, pointing to the sinner standing condemned, and usually being quite aware of it. It focused upon the results of sin for the sinner. The basic term is 'awon, and it is usually translated as "iniquity" or "guilt." It appears to me that iniquity is far too weak a translation for this word. Guilt is more emphatic and gives a better description of the actual meaning.

This emphasis is clearly set forth on numerous occasions. Jeremiah proclaimed: "For my eyes are upon all their ways; they are not hid from me, nor is their guilt concealed from my eyes" (Jer. 16:17, author's translation). Isaiah also cried out, "Woe to those who draw up guilt with cords of falsehood" (Isa. 5:18, author's translation). And in the beautiful song of the Suffering Servant, we are told:

> But he was wounded for our rebellions,
>   he was bruised for our guilts;
> upon him was the chastisement which made us whole,
>   and with his stripes we are healed (Isa. 53:5, author's
>   translation).

To indicate both the burden of this guilt and the sinner's consciousness of it, the psalmist cried out:

For my guilts have gone over my head;
>they weigh like a burden too heavy for me (Ps. 38:4,
>>author's translation).

The guilt which had been accumulated from a series of sins had become too heavy to bear. On the other hand, the relief when this burden was lifted is unmistakable.

>Blessed is he whose rebellion is forgiven,
>>whose sin is covered.
>Blessed is the man to whom the Lord imputes no guilt
>>(Ps. 32:1-2, author's translation).

There are times when this word for sin also appears to describe not only the guilt but also the punishment which accompanied it. Thus Cain cried out to God, "My guilt is greater than I can bear" (Gen. 4:13, author's translation). Here it appears from the context that Cain was referring to the punishment as well as to the sense of guilt. Both were a burden to him.

There was another term for guilt in the Old Testament, and that was *'asham.* This term was used almost entirely in the context of the ritual law and appears generally to refer simply to "uncleanness." This is the sense of unworthiness which overtakes the sinner when he has failed to be fit for worship. It did not necessarily include willful rebellion but might have been entirely accidental and unwitting. Nor did it ever seem to imply premeditation, and frequently arose through either ignorance or negligence. The guilt, however, was nonetheless real. Further, for ritual offenses, the sinner might have been unaware of his guilt, but he was still "unclean."

For its New Testament development, the basic emphasis here was upon guilt in the presence of a judge, not upon the ritual uncleanness. Paul's basic argument in Romans 1:18-23 was to establish the guilt of all men before God. Further, it appears that his amazement at Jesus' sacrificial death was the wonder of the fact that he died for the guilty!

While we were still weak, at the right time Christ died for the ungodly. Why, one will hardly die for a righteous man—though perhaps for a good man one will dare even to die. But God shows his love for us in that while we were yet sinners Christ died for us (Rom. 5:6-8).

There appears to be a sense of the interrelatedness of all these terms for sin which was set forth in the ritual for the Day of Atonement.

And Aaron shall lay both his hands upon the head of the live goat, and confess over him all the guilts of the people of Israel, and all their rebellions, all their sins; and he shall put them upon the head of the goat, and send him away into the wilderness (Lev. 16:21, author's translation).

Further, we have seen how each of these basic terms point to an aspect of sin that the others fail to describe. All of these terms fundamentally pointed out the fact that man had failed his Maker. At the same time, as we move from merely missing the mark through going astray, turning away, and rebellion, we sense a growing emphasis upon the personal aspect of sin. There man seeks to replace his maker. For all of these acts, there comes a resultant guilt upon the sinner. It is only as we confront this sense of guilt that we are brought up short. Where is the solution for this guilt? How can it be removed? Before we can turn our attention to the answer which the Old Testament gives to this question, there are two other questions which were raised about sin whose answers we must consider. The first of these is: where did sin come from? The second looks at the other end of the process: what are the consequences of sin; where does it lead?

The Origins of Sin

The prophets' attack upon the sins of Israel and of her neighbors forced two conclusions upon the people of Israel. First, God was more concerned with righteousness than with Israel. Second, sin was a universal problem for all men of all nations in all ages. We will pass over the first conclusion for a while. But the second one must be considered here, for it apparently caused these ancients to raise the question as to the origin of sin: from where did it come? Why was it a universal experience?

The Old Testament answer to this was set forth in three stages. The earliest answer was presented in the so-called Fall narrative in Genesis 3. The story is too familiar to need to be repeated. Further, its literary analysis can be found in any good critical commentary. The point we must make is that there are some very profound theological truths set forth in a very simple, nontheological narrative of the events in the Garden. It is from the interplay of these figures that we find our insights into sin and its origin.

This first sin is clearly portrayed as the revolt of the creature against his Creator. On the part of both Eve and Adam, there was the desire to be equal with God. This sprang from human pride, arrogance, and self-exaltation. It resulted in willful disobedience of the divine command. The root of sin is clearly painted as human pride expressing itself in a declaration of independence from God. It was the insidious whisper of the serpent, "You will be like God," that really set the whole thing in motion (Gen. 3:5).

The narrative also clearly indicates that the whole thing would have been impossible if Adam had not been created to exercise dominion over his world. (The Hebrew word for man is 'Adam.) He had been given freedom to choose, as well as an authority and a responsibility. But he was also given certain restrictions and limitations. Adam and his descendants were to rule over this world, but were not the central figures in it. God was central and if man insisted on usurping that place, he would surely die. But he did have the freedom to decide.

The one thing which had been denied to Adam in the Garden of Eden was the "tree of the knowledge of good and evil" (Gen. 2:17). This would be better translated as the "tree of the knowledge, both good and evil." It was not simply that man was being denied the knowledge of the difference between good and evil, but a special kind of knowledge which included both good and evil. It would appear that this knowledge was specifically God's, for to know it would be to become like God. Further, the God of the Bible is nowhere else revealed as simply tempting man for the sake of temptation alone. Therefore it is highly likely that since this tree was placed in the Garden, it was God's intent that man should have it sometime. It is quite possible that the biblical account reflects the fact that God intended man first to have life before he obtained this knowledge. At least, it is quite certain that mankind has always had a problem with getting knowledge before getting the character to use it properly.

For example, we learn to split an atom, and the first thing we do with this knowledge is make a bomb. Only later do we begin to develop nondestructive uses of atomic energy. Over and over again, our history shows us prostituting our knowledge because we do not have the character to use it properly. That character comes only from life in and with God.

Be that as it may, the fall story clearly reveals that in the Garden, Adam and Eve sought to get a knowledge which was God's. He could give it when and if he chose. But it was not man's place to seize it.

The next major feature of the story is the serpent. Satan disputed God's command and implied a low motive to God for giving it. This, too, is still a common thought in our world. God's commands are always considered to be prohibitive rather than protective, as an infringement upon man's freedom rather than as a safeguard against man's folly. Man's sin began with anxiety about himself. The serpent's sin began with open rebellion against God.

Adam and Eve's sin revealed an element of weakness. Man was too weak to resist, too foolish to realize what was going on. The Genesis writer was, in a sense, poking fun at Adam and Eve. So motivated with pride that they wished to be like God, they could not even think of a way to accomplish this until an outside whisper came. Man was just not great enough to discover sin for himself. The arrogant man thought he could look after himself better than God could, but he could not find anything to do differently until there was the subtle suggestion from outside himself. How funny! How tragic!

Furthermore, the figure of the serpent introduced the demonic element. There are other forces at work in our world which we did not introduce. The Genesis writer did not try to suggest from whence this evil force came. As far as he was concerned, it was simply there. In the serpent's rebellion against God, he sought to lead God's supreme creation astray. In this he succeeded, but not without an ultimate cost to himself.

The first consequence of Adam's sin was that he was suddenly stripped of all illusions. He was aware that he was self-exposed before God. Immediately, he wanted to hide from God. Long before God thrust man out of the garden, man was hiding himself from God's presence. The sinner cannot face God. It was just that simple.

When he could no longer hide from God, Adam then sought to argue his way out. He blamed his wife. He also blamed God for giving her to him. His wife, Eve, blamed the serpent. One of the consequences of sin is the attempt to cover it up by blaming someone else. This is still with us. Adam had stepped forth boldly in his quest for godlikeness. In the end, he who had been made in God's image was hiding from God and blaming God for his problem.

The ultimate end of the narrative was punishment and separation. But there was also hope. Adam, Eve, and the serpent all faced punishments in varying degrees. But there was a promise of ultimate victory given to man when God said,

I will put enmity between you and the woman,
>and between your seed and her seed;
he shall crush your head,
>and you shall crush his heel (Gen. 3:15, author's translation)

A crushed heel will create a limp. A crushed head is fatal. The final crushing of Satan by the seed of woman took place in the incarnation of God's Son in human flesh.

We should also note that even when man was thrust out of the garden, it was an act of mercy on God's part. He was driven out, "lest he put forth his hand and take also of the tree of life, and eat, and live forever" (Gen. 3:22). God did not intend that his creature should live forever in an alienated, rebellious state. Something had to be done to correct man's condition before God would allow him the opportunity of living on.

A second answer to the question of the origin of sin was given in Genesis 6:1-8. The "sons of God" in this story are not to be interpreted as godly men but as some sort of angelic beings. This story was of greater importance in post-Old Testament, nonbiblical books than it ever was in the Old Testament.

As the story stands, it tells of some spiritual beings who lusted for the women of earth, took upon themselves human form and sinned by marrying them. The result was a race of giants known as the Nephilim. It also introduced into mankind an evil imagination. In order to purge this, the Flood was sent by God. The details of the story can be analyzed by any good analytical commentary. That it does refer to fallen angels can be seen in the First Epistle of Peter which refers to the spirits who had been disobedient in the days of Noah (1 Pet. 3:19-20). Further, the very word *Nephilim* means "Fallen Ones."

The end result of the intermarriage is stated quite simply.

The Lord saw that the wickedness of man was great in the earth, and that every imagination of the thoughts of his heart was only evil continually (Gen. 6:5).

This narrative sets forth the basis for man's innate leaning toward evil. Even the Flood did not destroy it, for as soon as the waters receded, God said, "the imagination of man's heart is evil from his youth" (Gen. 8:21).

The preaching of the prophets clearly pointed to the many results of this evil imagination. Isaiah denounced his people, saying,

Woe to those who call evil good and good evil,
who put darkness for light and light for darkness,
who put bitter for sweet and sweet for bitter! (Isa. 5:20).

Although he did not specifically refer to the "evil imagination," it was obviously in the background of his thought. The same can be said of the warning of the psalmist.

Transgression speaks to the wicked
deep in his heart;
there is not fear of God
before his eyes.
For he flatters himself in his own eyes
that his iniquity cannot be found out and hated.
The words of his mouth are mischief and deceit;
he has ceased to act wisely and do good.
He plots mischief while on his bed;
he sets himself in a way that is not good;
he spurns not evil (Ps. 36:1-4).

The idea was also clearly in the background of the Proverbs when it said:

A worthless person, a wicked man,
  goes about with crooked speech,

. . . .

with perverted heart devises evil
  continually sowing discord (Prov. 6:12-14).

Thus, a basic part of man's sinfulness is his evil imagination. His heart is perverted, his life is twisted, and his every act is bent toward evil. This, then, lays the basis for human sin at the feet of the intervention of rebellious angels who bred into man a sense of evil. Although this idea of the origin of sin was not a major significance in the Old Testament and of less in the New, it played a significant part in the post-Old Testament thought on the matter.

The impact of this story on the New Testament was far greater in another area. With the intermarriage of the angels and the daughters of men, there was clearly laid a foundation for the belief in the possibility of the indwelling of flesh with spirit. This was a temporary thing in the Old Testament. On the other hand, it surely paved the way for the New Testament thought of the incarnation of the divine Son of God in human flesh. If one of the origins of human sinfulness is to be found in the story of lusting, rebellious spiritual beings, certainly the ultimate solution of this problem was only found in the pure incarnation of Spirit with flesh in Jesus of Nazareth.

A third stage in the Old Testament understanding of the origin of sin in the human race is found in the story of the tower of Babel (Gen. 11:1-9). Actually, this is not an origin story, but a narrative which tells that sin was still in the world after the Flood. As such, it set the final stage for the story of redemption which begins in Genesis 12.

Here, the story turns more upon the evil and arrogant pride of the human race. In direct disobedience to God's command to fill up the earth, mankind decided to stay in one place. Further, with no concern other than to "make a name for ourselves," they decided to build "a tower with its top in the heavens" (Gen. 11:4). At this point, the Genesis writer again poked a bit of fun at the best that arrogant man could do. When he built the highest skyscraper he could, God had to come "*down* to see the city and the tower" (Gen. 11:5, italics mine). At the same time, man's abilities were highly complimented by God, when he said, "This is only the beginning of what they will do; . . . nothing that they propose to do will now be impossible for them" (Gen. 11:6).

The message of Genesis here is that man's problem is that of arrogant, disobedient pride. He seeks to be upon the throne of his life, rather than submitting to God. In this story, there is no outside element at all. Man had now become devilish enough to think up his own disobedience.

From the first chapters of Genesis, then, comes a simple, but profound statement, contained in these three narratives. First, man has been a sinner from first to last. Second, his sin was rooted and grounded in his own pride. Third, there was an external power and presence which injected itself into the divine-human relationship, seeking to destroy it. Fourth, even though sin entered into the world through the rebellion of man, God was still sovereign. He was not overthrown by his creature. Fifth, even in the very midst of his sinful rebellion, man was offered a hope for the future by his sovereign Creator. The darkest stories carry this ray of light. Sin brought darkness to God's creation. But in the midst of man's darkness, God again said, " 'Let there be light'; and there was light" (Gen. 1:3). It was against the background of this idea that the Fourth Gospel could say, "The light shines in the darkness, and the darkness has not overcome it" (John 1:5). It never has. It never will.

IV. The Consequences of Sin

Given the fact of sin, the Old Testament also addressed a second question, what are the results of sin? Where does sin lead? The same narratives which we have considered for sin's origin set the stage for our consideration of its consequences.

First of all, sin was seen as destroying relationships. Adam and Eve hid from God in the garden (Gen. 3:8). Adam blamed both Eve and God for his condition, an obvious attack upon relationships (Gen. 3:12). Finally, God had to drive the pair from the garden (Gen. 3:24). In the tower narrative, the ultimate result was the breaking up of human relationships through the confounding of language (Gen. 11:7-9).

The prophets further underscored this result of sin. Hosea described the broken relationship in terms of a divorce between God and Israel (Hos. 2:2-13). Isaiah, on the other hand, described Judah's apostasy in terms of rebellious sons, saying,

> Sons have I reared and brought up,
>   but they have rebelled against me.
> The ox knows its owner,
>   and the ass its master's crib;
> but Israel does not know,
>   my people does not understand (Isa. 1:2-3).

Jeremiah was more direct, pointing to the turning away of God's people as foolish rejection.

> For my people have committed two evils:
>   they have forsaken me,
> the fountain of living waters,
>   and hewed out cisterns for themselves,
> broken cisterns,
>   that can hold no water (Jer. 2:13).

The second consequence of sin was clearly seen as punishment. Sin was disobedience and had to be punished. Adam and Eve were punished both immediately and over the long-term (Gen. 3:14-19,22-24). The Flood followed the sin of the sons of God and the daughters of men (Gen. 6:11-13). The thundering messages of the prophets were aimed at warning of this punishment. Examples can be found on almost every page of these books.

> Therefore because of you
>   Zion shall be plowed as a field,
> Jerusalem shall become a heap of ruins,
>   and the mountain of the house a wooded height
>   (Mic. 3:12).

> But rebels and sinners shall be destroyed together,
>   and those who forsake the Lord shall be consumed
>   (Isa. 1:28).

In addition, the books which record the history of Israel or of individuals within Israel give ample illustration of the

punishment which followed sin. Since sin had to be punished, the idea grew up quite early that all suffering was a
consequence of sin. The Book of Job dealt quite thoroughly
with this idea, coming to a final conclusion that suffering
may be the result of sin but was not necessarily so. Death,
also, was a consequence of sin. It might occur quickly or be
delayed, but sin initiated the death process.

Sin also had consequences for those round about the sinner. Achan's sin cost Israel a victory at Ai and his family
and servants their lives (Josh. 7:1-12,24-25). Jonah's sin
cost all the people on board the ship their goods, for they
cast "the wares that were in the ship into the sea, to lighten
it for them" (Jonah 1:5). The ultimate cost of sin for others
was set forth in the song of the Suffering Servant.

> But he was wounded for our transgressions,
>   he was bruised for our iniquities;
> upon him was the chastisement that made us whole,
>   and with his stripes we are healed.
> All we like sheep have gone astray;
>   we have turned every one to his own way;
> and the Lord has laid on him
>   the iniquity of us all (Isa. 53:5-6).

Sin also had the immediate consequence of the agony of
guilt. The sinner knows his sin, bears his guilt, and cannot
escape this burden. Let us hear the cry of such a one.

> Have mercy on me, O God,
>   according to thy steadfast love;
> according to thy abundant mercy
>   blot out my transgressions.
> Wash me thoroughly from my iniquity,
>   and cleanse me from my sin!
> For I know my transgressions,
>   and my sin is ever before me (Ps. 51:1-3).

The sinner cannot escape the knowledge of his sin. It is this
burden which breaks his heart.

The ultimate consequence of sin rests beyond this life.
But it remained for the New Testament to fully develop this
idea. For the people of the Old Testament, their prime concern was its present consequences. These loomed so large
that they seldom saw beyond them.

For the New Testament, the ultimate consequences of sin

are all grown from these same roots. Sin is clearly seen as destroying relationships. Paul pointed to the "dividing wall of hostility" which had separated Jew and Gentile but which had been broken down by Christ (Eph. 2:14). He also pointed to the divisions in the church at Corinth which produced dissension and disagreement (1 Cor. 1:10-13).

The punishment of sin is also clearly taught in the New Testament. There it is taught more in the sense of an ultimate punishment in hell, but there is also the very real sense of present punishment. Jesus, however, rejected the idea that all suffering must be the result of sin. When his disciples saw a man who had been blind from birth, they asked, "Rabbi, who sinned, this man or his parents, that he was born blind?" (John 9:2). Jesus responded that neither was the case. All suffering does not come as the result of sin.

Sin in the New Testament is also seen as the bringer of death, but here the emphasis is upon eternal death, the ultimate separation between man and God. Thus Paul admonished, "the wages of sin is death" (Rom. 6:23). He was taking the Old Testament thought and using it as a basis for preaching the gospel.

Ultimately, the main emphasis of the New Testament on the consequences of sin appear to be that the sinner cannot escape his sin by himself. Thus Paul, describing his sinful nature, cried out in agony, "Wretched man that I am! Who will deliver me from this body of death?" (Rom. 7:24). But, contrary to the Old Testament saints, he can also cry out in ecstasy, "Thanks be to God through Christ Jesus our Lord!" (Rom. 7:25).

If the Old Testament view of sin were the whole story, it would be quite tragic. On the other hand, we certainly know that the Old Testament did not have the cross of Christ to which to look back. Then, were they without hope? Trying to answer this question brings us to the next step in our study. What hope did the Old Testament offer to a sinner? It is to this which we must now turn.

7
Redeeming God and Penitent Man

INTRO

The beauty of God's creation had been spoiled by the tragedy of human sin. The righteousness of God demanded that sin be punished. But his steadfast, loyal love *(hesed)* would not let his rebellious creatures go. There had to be a way by which humanity could be salvaged. So the divine wisdom found a way. This brings us face to face with the real heart of the Old Testament message: redemption.

The salvation of man is, in fact, the heart of the entire biblical message. Genesis 1 to 11 set the stage. There we were introduced to God, man, and man's sinful rebellion. All the rest of the Bible is the story of God working out man's redemption. In the Old Testament we note the two main features in this story. First, history is the record of the sin of man. Second, God's acts in history center in salvation and redemption.

God is revealed in his acts as both just and loving. He is clearly the sovereign Judge. But he is also the sovereign Savior. Israel rebelled and violated the covenant. But the loyal love of God found a way to redeem and save. Throughout the Old Testament, then, we find a message of the hope of salvation. It was that hope onto which Israel held in the darkest days of their history. It was that hope which allowed the light of God's love to shine into the darkness of their sin. It is to that hope that we must now turn our attention.

I The Nature of Salvation

From our standpoint on this side of the cross, our concept of salvation is intimately bound up with the experience of the forgiveness of sin in its fullest New Testament sense. We think of salvation as primarily spiritual, relating to our eternal relationship with God. The Old Testament understanding of salvation also has this sense, but lesser conceptions are also found. In fact, it is the growth of the idea through these lesser conceptions which gives a richer, fuller meaning to the New Testament understanding of salvation. We shall begin to see both the limitations of the Old Testament ideas as well as the enrichment they bring to those in the New Testament as we consider the basic Old Testament vocabulary of salvation.

Salvation as Deliverance. The basic verb for salvation has as its root meaning the idea of "to be wide," "to be spacious," or "to have room." The idea appears to have developed from the thought that one who had been given room had been given victory. Whatever it was that crowded you or bound you, salvation removed it, delivering you from it. It is also quite fascinating that this verb occurs in only two stems (out of seven possible) in the Old Testament. One of these is a simple passive, with the idea of: "I have been given room," or "you have been given room." The other stem is a causative, carrying the force of: "He has caused you to have room," or simply "causing to have room." In general, the term usually referred to the idea of the victory which had been won or to the one who had caused it to be won. When such a victory had been won, the one who had been delivered had been saved. It was through this development that the noun form of this word came to mean "salvation." Further, the one who caused the deliverance came to be known as a savior.

As evidence of this development, consider Jonathan's statement to his armor-bearer:

Come, let us go over to the garrison of these uncircumcised; it may be that the Lord will work for us; for nothing can hinder the Lord from saving by many or by few (1 Sam. 14:6).

In this instance, Jonathan was obviously referring to a military victory as God's "saving" Israel. This is further illustrated in the Book of Judges, where we are told,

Whenever the Lord raised up judges for them, the Lord was with the judge, and he saved them from the hand of their enemies all the days of the judge (Judg. 2:18).

Such a person had the gifts and the strength to use them to effect a military deliverance for Israel.

But, since such gifts were from God and since he had raised up the human savior, it was only a step for the Hebrews to realize that it was God who was fundamentally the Savior. Furthermore, to Israel, God's greatest deliverance of Israel took place in the Exodus experience. Thus the prophets began to describe God as the Savior, pointing to the deliverance from Egypt as the proof of this. Through Hosea, God said,

> I am the Lord your God
> from the land of Egypt;
> you know no God but me,
> and besides me there is no savior (Hos. 13:4).

Furthermore, since Israel had placed so much trust in their human deliverers, they had to be reminded that such persons had been able to save only because God had empowered them. Israel had trusted in their human leaders and had forgotten God. Again, God spoke through Hosea, saying,

> Where now is your king, to save you;
> where are all your princes, to defend you—
> those of whom you said,
> "Give me a king and princes"? (Hos. 13:10).

To the prophets it was perfectly clear that if Israel really saw God as their Savior in the experience of the Exodus, then they would understand that in all subsequent victories, it was God who had wrought them. After all, it was Moses who had commanded the priests to encourage Israel in the future, whenever they stood on the threshold of battle, by saying,

Hear, O Israel, you draw near this day to fight against your enemies; let not your heart faint; do not fear, or tremble, or be in dread of them; for the Lord your God is he who goes with you, to fight for you against your enemies, to save you (Deut. 20:3-4, author's translation).

It was God who was supremely the Savior, even when the emphasis was upon military victory.

This thought of salvation in the terms of military victory or of national deliverance seems to have persisted throughout the entire period of the Hebrew kingdoms. The historical books of the Old Testament use it this way consistently.

On the other hand, the thought of salvation being a deliverance from one's enemies lent itself very precisely to the description of deliverance from the supreme enemy, sin. Thus the Book of Isaiah describes a salvation that is clearly more than military victory and a Savior who is more than a conqueror of national enemies.

> And there is no other god besides me,
> a righteous God and a Savior;
>   there is none besides me.
> Turn to me and be ye saved,
>   all the ends of the earth!
>   For I am God, and there is no other.
> By myself I have sworn,
>   from my mouth has gone forth in righteousness
>   a word that shall not return;
> "To me every knee shall bow,
>   every tongue shall swear" (Isa. 45:21b-23).

The psalmists also sang of a salvation which was obviously more than a military deliverance.

> Turn, O Lord, save my life;
>   deliver me for the sake of thy steadfast love (Ps. 6:4).

> Incline thy ear, O Lord, and answer me,
>   for I am poor and needy.
> Preserve my life, for I am godly;
>   save thy servant who trusts in thee.
> Thou art my God; be gracious to me, O Lord,
>   for to thee do I cry all the day.
> Gladden the soul of thy servant,
>   for to thee, O Lord, do I lift up my soul.
> For thou, O Lord, are good and forgiving,
>   abounding in steadfast love to all who call upon thee.
> Turn to me and take pity on me;
>   give thy strength to thy servant,
>   and save the son of thy handmaid (Ps. 86:1-5,16).

In this latter psalm, the plea for salvation is clearly connected with the assurance that God is forgiving and abounding in steadfast love.

However, the spiritualization of salvation from the standpoint of this particular word does not fully take place within the Old Testament. Its major emphasis was generally upon physical deliverance from an enemy. A careful scrutiny of the Old Testament use of this term points up several significant facts both about its use and its meaning.

First, the one who needed saving, whether it was an individual or the nation, was one who had either been threatened or oppressed by an enemy. In such cases, his salvation was deliverance from the danger, oppression, or impending catastrophe. Whatever the nature of the crisis, salvation was deliverance from it.

Second, the savior, whether he was king, judge, or God himself, was one who had power and was able to use it for the one in need or to give it to the one in need. Thus, the savior either acted in behalf of the saved or else he furnished the resources so that the saved could act for himself.

Third, in the last analysis, only God himself can always save like this. He alone is always strong enough to effect salvation. Remember again the magnificent statement: "Besides me there is no savior" (Hos. 13:4). When Israel turned to other saviors, the psalmist said of them,

> They forgot God, their Savior,
> who had done great things in Egypt (Ps. 106:21).

On the other hand, when victory came, they sang,

> O sing to the Lord a new song,
> for he has done marvelous things!
> His right hand and his holy arm
> have brought salvation for him
> (Ps. 98:1, author's translation).

Fourth, when anyone else acted the part of a savior he was completely dependent upon God. From God alone could come the strength and power to save others. Furthermore, only God can save the savior!

Fifth, there appears to be some sense in which salvation in the Old Testament was bound up with the covenant relationship. This becomes more obvious in those passages where the emphasis was not as much upon the victory as upon the purpose behind it and the ultimate results beyond it. In this sense, peace was frequently linked with salvation. This is the same peace which was also frequently linked with the covenant. (See chapter 4.) When used with salvation or with the covenant, peace always seems to include wholeness, completeness. It also appears to include health, prosperity, and the general well-being of the one who has been saved.

Furthermore, as the prophets began to focus upon a spiritual deliverance with spiritual consequences, they also saw a deepening understanding of the spiritual dimensions of the covenant. Issuing the divine call to repentance and presenting the divine offer of forgiveness, they set forth a broader understanding of salvation. For them, salvation came more and more to mean God's mighty acts of restoring the covenant relationship between Israel and himself. This was done by delivering Israel from the degradation brought about by their sinful rebellion and the rejection of the divine will.

In the end, salvation came to focus upon the renewed covenant relationship or upon a new covenant. Thus to be saved was to be brought into fellowship with God and to enjoy living in his will. (We shall consider this further in chapter 8, where we further consider the new covenant.)

Sixth, salvation ultimately was applied in the same full range of meaning to the life of the individual as it had been to the life of the nation. Thus it covered the entire range from physical deliverance to material prosperity to forgiveness of sins to spiritual fellowship with God. The end picture of the Old Testament shows the saved individual as one who knows the full joy of God's presence in his own life. As long as there was little hope of any kind of meaningful life beyond the grave, it is easy to understand why the ideas of salvation and material prosperity were linked. It was only as God was able to open the Hebrews' minds to the idea of something meaningful beyond death that they were able to realize that material prosperity in this world did not necessarily follow salvation. (To this, also, we shall return when we consider Israel's future hope, in chapter 8.)

It is quite easy to see how the New Testament picked up and enlarged upon these ideas as they came to understand the fullness of the title, "Savior," as applied to Jesus. The early Christians were quite aware of the fact that all men were under the domination of sin and were threatened by the imminent peril of their souls. Thus, when Jesus wrought our deliverance from sin and death, he quite clearly had saved us in the Old Testament sense of the term.

Further, Jesus was quite obviously the one who had the power to deliver us from such enemies, and he used it for benefit of all men. But not only was he able to deliver us from this enemy, he clearly set us free, giving us the power to be victorious over sin (1 John 3:4-10). In addition, that God alone is ultimately the Savior was clearly seen in that Jesus was the Son of God incarnate. Yet at the same time, Jesus showed his utter dependence upon God the Father through his prayers and his teachings.

It was also the point of the restored or renewed covenant relation that led Jesus to describe his own death and mission in terms of the new covenant. This relationship between God and man was effected by the forgiveness of sins wrought by Jesus in saving us. In the last analysis, all of this was wrapped up in his name. The name, Jesus, is the Greek form of the Old Testament verb, "He will save." It was this which was intended in the angel's statement:

> Joseph, son of David, do not fear to take Mary your wife, for that which is conceived in her is of the Holy Spirit; she will bear a son, and you shall call his name Jesus, for he will save his people from their sins (Matt. 1:20-21).

In the end, when John looked back over the entire Old Testament development and placed it alongside of his personal experience, he was able to state with an inspired conviction, "And we have seen and testify that the Father has sent his Son as the Savior of the world" (1 John 4:14). What a flower blossomed on that Old Testament root!

Salvation as Rescue. The second major word in the Old Testament vocabulary of salvation is usually translated as "ransom," less often as "redeem," and occasionally as "rescue." As we shall see, it is this latter meaning which comes closest to the ancient usage when applied to God's acts. With this word, we come to a far greater spiritual content than the preceding one.

This word is used frequently in legal contexts, which

help us come to understand its basic force. For instance, if a man had a dangerous ox which he allowed to remain at large and it gored someone, the following law applied. "If a price is laid on him, then he shall give for the redemption of his life whatever is laid on him" (Ex. 21:30, author's translation). In this case, the owner had the choice of being stoned or paying his "redemption" price. This was essentially the value of his life which the court established.

Still in a legal context, but also moving into the area of religious ritual, the firstborn of man and beast belonged to God. The reason for this was rooted in the Exodus experience and in ancient religion. But in Israel, they were told, "Every first-born of man among your sons you shall redeem" (Ex. 13:13). In ancient religions the firstborn male was frequently sacrificed to the chief god. This had been changed in Israel, where child sacrifice was prohibited. Abraham was told to substitute a ram for Isaac (Gen. 22:13). This practice of redeeming the life of a child by offering a redemptive sacrifice was still being practiced in the time of Jesus' birth. Mary and Joseph observed this ritual for Jesus.

And when the time came for their purification according to the law of Moses, they brought him up to Jerusalem to present him to the Lord (as it is written in the law of the Lord, "Every male that opens the womb shall be called holy to the Lord") and to offer a sacrifice according to what is said in the law of the Lord, "a pair of turtledoves, or two young pigeons" (Luke 2:22-24).

In these legal contexts, the idea of the redemptive price which was to have been paid was an integral part of the concept. But a greater emphasis came to be placed upon the result accomplished than upon the price paid.

This becomes particularly obvious in all those passages where the Old Testament speaks of God redeeming Israel. In these places the attention is directed to the result attained, with no mention being made of a ransom or a redemptive price being paid.

Rather than mentioning a price in these instances, the emphasis was turned upon his covenant love, his *hesed*. Here the Old Testament emphasis rested upon God's motive for redemption. God redeemed not by what he paid, but by what he is. Thus Israel was told,

The Lord has brought you out with a mighty hand, and redeemed you from the house of bondage, from the hand of Pharaoh king of Egypt. Know therefore that the Lord your God is God, the faithful God who keeps covenant and stead-fast love with those who love him and keep his command-ments, to a thousand generations (Deut. 7:8-9).

Further, the Book of Isaiah makes quite clear that the act of redemption by God was an act of deliverance, not an act of paying off Israel's oppressors.

> Is my hand shortened, that it cannot redeem?
> Or have I no power to deliver? (Isa. 50:2).

And the end result of his act of redemption is described in terms of the joyous return of those redeemed.

> And the rescued of the Lord shall return,
> and come to Zion with singing;
> everlasting joy shall be upon their heads;
> they shall obtain joy and gladness,
> and sorrow and sighing shall flee away
> (Isa. 51:11, author's translation).

The Old Testament also makes abundantly clear that it was not just the nation of Israel which was blessed by God's acts of redemption. There was a growing emphasis upon his acts of redemption for individuals. Thus the psalmist sang:

> But God will rescue my life from the power of Sheol,
> for he will receive me (Ps. 49:15, author's translation).

And Job was told by Eliphaz,

> In famine, he will rescue you from death,
> and in war from the power of the sword
> (Job 5:20, author's translation).

Further, when Jeremiah was overwhelmed by the opposi-tion he faced and the plight in which his ministry placed him, God encouraged him.

> And I will make you to this people
> a fortified wall of bronze;

> they will fight against you,
>> but they shall not prevail over you,
> for I am with you
>> to save you and deliver you,
>>> says the Lord.
> I will deliver you out of the hand of the wicked,
>> and redeem [rescue] you from the grasp of the
>> ruthless (Jer. 15:20-21).

Although the term for rescue offers a far more spiritual concept than that for salvation, it is obvious that its meaning is far less than that found in the New Testament. In almost every case, God's act of rescue was applied to deliverance from natural calamity, suffering, and death. However, there was an awareness that there were greater calamities than these. Upon this basis, the psalmist admonished his people to place their ultimate hope in God.

> O Israel, hope in the Lord!
>> For with the Lord there is steadfast love,
>> and with him is abundant rescue.
> So he will rescue Israel
>> from all his guilty acts (Ps. 130:7-8, author's translation).

God could be the basis for ultimate hope in that he could not only rescue from physical calamity, he could also rescue from spiritual calamity. He still can.

The New Testament development of this concept is closely bound up with the one which follows. Therefore we shall consider it before we turn again to the New Testament.

Salvation as Redemption. With the word translated as redemption, we move into the most significant area of the Old Testament vocabulary of salvation. As is usual with most words in the Old Testament, there was both a secular and a more spiritual use of this word. It is from the secular usage that we find our clearest insights into its spiritual meaning.

The first obligation of the redeemer was to buy back his brother from slavery. To perform such an act was to redeem the brother. For whatever reason the person might have become enslaved, the redeemer bore the obligation of paying off the debt and thus obtaining the freedom of his brother (Lev. 25:47-49). This obligation rested upon the nearest of living kin who was able to render this redemptive service.

Beyond this, the redeemer was also obligated to keep the property of a deceased relative in the family. The land had originally been the gift of God to each tribe, clan, and family. It was precious and must be retained in that family. For this reason, Naboth refused to sell his vineyard to King Ahab of Israel.

And after this Ahab said to Naboth, "Give me your vineyard, that I may have it for a vegetable garden, because it is near my house; and I will give you a better vineyard for it; or, if it seems good to you, I will give you its value in money." But Naboth said to Ahab, "The Lord forbid that I should give you the inheritance of my fathers" (1 Kings 21:2-3).

It was also this responsibility of the redeemer which served as the focal point of the Book of Ruth. There Boaz

said to the next of kin, "Naomi, who has come back from the country of Moab, is selling the parcel of land which belonged to our kinsman Elimelech. So I thought I would tell you of it, and say, Buy it in the presence of those sitting here, and in the presence of the elders of my people. If you will redeem it, redeem it; but if you will not, tell me, that I may know, for there is no one besides you to redeem it, and I come after you" (Ruth 4:3-4).

It was also very important in Israel that a man's family be saved from extinction. Thus if a man died childless, the nearest of kin was to marry his widow and the "first son whom she bears shall succeed to the name of his brother who is dead, that his name may not be blotted out of Israel" (Deut. 25:6). This, too, was a focal point in the story of Ruth.

Then Boaz said, "The day you buy the field from the hand of Naomi, you are also buying Ruth the Moabitess, the widow of the dead, in order to restore the name of the dead to his inheritance" (Ruth 4:5).

Upon the refusal of the nearest of kin, Boaz then took over the responsibilities of the redeemer, buying the land, and marrying Ruth.

There was also a fourth responsibility that the redeemer bore in ancient Israel. If a person was murdered, it was the responsibility of the next of kin to seek out and slay the

murderer. This was modified by the provision of cities of
refuge to which a person accused of murder might flee until
he was proven guilty or found innocent (Deut. 19:6-10;
Num. 35). The kinsman who bore this responsibility was
called the "avenger of blood." The Hebrew term is literally
the "redeemer of blood." Thus the redeemer was responsible to see that justice was done. In that ancient society, the
criminal was not to go unpunished. On the other hand, the
redeemer of blood could not merely unleash his fury in a
vengeful display of temper. He could not exact more from
the guilty than justice allowed.

In a brief digression, consider for a moment the famous
lex taliones (law of retaliation) in the Old Testament. Israel
was commanded:

> When men strive together. . . . If any harm follows, then
> you shall give life for life, eye for eye, tooth for tooth, hand
> for hand, foot for foot, burn for burn, wound for wound,
> stripe for stripe (Ex. 21:22-25; cf. Lev. 24:19-20).

It is needless to point out that this is far beneath the teachings of Jesus. Of course it is. In the Sermon on the Mount,
Jesus said,

> You have heard that it was said, "An eye for an eye and a
> tooth for a tooth." But I say to you, Do not resist one who is
> evil. But if any one strikes you on the right cheek, turn to
> him the other also; and if any one would sue you and take
> your coat, let him have your cloak as well; and if any one
> forces you to go one mile, go with him two miles (Matt.
> 5:38-41).

The point is not that the Old Testament demanded less than
Jesus later did. The New Testament is clearly a development far beyond the Old Testament. The point here is that
in the day when the *lex taliones* was given, vengeance was
the rule of the day. What the ancient Hebrews were being
told was that they could exact nothing more than justice.
This was a major step forward in their ethics. People had to
first learn about justice before they could begin to learn
about mercy. (We might well consider whether or not we
have really yet learned the lesson of justice, much less that
of mercy.)

In reviewing the ways in which the redeemer functioned
in the national life of Israel, one further thing stands out. In

every instance, the redeemer was the next of kin. He was the closest in blood relationship to the one who was in need. Thus, many interpreters call him the "kinsman-redeemer." While that term is not really necessary, we must remember that this relationship was always understood as belonging to the redeemer.

If this were the only way in which the term, redeemer, was used in the Old Testament, it would be of both interest and significance. But the fact that this term was then applied to God makes it of extreme importance. This use of it for God makes several very bold claims about God and his relation to Israel. First of all, God had assumed the relationship of Israel's next of kin. There was never any idea that God was related to Israel naturally. Rather, he had assumed a relationship through the covenant. Israel had been adopted as God's firstborn (Ex. 4:22-23; Ezek. 16:1-14).

Second, God, as Israel's Redeemer, had taken upon himself the responsibility of delivering Israel from slavery. This voluntary act of redemptive grace was carried out regardless of what kind of slavery Israel had sold herself into. God delivered Israel from bondage in Egypt and ultimately from her bondage to sin. Third, as Israel's Redeemer, God had assumed the responsibility of making Israel fruitful, of producing offspring. The good fruit which Israel produced was the product of God's redemptive acts. Closely related to this was the concept that God, as Israel's Redeemer, would preserve their heritage on the land. The final responsibility which God as Israel's Redeemer voluntarily assumed was that of seeing that justice was executed upon those who oppressed her. Thus it was that Israel was told,

> Vengeance is mine, and recompense. . . .
> For the Lord will vindicate his people
>   and have compassion on his servants
>   (Deut. 32:35-36).

And based upon this idea, Paul urged,

> Repay no one evil for evil, but take thought for what is noble in the sight of all. . . . Beloved, never avenge yourselves, but leave it to the wrath of God; for it is written, "Vengeance is mine, I will repay, says the Lord" (Rom. 12:17-19).

Against this secular background and its implications for God's redemptive relation with Israel, we can now comprehend some of the depth of its meaning. Thus God promised through Hosea, "From the power of Sheol I will rescue them, and from death I will redeem them" (Hos. 13:14, author's translation). Jeremiah further emphasized the spiritual significance of the term, proclaiming,

> Their Redeemer is strong; the Lord of hosts is his name. He will surely plead their cause, that he may give rest to the earth, but unrest to the inhabitants of Babylon (Jer. 50:34).

He also connected it with the idea of rescue, just as Hosea had done.

> For the Lord has rescued Jacob,
>   and has redeemed him from hands too strong
>   for him (Jer. 31:11, author's translation).

The concept really came to the forefront in the passages of the book of Isaiah known as the great redemption (Isa. 40—55). As an encouragement, the feeble community was told,

> But now thus says the Lord,
>   he who created you, O Jacob,
>   he who formed you, O Israel:
> "Fear not, for I have redeemed you;
>   I have called you by name, you are mine" (Isa. 43:1).

There should be no fear when God is Redeemer. This thought was repeated again and again, to offer hope to the people of Israel. Their God, the Holy One of Israel, had become their Redeemer! (Isa. 43:14; 44:6,24; 47:4; 48:17; 49:7,26; 54:5,8). But this section also makes it abundantly clear that God's redemption was not limited to physical deliverance. In a magnificent statement, Israel was told,

> I have swept away your transgressions like a cloud,
>   and your sins like mist;
> return to me, for I have redeemed you (Isa. 44:22).

Further, lest anyone get the idea that God was paying a ransom to redeem Israel, he boldly stated, "You were sold for nothing, and you shall be redeemed without money" (Isa. 52:3).

The psalmist also sang of the spiritual dimension of God's redemptive activities.

> For he delivers the needy when he calls,
>   the poor and him who has no helper.
> He has pity on the weak and the needy,
>   and saves the lives of the needy.
> From oppression and violence he redeems their life;
>   and precious is their blood in his sight (Ps. 72:12-14).

Even if this refers to physical calamity, the implication is broader than that alone. Much more pointed was the assertion,

> Bless the Lord, O my soul;
>   and all that is within me,
>   bless his holy name!
> Bless the Lord, O my soul,
>   and forget not all his benefits,
> who forgives all your iniquity,
>   who heals all your diseases,
> who redeems your life from the Pit,
>   who crowns you with steadfast love and mercy,
> who satisfies you with good as long as you live
>   so that your youth is renewed like the eagle's
>   (Ps. 103:1-5).

Here the obvious reference to forgiveness is tied in with the idea of physical health. To the psalmist, these regularly appear to be tied together.

Further, the concept of God as Redeemer took on an additional personal dimension in the Book of Proverbs. There it is asserted that God was especially involved in redeeming the fatherless, an example of those who have no one else as kinsman.

> Do not remove an ancient landmark
>   or enter the fields of the fatherless;
> for their Redeemer is strong;
>   he will plead their cause against you (Prov. 23:10-11).

God cares for those for whom no one else cares. Further, he protects and redeems them.

Perhaps the greatest Old Testament vision of God as Redeemer is found in the book of Job. There the sore tried saint had found no comfort from his friends and no hope in this life. Then he had the magnificent revelation that God was his Redeemer. So he cried,

Oh that my words were written!
  Oh that they were inscribed in a book!
Oh that with an iron pen and lead
  they were graven in the rock for ever!
For I know that my Redeemer lives,
  and at last he will stand upon the earth;
and after my skin has been thus destroyed,
  then from my flesh I shall see God,
whom I shall see on my side,
  and my eyes shall behold, and not another (Job 19:23-27).

For Job, the concept of God as his Redeemer gave him a hope which stretched beyond his life. It laid hold on the hope of individual immortality, of life beyond life. When no one else could or would vindicate him, he could rest in the assurance that God would do so.

It is quite easy to see how the New Testament writers picked up this image of God as rescuing or redeeming. Identifying Christ as the one who has redeemed us proclaims a depth of meaning which can be missed if this Old Testament root is ignored (Gal. 3:13; 4:5; Col. 1:14; Titus 2:14; Rev. 5:9). By this act, Jesus has become our closest of kin, our elder Brother (Rom. 8:29; Heb. 2:11). At the same time, by making himself our nearest of kin, he also made it possible for us to be adopted into the family of God (Rom. 8:15; Eph. 1:5). Further, lest there be any question that Paul connected our adoption with Christ's redemptive acts, he specifically tied them together. On one occasion, he said, "We ourselves . . . groan inwardly as we wait for adoption as sons, the redemption of our bodies" (Rom. 8:23). He also wrote to the Galatians,

But when the time had fully come, God sent forth his Son, born of woman, born under the law, to redeem those who were under the law, so that we might receive adoption as sons (Gal. 4:4-5).

In addition, in redeeming us Jesus delivered us from our slavery to sin and Satan. Thus the author of Hebrews wrote,

Since therefore the children share in flesh and blood, he himself likewise partook of the same nature, that through death he might destroy him who has the power of death, that is, the devil, and deliver all those who through fear of death were subject to lifelong bondage (Heb. 2:14-15).

And Paul admonished the Galatians, "For freedom Christ has set us free; . . . do not submit again to a yoke of slavery" (Gal. 5:1). From whatever enslaved us, Christ has set us free.

The concept of redemption also came to bear in the New Testament insistence that he who has been redeemed by Christ should bear fruit. Jesus himself said, "By this is my Father glorified, that you bear much fruit, and so prove to be my disciples" (John 15:8). He also insisted that he himself produced the fruit in his redeemed (John 15:16). The entire New Testament conception of Jesus as our Redeemer takes on a far deeper and richer meaning when we realize the Old Testament roots from which it has grown.

In looking back over the Old Testament treatment of salvation, several things stand out. There is the fact that the Old Testament teaches that salvation always rests upon the initiative of God. Further, the major emphasis is upon the actual deliverance accomplished. The idea of a ransom paid by God is hardly present, if it is there at all.

Beyond this, there is a growing development of thought placing the emphasis more on the spiritual and less on the physical. However, in the Old Testament, the emphasis upon the physical aspects of salvation and redemption clearly predominate. But before we overemphasize this, we must remember that, to the Hebrew, there was always a close relation between spiritual salvation and physical prosperity.

There was also a major emphasis upon the salvation of the nation Israel. However, we must recognize that there was a growing emphasis upon individual salvation. This, however, did not reach full fruition until the New Testament.

Finally, we must recognize that the ultimate purpose of God's redemptive activities was always two-pronged. He sought to create a righteous, obedient people. But the purpose of this was that they might fully enjoy fellowship with him. The only full life was found in the restored covenant relation. God's purposes have not changed. He still seeks to bring us into a right relation with him for our own benefit.

II. God Forgiving Man's Sin

To thoroughly understand the Old Testament concept of salvation, we must understand the conception of divine forgiveness. Forgiveness without salvation would be meaningless. So we considered salvation first. On the other hand, salvation without forgiveness is impossible. Therefore, we shall now direct our attention to the Old Testament teachings concerning God's forgiveness of our sins.

The Covenant Background. The covenant relation between God and Israel is absolutely at the center of all Old Testament thought about divine forgiveness. So much so, in fact, that it would appear that forgiveness can hardly be understood outside of the covenant context. This is true due to the fact that even though God was seen as a Judge, he was never understood as cold, harsh, or unimpassioned. He was never viewed as disinterested or uninvolved. To the contrary, even as a Judge, he was still described in covenant terms such as Husband, Father, or King.

Thus Hosea, through whom God revealed himself as both Husband and Father, called Israel to a covenant lawsuit before God.

> Hear the word of the Lord, O people of Israel;
> for the Lord has a controversy with the inhabitants
> of the land.
> There is no faithfulness or kindness,
> and no knowledge of God in the land (Hos. 4:1).

But this was the same God who also said,

> How can I give you up, O Ephraim!
> How can I hand you over, O Israel!
> How can I make you like Admah!
> How can I treat you like Zeboiim!
> My heart recoils within me,
> my compassion grows warm and tender (Hos. 11:8).

The God who was Judge, was also involved with the accused people of Israel through the covenant relation. Therefore, because of this involvement, and because of God's commitment, his steadfast love would not let Israel go. He would be loyal to his own election of Israel, to the love which chose them.

It was upon this basis that God sought for a way to restore

the covenant. At the same time, as we have seen, his righteous demands must be met. Thus the covenant background made repentance necessary from Israel before forgiveness could come from God.

At one and the same time, two factors must be operative. First, God's righteousness made strict moral demands upon man in general and his people in particular. But at the same time, his steadfast love must be victorious. It was at this point that the conflict arose. It is at this point that we confront the dilemma of faith. Therefore, God's steadfast love, his covenant love, sought to lead Israel to repent.

The righteous demands of God were not lowered. They never have been. They never will be. But he would not let Israel go. He struggled with them, drawing them to repentance with the cords of his steadfast love. It was the vision of this steadfast love behind his judgment which was intended to move Israel to repentance and to obedience. Thus Jeremiah was told:

> Stand in the court of the Lord's house, and speak to all the cities of Judah which come to worship in the house of the Lord all the words that I command you to speak to them; do not hold back a word. It may be that they will listen, and every one turn from his evil way (Jer. 26:2-3).

Amos also steadily pointed to God's acts of judgment which had been intended to lead Israel to repent (Amos 4:6-11). Repentance and obedience on Israel's part were the only conditions which they needed to meet in order for the divine covenant to be restored (Isa. 1:16-20). But they had to be met. Unless there was repentance and obedience, God's forgiveness would not operate and the covenant would not be restored. So God pled with Israel to repent. He also led Israel to repent.

The initiative was always God's. He was determined to save his people. So the major theme of the prophets was a call to repent. This was God's demand. It was his expectation. The constant prophetic refrain was that Israel would see with their eyes, hear with their ears, understand with their minds, and "turn and be healed" (Isa. 6:10). The healing meant the restoration of the covenant relation between Israel and God.

Repentance as Man's Act. Perhaps the most important

thing to note first about the Old Testament concept of repentance is that it is always referred to by a verb and never by a noun. When the concept is dealt with, it is an action that is demanded and expected. The prophets never called upon Israel to exist in a condition of repentance. Rather, they demanded that Israel repent.

The verb which was used to describe man's repenting is the verb which also means "to return," *shubh*. Thus, whenever we find the word *return*, it can also mean—and frequently does mean—"repent." Hosea's plea is a case in point.

> Return, O Israel, to the Lord your God,
>   for you have stumbled because of your iniquity.
> Take with you words
>   and return to the Lord;
> say to him,
>   "Take away all iniquity;
> accept that which is good
>   and we will render
>   the fruit of our lips" (Hos. 14:1-2).

The prophet was obviously calling upon his people to repent. Further, his call demanded both spiritual and physical action on their part.

God's offer to Judah through Jeremiah also illustrates this use. There he said,

> Return, O faithless sons,
>   I will heal your faithlessness.
> Behold, we come to thee;
>   for thou art the Lord our God.
> Truly the hills are a delusion,
>   the orgies on the mountains.
> Truly in the Lord our God
>   is the salvation of Israel (Jer. 3:22-23).

It becomes quite obvious that for the Old Testament, repentance was never just a passive state of being sorry for sin. Neither was it merely being sorry for the consequences of sin which had befallen the sinner. Sorrow for either or both these things might have been present. But this was never confused with or substituted for repentance in the minds of the prophets. One thing was quite clear to the prophets. Repentance described a positive, specific act of turning away from sin and turning to God, accepting his will as the new purpose and new direction of life.

It becomes quite obvious, as we examine this steady prophetic call to repentance, that the prophets never considered repentance as a simple act. It was, to the contrary, quite complex, demanding a number of specific responses on the part of the repentant sinner. Consider what Hosea said the Lord expected from his people in their repentance.

I will return again to my place,
  until they acknowledge their guilt and seek my face,
  and in their distress they seek me, saying,
"Come, let us return to the Lord;
  for he has torn, that he may heal us;
  he has stricken, and he will bind us up.
After two days he will revive us;
  on the third day he will raise us up,
  that we may live before him.
Let us know, let us press on to know the Lord;
  his going forth is sure as the dawn;
he will come to us as the showers,
  as the spring rains that water the earth" (Hos. 5:15 to 6:3).

In his description, the repentance of Israel included turning to God, acknowledging their present condition, expecting healing from God, hoping for both new life and a new fellowship, desiring to know God through personal experience, and depending on his steadfast loyalty.

Jeremiah described this experience in slightly different terms.

"If you return, O Israel," says the Lord,
  "to me you should return.
If you remove your abominations from my presence,
  and do not waver,
and if you swear, 'As the Lord lives,'
  in truth, in justice, and in uprightness,
then nations shall bless themselves in him,
  and in him shall they glory"
    (Jer. 4:1-2, punctuation modified).

Here repentance clearly included not merely a confession of sin, but giving up sinful practices. It also included a steady following of God, a genuine dependence upon him. Furthermore, the end result of Israel's repentance would be that other nations would find blessing in Israel's God. Their repentance would serve as a positive, winning witness to others. In addition, God further urged his people to return to him and find forgiveness by turning away from sinful acts and thoughts.

Seek the Lord while he may be found,
  call upon him while he is near;
let the wicked forsake his way,
  and the unrighteous man his thoughts;
let him return to the Lord, that he may have mercy on him,
  and to our God, for he will abundantly pardon (Isa. 55:6-7).

In examining the multiple references to this complex act, it becomes quite apparent that the concept of repentance in the Old Testament involved a number of interrelated actions on the part of the sinner. He had to recognize and accept the righteous demands of God. He had to acknowledge his own sinful condition, turning from it to God in obedient loyalty. He had to seek God's will, both to know and to do it. And finally, he had to accept whatever God gave to him in response.

Digression: the Repentance of God. Before we proceed, let us turn briefly to what has been a problem to numerous students of the Old Testament, the repentance of God. There are many references in the Old Testament which describe God as repenting. This is quite difficult to understand if we believe that the Bible teaches that God is righteous. Why then should he repent, or even need to do so?

Two things must be understood at the very outset. First, we must remember that God is different from man.

God is not man, that he should lie,
  or a son of man, that he should repent.
Has he said, and will he not do it?
  Or has he spoken, and will he not fulfil it? (Num. 23:19).

The second thing that we must grasp is that the word which is used of man's repentance, *shubh*, is never used of God's repentance. Rather a quite different word is used to describe what God does. This word is *nacham*, and literally means "to groan," "to feel deeply," or "to be deeply moved." Thus, whatever God does, it is different from what man does when he repents. Man makes a moral turn-around. God, on the other hand, keeps his same purposes. His will does not change.

When the Old Testament describes God as "repenting," it is saying that he is deeply moved over what one or more of his people have done. They have rejected his perfect will and therefore will experience something other than what God originally intended. But the divine purpose remains unchanged. The divine action toward his people changes because they have not responded in the way he desired. An example of this can be seen in Genesis 6:6. God was deeply distressed over the evil imagination of his people on earth. The King James Version translated this verse:

> And it repented the Lord that he had made man on the earth, and it grieved him at his heart.

On the other hand, the Revised Standard Version translated it:

> And the Lord was sorry that he had made man on the earth, and it grieved him to his heart.

Both translations are accurate. But it is obvious that God was not changing his purpose. Rather he changed his action in response to what man had done, that he might still fulfill his unchanged purpose. Thus God feels deeply, groans within himself, and is deeply moved over the fact that his creatures have failed. But he does not change his ultimate purpose.

Forgiveness as God's Gift. Turning our attention back to human repentance, we need to note the other side of the coin. Man's repentance was demanded by God because he wished to do something about man's sin problem. To repent is the human act. To forgive is the divine response. God desired to forgive the sin of man. But what did the Old Testament consider God's forgiveness to be? It is that which we must now consider.

There are three basic words used in the Old Testament vocabulary of divine forgiveness. The first of these means "to forgive," or "to pardon." It is only used of God's grace. However, it is not always unconditional or unlimited. Thus, when the Hebrews in the wilderness had been disobedient at Kadesh, and Moses pled for God to pardon their sin, God responded,

I have pardoned, according to your word; but truly, as I live, and as all the earth shall be filled with the glory of the Lord, none of the men who have seen my glory and my signs which I wrought in Egypt and in the wilderness, and yet have put me to the proof these ten times and have not harkened to my voice, shall see the land which I swore to give to their fathers; and none of those who despised me shall see it (Num. 14:20-23).

The disloyalty was forgiven. But at the same time, none of the older generation was allowed to enter the land of Canaan. Yet the psalmist could sing of God's forgiveness which allowed the nation to continue to exist.

> Yet he, being compassionate,
>   forgave their iniquity,
>   and did not destroy them;
> he restrained his anger often,
>   and did not stir up all his wrath (Ps. 78:38).

The Book of Isaiah clearly tied God's forgiveness to human repentance.

Let the wicked forsake his way,
  and the unrighteous man his thoughts;
let him return to the Lord, that he may have mercy on him,
  and to our God, for he will abundantly pardon (Isa. 55:7).

Jeremiah pointed to the divine gift of the new covenant as being the means whereby God's forgiveness would ultimately be effected.

Behold, the days are coming, says the Lord, when I will make a new covenant with the house of Israel and the house of Judah, . . . for I will forgive their iniquity, and I will remember their sin no more (Jer. 31:31-34).

In each instance, God's forgiveness was a gift. It was never viewed either as something automatic which followed the human fulfillment of certain acts or ritual steps. Neither was it viewed as something which man could earn. It was God's gift, based on his steadfast love, arising from his own nature.

The second word in the Old Testament vocabulary of divine forgiveness also has a variety of translations. It is translated "to cover," "to forgive," or "to atone." It, too, was used only of God's act, never of man's. It referred to

God's covering man's sin. Man could never cover his sin for himself. But God could cover it. And he did.

This word is used in the ritual of the great Day of Atonement (Lev. 16). It was from there, of course, that the New Testament picked up much of its imagery concerning the atonement of Christ.

The third word in the vocabulary of forgiveness means "to bear," "to lift up," "to remove," and "to take away," and in this context was applied to guilt. It is a very common word and is used in the Old Testament of both God and man. It can describe lifting up and carrying off a burden. It is thus particularly appropriate of God's forgiveness. In his forgiveness, what he does is to lift up and carry away human guilt. The prophet Micah praised God for this.

> Who is a God like thee, removing guilt,
>   and passing over transgression
>   for the remnant of his inheritance?
>   (Mic. 7:18, author's translation).

And the psalmist, having experienced God's forgiveness, sang of him in adoration.

> I acknowledged my sin to thee,
>   and I did not hide my iniquity;
> I said, "I will confess my rebellions to the Lord";
>   and you did remove the guilt of my sin
>   (Ps. 32:5, author's translation).

The Old Testament concept of forgiveness is obviously quite profound. In the use of all three of these terms, God's forgiveness was always based upon his abundant mercy and his steadfast love. Further, when God forgave, he removed the guilt from the sinner. Thus the forgiven sinner could truly sing, "All my sins are gone." Furthermore, when God forgave, some of the consequences of sin were removed, though not necessarily all. Even when he forgave, God did not rewrite history. He still doesn't. The past is still there. The evil example had been set and its influence continued to work. This is still true.

The forgiveness of God also appears to have always presupposed a genuine, earnest repentance on the part of the sinner. He had truly to desire to be restored into the divine favor, to give up his sin, and to seek to obey and serve God.

Finally, the forgiveness of God restored the sinner into the covenant relationship or brought him into a new covenant. When this happened, the forgiven sinner was given a new vision of God. The forgiven sinner saw the larger dimension, recognizing that God forgave because he loved. This forgiveness motivated the forgiven sinner to serve the God who had forgiven. Thus it was not until Isaiah's sin had been covered by God that he became aware of God's desire to have a messenger represent him to his people. At this, the prophet volunteered (Isa. 6:7-8).

Savior and Redeemer

It was the Old Testament's understanding of salvation and forgiveness that enabled Israel to grasp the revelation of God as Savior and Redeemer. They looked back to the great experience of the Exodus for the supreme example of God as Redeemer. In the context of human repentance and divine forgiveness, the psalmist sang:

> They remembered that God was their rock,
> the Most High God their redeemer (Ps. 78:35).

But, in thinking about the apostasy of Israel, they could also describe it in song, by saying, "They forgot God, their Savior" (Ps. 106:21). In looking back to what God had done for their fathers, they were sure that God was both Savior and Redeemer. But it was also this past memory that gave Israel hope for the present and the future.

At times Israel forgot that their salvation in the Old Testament was conditioned upon their response. The people seem to have thought that just because they were descendants of Abraham and a part of the covenant community, salvation should come automatically. Thus their cry when this did not happen bordered on despair.

> The harvest is past, the summer is ended,
> and we are not saved (Jer. 8:20).

It remained for the prophets to reassure Israel that God was both Savior and Redeemer. In that reassurance, however, they also made clear that his acts in saving, redeeming, and forgiving were not automatic. They were offers of grace which sprang from his nature. They were intended to give Israel hope. But they were never intended to assure Israel of an automatic blessing.

God was the Savior. Beside him, there was no hope. Thus Israel was told,

> I, I am the Lord,
> and besides me there is no savior (Isa. 43:11).

But as he acted graciously toward Israel, the ultimate purpose was to offer grace to all men.

Then all flesh shall know
that I am the Lord your Savior,
and your Redeemer, the Mighty One of Jacob (Isa. 49:26).

So Israel saw God as Savior and Redeemer, no matter where they looked in history. It was this insight, given by God's own self-revelation, which gave them a real hope for their future. There was something better beyond their present.

8
God's Promises and Man's Hope

INTRO

Israel had no glorious past to which her people could look back. Their past portrayed them as slaves in Egypt, delivered through no virtue or strength of their own. Neither did they normally have much of a present. With only a few exceptions, most of their history was lived under foreign threat or domination. In general, they did not have much of a future to which to look forward. Both kingdoms were told by the prophets that their future was one of defeat, captivity, and exile.

Yet, in spite of this, Israel did develop a quite definite hope for the future. Their hope was not based upon their own achievements but upon the gifts of God. It was certainly not derived from their own insights into the future but upon the revelation which God gave them. Their hope was not an empty optimism but a hardy realism, for it was based upon the character of God as he had revealed himself and his purposes. In short, their hope was based upon God's promises. Their future had to be good, because God was in it. And it would come, because God had promised it. To that hope and its development we shall now turn our attention.

I. The Sovereignty of God

We have from time to time pointed out the Old Testament's firm conviction of the absolute sovereignty of God.

In order really to understand Israel's hope for the future, we must first comprehend their belief in the total sovereignty of God. For it was upon the foundation of their belief in God's sovereignty that God built a hope for their future.

 Sovereign over Nature. As we have seen, the Old Testament points to the God of Israel as the divine Creator of the universe. It was he and he alone who brought all things into being. He did it through the power of his spoken word. He was in absolute control of all the creative forces of the universe. The Books of Genesis, Psalms, Job, and Isaiah all give a full treatment to this thought.

But not only was God seen as sovereign through his creative power, he was also seen as sovereign through his sustenance of the universe. It was God's promise to Noah that,

> While the earth remains, seedtime and harvest, cold and heat, summer and winter, day and night, shall not cease (Gen. 8:22).

All the forces at work in the world of nature were seen to be under his control. He caused the earth to quake, wind to blow, locusts to come, manna to fall, rain to cease, and anything else to occur in the world of nature which pleased him and accomplished his purposes. Israel never viewed God as the unmoved Mover, as some of the Greeks described him. They thought he set his world in motion and then departed and let it run on its own. Neither was God viewed as one who let the forces of nature get out of his control, as the Babylonians described their gods. The Old Testament was perfectly clear that God was sovereign over nature.

A further evidence of the Old Testament's understanding of God's sovereignty over nature is seen in Israel's concept of miracle. As we have seen, not nearly all of the miracles of the Old Testament were viewed as supernatural. But all were seen to be totally under God's control, whether supernatural or merely abnormal. Further, all Old Testament miracles were seen as pointing to his power, and being the result of his power. Thus, every miracle pointed to the absolute sovereignty of God. Nature was under his control.

Sovereign over History. We have also seen how the Old Testament teaches God's sovereignty over history. He not only controlled the natural features of the world, he con-

trolled the men and nations who walked upon it. All the nations of the earth were seen to be under his sovereign will.
In particular, the Old Testament teaches that God could and
did use the other nations in Israel's world. Furthermore, he
could use them without either their knowledge or their will
in order to effect his sovereign purposes. He held those nations responsible for their actions, and called prophets to
specific ministries to them. But all this was a relatively
minor aspect of God's sovereignty over history.

The major emphasis of the Old Testament concept of
God's sovereignty over history was directed to his sovereignty over Israel. It was quite common in the ancient Near
East for people to believe that their god, or if they worshiped more than one god, that their chief god was "king"
or "lord." That Israel held this belief in common with her
neighbors is beyond question. This idea that God was Israel's King appeared quite early in her history as a nation.
There is no way of actually knowing where it first appeared. When the people asked Samuel for a king, it was
considered to be a rejection of God's kingship (1 Sam. 8:4-9).
Further, as we have seen, the very form of God's covenant
with Israel was a declaration of his kingship over them.

Beyond this, when Israel was given a human king, his
authority was considered to have been derived from the
sovereign authority of God. Ideally, the king was to have
been an instrument in the hands of God for establishing his
purposes, fulfilling his promises, and making Israel into
the kind of people which God had intended. As it became
more and more obvious how the kings were failing, the
eighth-century prophets began to reemphasize the divine
King. Even though Israel and Judah had human kings, God
alone was the ultimate King.

In the post-Exilic period, when there was no longer any
human king in Israel at all, there was an even stronger
emphasis upon the divine kingship and sovereignty. In that
period we can see a growing emphasis upon the fact that
God was in charge of world history not so much through,
but in spite of, Israel. Without any question, there was
never any era but that Israel was clearly shown that God
was sovereign over history.

Sovereign over the Future. Based upon the Old Testament teachings of God's sovereignty over nature and over

history, God began to reveal to Israel that he was also sovereign over the future. As the people became increasingly aware of the frailties and failures of human kingship, God began to show them that there was to be an idealized Ruler from the Davidic line. It is this that we call their messianic hope. The future King was the Messiah. To this we shall return later in greater detail. But the prophets and song writers of Israel gave magnificent expression to this development.

As a parallel development, we can also see the Old Testament teachings about a future, supernatural kingdom of God. These teachings were both parallel to the idea of a Messiah and intertwined with it. The vision of the future kingdom was sometimes temporal and sometimes eschatological, having to do with the end of the age. This vision of the future kingdom was rooted both in the concept of God's sovereignty and in the concept that he alone knew the future. Accepting both of these as true, it was but a step for God to show Israel that therefore, he alone was in control of the future. Part of this control was seen as being exercised through the nation of Israel. But this was not the whole story. God also controlled the future in spite of Israel. They could not thwart his control either through disobedience or rebellion.

In most of the Old Testament visions of this future kingdom, the Day of the Lord was seen as the time of the inauguration of the kingdom. We shall return to a detailed discussion of "that Day." Insofar as it affects our consideration of that future kingdom, there are several significant features for which we must watch. At the Day of the Lord, the divine purposes were to be vindicated upon the stage of human history. Further, a new era was to be inaugurated upon the earth. Even the animals would share in the glory of this coming kingdom.

In that future kingdom of God, justice and peace were to abound, for God will reign supreme. Redeemed men were to share in that future kingdom. These redeemed men would be a saved remnant. To this, too, we shall return.

In the last analysis, all of Israel's hope for the future rested in the absolute sovereignty of God. He had been sovereign in the past. He was sovereign in their present. And he would be sovereign in the future. To his sovereignty there was no ultimate challenge which would stand. Upon the assurance of that sovereignty, Israel was given a hope for the future.

II. The Judgment and Wrath of God

We have already given some attention to the judgment and wrath of God in chapter 3, where we considered the acts of God. We must return to these concepts now, for they also played a very real and vital part in Israel's future hope. God's acts of salvation and grace have been displayed within history against a background of wrath and judgment. Israel's salvation depended upon her recognition that God's wrath was manifested against sin and uncleanness. Thus, as Israel's thoughts turned more and more from present to future salvation in her hope, it was firmly grounded upon the Old Testament teachings of present and future judgment and wrath.

The Nature and Purpose of God's Judgment. The judgment and wrath of God are clearly taught as realities within the Old Testament. The ideas have been dismissed by some interpreters as outworn anthropomorphisms. Anthropomorphic, they may be. Outworn, they most certainly are not. It is a major emphasis which would make nonsense out of much of the Old Testament if it were removed.

The wrath of God clearly had a moral emphasis, for the prophets proclaimed that it was directed toward moral sin. Furthermore, the prophets were equally as clear about the fact that God's wrath was directed primarily toward Israel, due to their treacherous betrayal of the covenant relationship. But beyond this, the prophets also saw that God's wrath was directed toward all human pride, whether Israel's or some other nation's. Inhumanity of any people toward another was just as surely under God's wrath.

Thus when the Spirit of God is grieved by man's sin, he becomes the enemy of the sinner, whoever he may be. So we are told,

> But they rebelled
> and grieved his Holy Spirit;
> therefore he turned to be their enemy,
> and himself fought against them (Isa. 63:10).

But we have also noted that God's wrath had an evangelizing aim. The prophets were firmly convinced that God's wrath was tempered by mercy, and that his steadfast love was his prevailing characteristic. So judgment and wrath always were products of his love. Amos declared that God's purpose in judgment was to bring Israel to repentance, thus turning them back to God (Amos 4:6-11).

The prophets were also sure that God's judgment was inescapable. No one could flaunt the righteous demands of God. Such acts kindled his wrath and made his judgment sure.

Further, judgment was seen as falling upon nations, groups within nations, families, and individuals. There was a real sense of corporate responsibility for sin. But it is equally as true that there was a sense of personal responsibility. Even Deuteronomy says,

> The fathers shall not be put to death for the children, nor shall the children be put to death for the fathers; every man shall be put to death for his own sin (Deut. 24:16).

However, this does not mean that children can escape the historical consequences of their fathers' sins. That, however, is neither wrath nor judgment.

On the other hand, it was the inescapable nature of God's temporal judgment and its evangelizing aim which gave Israel hope. God was not merely punishing, he was seeking to redeem. He was not merely striking out at sin, he was purposing to deliver the sinner. But this brings us to consider the Day of the Lord and God's judgment and wrath.

The Day of the Lord and God's Judgment. One of the features of the Old Testament's understanding of God's wrath and judgment was that it was clearly linked with the Day of the Lord. Amos was the first prophet to refer to this event.

> Woe to you who desire the day of the Lord!
>   Why would you have the day of the Lord?
> It is darkness and not light;
>   as if a man fled from a lion,
>   and a bear met him;
> or went into his house and leaned with his hand
>   against the wall,
>   and a serpent bit him.
> Is not the day of the Lord darkness, and not light, and gloom
>   with no brightness in it? (Amos 5:18-20).

Although there are no biblical references to the Day of the
Lord prior to Amos, the very way he dealt with the idea
made it quite clear that it was already a part of the popular
theology. He was not presenting a new idea but correcting
an old one. The people were expecting the Day to be a time of
judgment upon God's enemies. Amos said that this was
true, but Israel was one of the enemies! Judgment was already an essential part of the concept of the Day. What
Amos added was that the judgment would be a moral judgment upon the covenant people.

The obvious question which we must face is how did the
concept of the Day of the Lord arise? Where did the idea
enter Israel's faith? By this avenue, perhaps we can discover what the Day actually meant. Before pursuing that
question, we should note that the Day of the Lord was regularly identified as "that day," "the day of his coming," "the
day of punishment," or such similar expressions (Isa. 12:1;
Mal. 3:2; Isa. 10:3).

There appears to be two essential roots behind the concept of the Day of the Lord. The first and more basic arose
from Israel's time-consciousness. They viewed time as
important because of what happened in it, not merely because it passed. Thus months were named by what happened, such as "barley harvest," "early planting," "flax
harvest," and such. Therefore, any day which was specially
filled with God's activity could have been called the Day of
the Lord. Quite naturally, the idea that any future day of
judgment or deliverance was the Day of the Lord could have
arisen. It would have been quite easy for this to have been
transferred to the ultimate time of judgment. Such would
have been the Day of the Lord in a very special way.

The second root idea behind this concept probably came
from the idea that God was a warrior who fought for Israel.
He is so described in many of the earlier books in the Old
Testament. He fought for them in Egypt and he fought for
them in Canaan. From this standpoint, the Day of the Lord
would have been the day of his particular victory over his
and Israel's enemies. Then Amos would have been pointing
out that while this was true, Israel was among the enemies.
Here again, it is quite easy to see how this could have transferred itself to the idea of the ultimate victory of God over all
who were his enemies.

Although other suggestions have been made, there are none which really seem to fit the descriptions of the Day as it is used in the Old Testament. It was seen as the Day of God's activity in judgment. It was also seen as the Day of God's ultimate victory over his enemies.

In considering the significance of the Day of the Lord for Israel's future hope, we need to note several things. First, it was a major part of Israel's future hope. Almost every prophet had something to say about it. There are frequent references among the Psalms, also.

Second, in the pre-Exilic period, the main idea of "that Day" was judgment. This judgment would fall upon Israel, for her privilege in the covenant carried a concurrent responsibility. However, the judgment was also seen as falling upon the surrounding nations. They, too, were held responsible for their actions (Amos 1:3 to 2:3). But even though the emphasis was upon judgment, there was also an awareness that God would deliver a remnant of his people. So Isaiah proclaimed:

> In that day the remnant of Israel and the survivors of the house of Jacob will no more lean upon him that smote them, but will lean upon the Lord, the Holy One of Israel, in truth. A remnant will return, the remnant of Jacob, to the mighty God. For though your people Israel be as the sand of the sea, only a remnant of them will return (Isa. 10:20-22).

Third, in the post-Exilic period, there appears to have been a slight change of emphasis. There was a new focus upon the fact that the Day was to be a time of deliverance from Israel's enemies. It is almost as if to some extent the Exile itself was seen as primarily directed against Israel as the Day of the Lord. Then there would be a future Day of the Lord to be directed against her oppressors. But this is not the whole story. For in this period, the Day was also seen as a day of salvation both for Israel and for her enemies. The great Day of the Lord was to be a day of redemption as well as judgment.

It should be noted that Israel never saw herself as ushering in the Day. It was always viewed as being brought in by God himself. Israel was seen to be quite passive.

We have a tendency to want a timetable for all God's events. This was apparently not true of the Hebrew prophets. The Day of the Lord was usually described in the Old Testament with a verb form known as a prophetic perfect. This makes it sound as if it had already happened. But what these ancient spokesmen for God were describing was the fact that it was already set and certain in the mind of God. He had it planned out and could describe it as if he had seen it. Thus the prophets knew it was coming. They knew it was sure. They did not spend much time asking, "When?" Rather, it was their task to use the certainty of its coming as a means to call people to repentance.

C - *The Remnant and God's Judgment.* The concept of the remnant was also a major part of Israel's future hope which was intimately related to the idea of judgment. There are five basic words which the Old Testament used to describe this group. Each of these is translated "remnant," but each has a slightly different background. First, the remnant was to be the remainder, the ones left over after judgment. The second term focused upon the fact that this remnant had escaped from the judgment. The third described the residue left at the bottom of a cup or a bowl. The fourth term emphasized the fact of survival. And the last one directed attention to the scraps which are left over when something has been made. All of these terms point to the fact that only part of Israel would be left after the wrath of God had issued in judgment. Thus Isaiah offered hope, saying,

And the surviving remnant of the house of Judah shall again take root downward, and bear fruit upward; for out of Jerusalem shall go forth a remnant, and out of Mount Zion a band of survivors (2 Kings 19:30-31; Isa. 37:31-32).

The concept of a surviving remnant is found throughout the Old Testament. Noah and his family were the remnant which survived the Flood (Gen. 7:21-23). Lot and his daughters were the remnant which survived the destruction of Sodom (Gen. 19:29). God told Elijah that there was a faithful remnant still in Israel during his lifetime (1 Kings 19:18).

But it remained for the prophets to sharpen and develop the concept for Israel's future hope. Their development had several different emphases. In some instances, the remnant appears only to be those who survive judgment. There was no thought here that this was a righteous remnant. Rather, their survival was sheer grace. The prophets seem to hope that, in response to their gracious survival, this remnant would gratefully turn to God for forgiveness and mercy. It was of these that Isaiah spoke.

> If the Lord of hosts
>   had not left us a few survivors,
> we should have been like Sodom,
>   and become like Gomorrah (Isa. 1:9).

Yet, there also seem to be some instances where the prophets described the remnant as surviving because they were righteous and in a right relationship to God. In this case, those in the remnant were seen as being there by deliberate choice. To these, God lovingly called.

> I will surely gather all of you, O Jacob,
>   I will gather the remnant of Israel;
> I will set them together
>   like sheep in a fold,
> like a flock in its pasture,
>   a noisy multitude of men (Mic. 2:12).

Jeremiah added a new dimension with his vision of the new covenant (Jer. 31:31-34). To him, the remnant would be made up of those individuals who entered into that new relationship with God. His hope of the remnant was based upon God's acts of grace and man's free response, a response made possible by the gracious act of God. (We shall deal with the new covenant in more detail later in this chapter.)

The prophetic hope thus offered a vision of a remnant saved both through and by judgment. Unfortunately, when Israel came back from the Exile, this hope was almost dashed. Those who returned seem to have considered themselves the remnant. But things were not better. Thus Nehemiah was told,

The survivors there in the province who escaped exile are

in great trouble and shame; and wall of Jerusalem is broken down, and its gates are destroyed by fire (Neh. 1:3).

The people who returned had the same old problems with sin and disobedience. Thus it was that the prophets saw their hope for a remnant deferred, but not abandoned. It was at this point that God caused them to look farther down the corridors of time to the future remnant of God, to whom all God's promises would be fulfilled.

It was upon this deferred hope that Paul built in his letter to the Romans. To them he wrote:

I ask, then, has God rejected his people? By no means! I myself am an Israelite, a descendant of Abraham, a member of the tribe of Benjamin.
So too at the present time there is a remnant, chosen by grace (Rom. 11:1,5).

In reviewing Israel's concept of God's judgment, we note that it, in itself, was a basis of hope. Judgment by itself offered hope, because it assured them that God cared. He was concerned with what they did. Even more, it offered hope because his judgment had a redemptive dimension. Within time, it sought to bring Israel back to God. In the ultimate Day of the Lord, his judgment would produce a purified, redeemed remnant. The people in that remnant would be the participants in the new covenant. As such, they would be the new people of God. It is this new people of God whom Jesus has saved and called unto himself. Here is another glorious New Testament flower from an Old Testament root.

III.   The Messiah

For the Christian, perhaps the most significant area of Israel's future hope lies in their expectation of the Messiah. At the same time, this is frequently one of the more confused and confusing areas. Most of the confusion lies in a hazy conception of what the various terms used by interpreters mean. However, some of the confusion also lies in the fact that interpreters use these terms in different ways. Therefore, there is no consistency. Let us be well aware that lack of clarity concerning the key words can bring about total confusion as we try to bring these concepts into some kind of order.

It is imperative, therefore, that you understand these key words as I am using them. The following definitions should help clarify this.

The first word used so frequently in this context is **eschatology.** It also shows up regularly as an adjective, eschatological. The word is derived from a Greek word which means last, or end. Old Testament eschatology therefore refers to the Old Testament concept of last things. It directs attention to those things which will accompany the end of the age as it was viewed by the Old Testament writers.

The second term which needs to be more closely defined is **future hope.** I use this term in referring to those events which the Old Testament writers viewed as coming to pass in their future and which were a basis for hope. From our historical vantage point, much of their future hope is past. For example, some of the future hope of the prophets of the Hebrew kingdoms came to pass in the return from the Exile. Other parts of it came to pass in the ministry of Jesus Christ. Israel's future hope could and did involve things which were both good and bad, as long as they offered some kind of hope. Thus, Israel's eschatology was clearly a part of their future hope. But their future hope involved far more than their eschatology.

The third idea which we must understand more precisely actually shows up in two forms, **messiah**, and **messianic prophecy.** These are a bit more difficult for us to grasp clearly. By definition, I am limiting messianic prophecy to those parts of Israel's future hope which speak specifically about the messiah. Therefore, any view of the future which does not deal with the work of the messiah should not, and will not, be called messianic prophecy.

Before we can define *messiah*, we must consider some other factors. The word, *messiah*, is actually a transliteration of a Hebrew word. It specifically means the "anointed thing" or the "anointed one." It was used in the Old Testament to refer to a number of different objects and people.

Occasionally the term was specifically applied to inanimate objects, such as the altar, or armor (Num. 7:10; Isa. 21:5). These were objects which were anointed or set apart for the use of God. They were specifically designated for the accomplishment of his purposes.

The term is also frequently used of persons who were appointed to historical offices. These were positions in which they were to serve God and minister to his people. Thus we are told of Saul,

> Then Samuel took a vial of oil and poured it on his head, and kissed him and said, "Has not the Lord anointed you to be prince over his people Israel?" (1 Sam. 10:1).

This could also be translated, "Has not the Lord made you messiah, to be prince." It was applied to David (1 Sam. 16:13), and generally to the kings who ruled in either Israel or Judah.

In addition, priests and prophets were also described as anointed ones (Lev. 4:5; 6:22; Isa. 61:1). They were either anointed to serve at the altar or to proclaim God's word. Furthermore, even a pagan king, Cyrus, the Persian conqueror, is called by this title.

> Thus says the Lord to his anointed [his messiah],
>   to Cyrus,
>   whose right hand I have grasped,
> to subdue nations before him
>   and ungird the loins of kings,
> to open doors before him
>   that gates may not be closed (Isa. 45:1).

In one instance, the term was even applied to the entire nation of Israel,

> Thou wentest forth for the salvation of thy people,
>   for the salvation of thy anointed (Hab. 3:13).

In these instances, the term frequently referred to the anointing with oil before someone or something could be used for God's service. But in every instance, the anointed thing or person was specifically devoted to the service of God.

But the term, *messiah*, was ultimately applied to the ideal Davidic ruler of the future. It is here that we actually come to what we generally mean by *messiah*. It is here that we come to grips with actual messianic prophecy.

The term *messiah* is never used in the Old Testament with a definite article. There is not a single reference to "the messiah." Neither does it ever seem to be used as a proper name. Rather, the term seems always to focus upon a function, the duty or service which one who is messiah will render to God. Thus, we shall define messiah as: one who has been set apart for the specific service of God. It will focus itself as pointing to a descendent of David. We must keep this definition before us as we direct our attention to the Old Testament development of the hope for a messiah.

The Background of the Messianic Concept. As we have noted, there was no glorious past in Israel's history. The peoples surrounding her always looked back to a real or imagined past which was a golden age. Israel could only look back to a past which included Egyptian bondage, wilderness wanderings, and the rebellions and oppressions of the period of the judges. Since they had no golden age to give them a backward pull, they were more open to the possibilities of the future. It was into this openness toward a forward look that God poured his revelation.

In Israel's past, the work of Moses was just about the brightest spot, and it was not all that attractive. The reign of David became the next bright spot. But he, too, had feet of clay. Aside from his personal, human failures however, there was an assurance that God had chosen him for special service. Further, God had used David to bring about the only truly great achievements in Israel's national history. Further, to David had been promised future blessings for his family and, through them, to his people.

This brought about a dilemma for the people of Israel. As they contrasted those promises of future blessings with the present realities of most of their reigning monarchs, the Davidic successors, there was an obvious discrepancy. What they had expected and what actually was were far apart. Thus they were led to lift their eyes and look to the future for a son of David who would reign over them as they both expected and hoped. It was this difference between that for which they hoped and that which they actually experienced which established the first part of the background against which their messianic hope was built.

Related to this, but adding a somewhat different dimension, was the Old Testament concept of kingship. The royal ideology of the ancient Near East may have played some part here. In the nations which were Israel's neighbors, the king was seen as being the god's representative, the god's son, and sometimes was even identified with the god. They had great celebrations at an annual enthronement ceremony, where the king acted the part of god in elaborate rituals celebrating creation, the annual renewal of nature, and sometimes the establishment of their own nation. Now it is quite apparent that in Israel there never was any such emphasis placed upon the king or upon his specific relationship to God. However, Israel was surely aware of these observances and of their meaning.

It is quite possible that Israel's emphasis upon the humanity of their king was a reaction against this kind of pagan observance. It is also quite possible that some of their emphasis upon the ultimate kingship of God was a similar reaction. But it is also likely that Israel used some parts of those ancient rituals in a quite different way from the way they were used by her nieghbors. Certainly, Israel looked for some things from the future messiah of God that the surrounding nations claimed for their reigning kings. Thus Israel was saying to her neighbors, "You think your present king is an ideal ruler with an ideal relationship to your god. You are wrong. But we are going to be given a future ideal ruler who will have an ideal relationship with our God." In a sense, Israel may have been using her neighbors' rituals and beliefs as a basis of preaching her faith.

This is precisely the kind of thing which Paul did in Athens (Acts 17:16-31).

More to the point, Israel's own ideal of kingship clearly played a part in the development of their messianic hope. The Israelite ideal of kingship began with the concept of the king as God's anointed. As such, he was set apart for a special service to God (Deut. 17:14-20; 1 Sam. 8:4-22; 12:13-25). At the same time, the king was never above the law. He was always to be obedient to the law and to God. He was to lead the people forth to battle, to defend them, and to rule over them, thus ensuring peace. He was also considered to have been given special talents or gifts by God to enable him to fulfill his responsibility. Furthermore, he was considered to possess a special relationship to God as the representative of his people. It is quite obvious that this, too, was surely in the background of the developing messianic hope in Israel. They looked for a future king who would be what every actual king should have been but was not.

It was in the prophetic preaching that these strands came together. In spite of the overwhelming predominance of judgment in their preaching, they had great visions of a future for the nation. God's judgment was both redemptive and purifying. Further, there was to be a remnant which would survive. As they looked to this future, they envisioned an ideal king who would be a descendent of David. It is to that vision which we must now turn.

The Future Ministry of the Messiah. In the Old Testament descriptions of the coming deliverer, the ideal future king, there are a number of titles and names by which he is called. These help us get a picture of his function as the Old Testament viewed it. It is worth noting that the actual term, *messiah,* is seldom if ever used to apply to this ideal ruler in the Old Testament. It was the New Testament which actually did this by calling Jesus, "Christ." (This is a transliteration of the Greek word for *messiah.*) However, the Old Testament hope clearly points to an ideal ruler who was the descendent of David.

Among the terms which were used to apply to this ideal

future ruler are those which clearly identified him as great David's greater Son. Among these are "shoot," "branch," and such. Thus Isaiah promised.

> There shall come forth a shoot from the stump of
>   Jesse,
>   and a branch shall grow out of his roots (Isa. 11:1).

Jeremiah added to the picture.

> Behold, the days are coming, says the Lord, when I will raise up for David a righteous Branch, and he shall reign as king and deal wisely, and shall execute justice and righteousness in the land (Jer. 23:5).

Furthermore, after the Exile, Zechariah offered hope to his people with the divine promise, "Behold, I will bring my servant the Branch" (Zech. 3:8). It would appear that Isaiah was merely being descriptive of the relationship which existed between the messiah and David. He was to be an offspring, a descendant. But probably by the time of Jeremiah and certainly by the time of Zechariah, the term had actually become a title for the expected deliverer. It was clearly upon this basis that the announcement was given in the New Testament concerning the birth of Jesus:

> He will be great, and will be called
>   the Son of the Most High;
> and the Lord God will give to him the
>   throne of his father David (Luke 1:32).

However, other titles and names for the messianic deliverer in the Old Testament are far more descriptive. In Isaiah 7:14, he was given the name Immanuel. This name simply means, "God with us." What a promise of hope was contained in that name! However, the most familiar list of messianic names is found in the statement,

> and his name will be called
> "Wonderful Counselor, Mighty God,
>   Everlasting Father, Prince of Peace" (Isa. 9:6).

Where earthly kings had failed in wisdom the ideal king would possess miraculous wisdom. (The word *wonderful* is

the same Hebrew word which is used in the Old Testament
vocabulary of miracle, referring to a wonder.) Where Israel's earthly kings had been seen over and over as weak
and human, the coming one would have the power of God.
(This title might even have hinted of more to Isaiah than we
have dared consider. The word for *mighty* in every other
occurrence in the Old Testament except in this title referred to a mighty man. Could it be that God was giving
Isaiah a glimpse into the incarnation? I cannot prove this.
But based upon its other usage, it would appear to be quite
legitimate to translate it as "Mighty Man-God." Obviously,
if this was intended to be a prediction of the incarnation, the
people of the Old Testament missed it. This idea did not become a part of their messianic hope. But we have abundant
evidence that they missed seeing many such things until
Jesus made them obvious.)

The other two titles also pointed out the substance of Israel's messianic hope when contrasted with their present
reality. The king who was always expected to be a father to
his people often oppressed them. Even when one fulfilled
this ideal, he soon died. The messiah would be an Everlasting Father. Further, there was seldom any length of time
when the Hebrew kingdoms were not at war or threatened
by war. The messiah would truly be a Prince of Peace.

In addition to the broad hints of the ministry of the messiah given by his titles, there are more specific statements.
Thus Israel was promised:

> And he shall stand and feed his flock in the strength
>   of the Lord,
>   in the majesty of the name of the Lord his God.
> And they shall dwell secure, for now he shall be great
>   to the ends of the earth (Mic. 5:4).

The messiah would lead his people as a shepherd, nourish-
ing and protecting them. Furthermore, his greatness and
authority would extend over the entire world.

Isaiah enlarged upon this vision, promising,

> For to us a child is born,
>   to us a son is given;
> and the government will be upon his shoulder,

. . . .

Of the increase of his government and of peace
  there will be no end,
upon the throne of David, and over his kingdom,
  to establish it, and to uphold it with justice and with righ-
    teousness
from this time forth and for evermore (Isa. 9:6-7).

The messiah was to come into the world through birth, a
natural process. He would assume the authority of government over his people. But this authority would increase to
the end of time. It would bring in peace and be a reign of
righteousness and justice. To this point, it might seem that
the primary emphasis upon the messianic ministry was political. But it did not remain so.

> And the Spirit of the Lord shall rest upon him,
>   the spirit of wisdom and understanding,
>   the spirit of counsel and might,
>   the spirit of knowledge and the fear of the Lord.
> And his delight shall be in the fear of the Lord.
>
> He shall not judge by what his eyes see,
>   or decide by what his ears hear;
> but with righteousness he shall judge the poor,
>   and decide with equity for the meek of the earth;
> and he shall smite the earth with the rod of his
>   mouth,
>   and with the breath of his lips he shall slay the
>   wicked.
> Righteousness shall be the girdle of his waist,
>   and faithfulness the girdle of his loins.
>
> The wolf shall dwell with the lamb,
>   and the leopard shall lie down with the kid,
> and the calf and the lion and the fatling together,
>   and a little child shall lead them (Isa. 11:2-6).
>
> They shall not hurt or destroy
>   in all my holy mountain;
> for the earth shall be full of the knowledge of the
>   Lord
>   as the waters cover the sea.

In that day the root of Jesse shall stand as an ensign to the
peoples; him shall the nations seek, and his dwellings shall
be glorious (Isa. 11:9-10).

Here is clearly described a spiritual and an ultimately eschatological ministry. The messiah would find spiritual resources from God himself. Further, his pleasure would be in the personal experience with God, as well as in the authoritative revelation from God. (See chapter 1 for the meaning of "the fear of the Lord.") In addition, he would exercise his authority with righteousness and fairness, but he would also see that the poor got a fair deal. Finally, there would result a transformed world where all creatures were at peace with one another, a time when fear was absent. In the end, he would bring a personal experience with God to the entire earth, attracting peoples from all nations to himself.

One last description will complete the picture. Here, another dimension was added to the messiah's portrait which we have not seen before.

> Rejoice greatly, O daughter of Zion!
>   Shout aloud, O daughter of Jerusalem!
> Lo, your king comes to you;
>   triumphant and victorious is he,
> humble and riding on an ass,
> on a colt the foal of an ass (Zech. 9:9).

Here we see the messiah still pictured as a king. But he is a different kind of king. Although coming in absolute victory, he is coming with genuine humility. He was not portrayed as riding upon the traditional white stallion of the conquering hero. Rather he was riding upon a donkey, unassuming and with genuine humility.

It is so easy to see how each of these strands of the Old Testament picture played their part in the ministry of Jesus. Many of the features he fulfilled in his earthly ministry. Some have yet to be fulfilled in his final return and ultimate victory when he assumes authority over his kingdom. Yet it was the picture of the king on the donkey that gave his contemporaries their most trouble. When Jesus thus rode into Jerusalem, he did it in deliberate fulfillment of this prophecy (Matt. 21:1-10; Mark 11:1-10; Luke 19:29-38; John 12:13-15). It was the specific kind of act that the priests and religious leaders of Jerusalem could not fail to understand. It was his deliberate claim to be the coming King. At the same time, however, it was an act which Pilate and the Roman government could not take seriously. If he had ridden upon a stallion, he would have been acting like an earthly king, and Pilate would have reacted at once. As it was, Jesus deliberately made a claim to Israel that offered no threat to the temporal power of Rome. Such was the wisdom of God. Jesus claims the allegiance of the hearts and minds of men without overthrowing their governments. It is as people turn to him that their governments will also bow before him.

C - **The Messiah and the Son of Man.** There is yet another aspect of Israel's messianic hope to which we must turn our attention, the enigmatic Son of man. This is really not a major aspect of the Old Testament messianic hope, but it did have a major impact upon the New Testament.

Among the visions of Daniel, the Son of man appears in the messianic tradition.

> I saw in the night visions,
>   and behold, with the clouds of heaven
>   there came one like a son of man,
> and he came to the Ancient of Days
>   and was presented before him.
> And to him was given dominion
>   and glory and kingdom,
> that all peoples, nations, and languages
>   should serve him;
> his dominion is an everlasting dominion,
>   which shall not pass away,
> and his kingdom one
>   that shall not be destroyed (Dan. 7:13-14).

The Son of man in this passage obviously appears to be connected with the Messiah, for the concept of a king with dominion and authority is messianic. That is what a king does. He rules.

At the same time, this is the only reference in the Old Testament to the Son of man in this way. However, we must be aware that in other, extrabiblical literature of late Old Testament times, the idea was picked up and quite thoroughly developed. (This was done in the Ethiopic Book of Enoch 37—71, in the Ezra Apocalypse, and in the Syriac Apocalypse of Baruch, as well as in the Targums and other minor references.) This development would not have been significant if Jesus had not picked up the concept and used it so thoroughly. He at one time warned his disciples, saying,

the Son of man is to come with his angels in the glory of his Father, and then he will repay every man for what he has done. Truly, I say to you, there are some standing here who will not taste death before they see the Son of man coming in his kingdom (Matt. 16:27-28).

Furthermore, when he was on trial before the high priest, there was a confrontation over this very phrase. The high priest said to him,

"I adjure you by the living God, tell us if you are the Christ [Messiah], the Son of God." Jesus said to him, "You have said so. But I tell you, hereafter you will see the Son of man seated at the right hand of Power and coming on the clouds of heaven." Then the high priest tore his robes, and said, "He has uttered blasphemy. Why do we still need witnesses?" (Matt. 26:63-65).

The claim to be the Son of man was considered both to be a claim to messiahship and to be a claim to divinity. The high priest so understood it and led the Sanhedrin in condemning Jesus at this point.

To return to the passage from Daniel, there the Son of man was clearly seen in an eschatological context. He was given, by God, a kingdom over all peoples. That kingdom was without end, either geographically or chronologically. In Daniel, the Son of man was not identified as divine. Neither can we say that he was just presented as a human, for there was clearly a superhuman dimension about him. But in the extrabiblical material he was clearly identified as being divine. Thus, when Jesus called himself the "Son of man," it was not a claim to humanity. His humanity was obvious. To Caiaphas and the Sanhedrin, his claim to be Son of man was clearly a claim to be divine. That was what made it blasphemy in their eyes.

Apparently, then, the Son of man concept in Daniel was the final dimension of the Old Testament messianic hope. It had moved from a purely physical, political concept to that of a spiritual ministry. To this was added the idea that he was to be the conquering, supernatural King of the ages. It was precisely this that Jesus came to be.

Men expected him to be a political king, restoring the kingdom of Israel. His kingdom turned out to be over the hearts of men, without territorial or temporal limits. Ultimately, he will be the all-conquering King, coming in the clouds of glory.

The Suffering Servant

Israel's future hope extended far beyond the Messiah and the messianic kingdom. Another major dimension is found in their portrait of the Suffering Servant. It has long been recognized that there are four passages in the book of Isaiah which are significantly different in content from the rest of the book. These have been called "The Servant Songs," or "The Songs of the Suffering Servant." Whole volumes have been written about these, and a detailed analysis can be found in any good critical commentary.

The Nature and Ministry of the Servant. In the first of these songs, God described his servant.

> Behold my servant, whom I uphold,
>   my chosen, in whom my soul delights;
> I have put my Spirit upon him,
>   he will bring forth justice to the nations.
> He will not cry or lift up his voice,
>   or make it heard in the street;
> a bruised reed he will not break,
>   and a dimly burning wick he will not quench;
>   he will faithfully bring forth justice.
> He will not fail or be discouraged
>   till he has established justice in the earth;
>   and the coastlands wait for his law (Isa. 42:1-4).

The Servant had been called by God, filled with his Spirit, and given a worldwide ministry. He was gentle and undiscouraged. He would be successful in his ministry.

In the second song, the servant himself spoke (Isa. 49:1-6). There he described his call from God. He also indicated that to all outward appearances, his ministry had been unsuccessful. He was aware of the honor which God had given him and of the strength by which he was sustained. God responded to him that the servant was to be God's gift to all men, bringing salvation.

> I will give you as a light to the nations,
>   that my salvation may reach to the end of the
>   earth (Isa. 49:6).

It is in the third song that the Servant was first described as suffering (Isa. 50:4-9). The Servant had been taught by God and had been obedient to those teachings. Therefore, he endured his sufferings.

> I gave my back to the smiters,
>   and my cheeks to those who pulled out the beard;
> I hid not my face
>   from shame and spitting (Isa. 50:6).

In spite of this maltreatment and opposition, the Servant continued to trust in God. He knew that God would not allow him to endure ultimate defeat.

It has been well said that the fourth song is the climax of divine revelation in the Old Testament (Isa. 52:13 to 53:12). God had promised that his Servant should be ultimately successful. Yet everything appears to indicate otherwise. The people of the nation are portrayed as speaking concerning the Servant.

Who has believed what we have heard?
    And to whom has the arm of the Lord been revealed?
For he grew up before him like a young plant,
    and like a root out of dry ground;
he had no form or comeliness that we should look at him,
    and no beauty that we should desire him.
He was despised and rejected by men;
    a man of sorrows, and acquainted with grief;
and as one from whom men hide their faces
    he was despised, and we esteemed him not.

Surely he has borne our griefs
    and carried our sorrows;
yet we esteemed him stricken,
    smitten by God, and afflicted.
But he was wounded for our transgressions,
    he was bruised for our iniquities;
upon him was the chastisement that made us whole,
    and with his stripes we are healed.
All we like sheep have gone astray;
    we have turned every one to his own way;
and the Lord has laid on him
    the iniquity of us all.

He was oppressed, and he was afflicted,
    yet he opened not his mouth;

like a lamb that is led to the slaughter,
  and like a sheep that before its shearers is dumb,
  so he opened not his mouth.
By oppression and judgment he was taken away;
  and as for his generation, who considered
that he was cut off out of the land of the living,
  stricken for the transgression of my people?
And they made his grave with the wicked
  and with a rich man in his death,
although he had done no violence
  and there was no deceit in his mouth (Isa. 53:1-9).

The nation was astounded at the suffering of the Servant. But the fact that the suffering was vicarious was beyond comprehension. He had suffered for the sins of others. This was the new dimension, the greatest revelation ever given.

The ministry of the Servant appeared to end in defeat, since it ended in death. Yet, that was not the end of the story. The fourth song goes on:

Yet it was the will of the Lord to bruise him;
  he has put him to grief;
when he makes himself an offering for sin,
  he shall see his offspring, he shall prolong his days;
the will of the Lord shall prosper in his hand;
  he shall see the fruit of the travail of
    his soul and be satisfied;
by his knowledge shall the righteous one,
    my servant,
  make many to be accounted righteous;
  and he shall bear their iniquities (Isa. 53:10-11).

The Servant died in obedience to God. But death was not defeat but victory. The Servant himself, though dead, yet shall live to see that what he accomplished brought freedom from sin to his people. The Servant shall ultimately be satisfied by his ministry.

The total picture of the Suffering Servant of God is of one who was patient and gentle in spirit, conscious of being a chosen instrument in the hand of God, and sustained by the fellowship of God himself. His task was to bring all men to God. He accomplished this through undeserved, vicarious suffering. He became both priest and sacrifice, offering himself as the guilt offering of his people. The end was victory of which the Servant was both aware and satisfied.

There are also a few psalms which point to this portrait of the Suffering Servant. However, they are neither as exalted nor as beautiful. Neither do they really add anything to the portrait already painted.

The Teachings of the Servant Songs. There are three major teachings in the Songs of the Suffering Servant, beyond their basic presentation of the Servant himself. We at least need briefly to give attention to them.

The first of these teachings is the concept of representative suffering. For the first time in the Old Testament, there is the profound revelation that a worthy sacrifice can bear the moral sins of others. Although we shall consider it in more detail in chapter 9 where we will consider the sacrificial system, there was little or no provision in Israel's ritual for any sacrifice for moral sins. Rather, the primary emphasis was upon ritual sins. When the psalmist confessed his great sins, he also added,

> For thou hast no delight in sacrifice;
>> were I to give a burnt offering, thou wouldst not
>> be pleased (Ps. 51:16).

And in the very midst of the sacrificial regulations, the Hebrews had been told that there was no offering for sin committed "with a high hand" (Num. 15:29-31).

Yet, in the Servant Songs, there was a substitutionary sacrifice which could remove or carry away the sins of the people. The sacrifice was not an animal but God's Servant himself.

The second major teaching of these songs is closely related to the first. Although all sins could now be removed by the representative who suffered, this could only be accomplished as the guilty sinners entered into a personal relationship with the Servant.

> By his knowledge, shall the righteous one, my servant,
>> make many to be accounted righteous;
>> and he shall bear their iniquities (Isa. 53:11).

We must remember that knowledge in the Old Testament involved intimate personal relationship. It is as the guilty enter this relationship with the Servant that their sins are borne away.

The third major teaching of these passages is more of an

implication than an actual teaching. Much of Israel's future hope, as we have seen, was wrapped up in the nation. Here this is not so. In no way can these words be limited to Israel alone. It was a hope clearly offered to all peoples and nations. Certainly, Israel was included in this (Isa. 49:5). But so were all others (Isa. 42:1,4; 49:6). The Suffering Servant extended God's salvation to the ends of the earth.

The Suffering Servant and the Messiah. The last question which must be raised concerning the teachings about the Suffering Servant is his relationship to the Messiah. The question is simply this: Is the Suffering Servant to be identified with the Messiah?

From our standpoint, on this side of the cross, the answer would appear to be so simple as to make us wonder why the question was ever asked. Anyone who has known the life and ministry of Jesus Christ would surely answer the question with a resounding yes! Jesus was clearly the Messiah of Israel. He was just as clearly God's Suffering Servant. But we are considering this from its Old Testament position, not from its New Testament fulfillment.

Perhaps our first hint that the question is not so easily answered comes from the New Testament itself. Even those closest to Jesus had trouble understanding the kind of Messiah he was to be. This was such a problem that John the Baptist, while he was in prison, took action.

And John, calling to him two of his disciples, sent them to the Lord, saying, "Are you he who is to come, or shall we look for another?" (Luke 7:19).

Jesus also recognized the problem. Thus he did not rebuke the questioners or reject the question. Rather, he gave it a serious answer, saying,

Go and tell John what you have seen and heard: the blind receive their sight, the lame walk, lepers are cleansed, and the deaf hear, the dead are raised up, the poor have good news preached to them. And blessed is he who takes no offense at me (Luke 7:22-23).

So it appears quite obvious that, in Jesus' own lifetime, the people of Israel had in no way connected the Messiah and the Suffering Servant in their own minds. Further, Jesus was not surprised at this, even from one with the insights of John. (A different possible interpretation of John's question will be considered in chapter 11.)

At the same time, we need to be honest with the evidence and note that shortly after the final Servant Song, the book of Isaiah made a tentative connection with the Davidic hope.

> Ho, every one who thirsts,
>   come to the waters;
> and he who has no money,
>   come, buy and eat!
> Come, buy wine and milk
>   without money and without price (Isa. 55:1).
> Incline your ear, and come to me;
>   hear, that your soul may live;
> and I will make with you an everlasting covenant,
>   my steadfast, sure love for David (Isa. 55:3).

We must remember that the messianic hope was clearly looking to an offspring of David. Thus a hope based in the Davidic covenant would be messianic. However, it is quite questionable that this messianic passage was intended to be connected with the concept of the Suffering Servant which preceded it. Even if it was intended to be so connected, apparently no one else ever made this connection within the Old Testament.

It remained for Jesus himself, in his own life and ministry to identify the Messiah and the Suffering Servant. The final revelation of God's Suffering Servant and of his Messiah are uniquely seen in Jesus himself. He gave full meaning to both ideas. He clearly combined them. And when he did, he also tied in the portrait of the Son of man. It is only in him that we see all the strands of Israel's hope for the Messiah, the Son of Man, and the Suffering Servant coming together.

The New Covenant

Another major aspect of Israel's future hope was the outgrowth of their covenant relation with God. God had clearly promised that he would be steadfastly loyal to the covenant. Yet at the same time, Israel had treacherously violated the covenant, betrayed their commitments, and rebelled against God. What could be done about it?

Hosea was apparently the first to be given an insight into

the way by which God was going to solve this dilemma of love. In looking beyond the judgment which God was going to visit upon Israel, Hosea heard God affirm his promised loyalty in terms of another or renewed covenant (Hos. 2:18-20).

This concept was later picked up and enlarged by Jeremiah. He specifically called it a "new covenant" (Jer. 31:31). The new covenant was to be different from the old. First, it was to be an inner covenant, made from within man rather than established outwardly by laws. God promised, "I will put my law within them, and I will write it upon their hearts" (Jer. 31:33). The inwardness of the covenant obviously meant that it would be individual, rather than national. Each person would participate in it for himself.

The second feature of the new covenant was that it would establish a new relationship between God and his people. "I will be their God, and they shall be my people" (Jer. 31:33). Again, it would appear that the emphasis at this point was upon the personal nature of this relationship. The purpose of this new relationship which God was creating was "that they may walk in my statutes and keep my ordinances and obey them" (Ezek. 11:20). The old covenant had failed because Israel had found it impossible to be loyal. By virtue of the new relationship, God was going to enable them to be obedient.

Furthermore, the new covenant was to lead to an experiential relationship with God for all peoples, "for they shall all know me, from the least of them to the greatest" (Jer. 31:34). The new covenant was not to be passed on through teaching about God. It would come about through direct confrontation between each individual and God.

The fourth emphasis of the new covenant was upon its foundation. The old covenant had been established following God's deliverance of Israel from Egypt. The new covenant was to be established through God's deliverance from sin. It was to be based upon divine forgiveness. "I will forgive their iniquity, and I will remember their sin no more" (Jer. 31:34). Jeremiah did not point out how this forgiveness was to be achieved. We have already seen that it was to be accomplished through the ministry of the Suffering Servant.

This concept of the new covenant became a real part of Israel's future hope. However, here as elsewhere, it remained for Jesus to give it its ultimate meaning. On Jesus' last night on earth, when he was seeking to describe the real meaning of his mission, this was the term he chose to describe it.

He took a cup, and when he had given thanks he gave it to them, saying "Drink of it, all of you, for this is my blood of the new covenant, which is poured out for many for the forgiveness of sins" (Matt. 26:27-28, author's translation).

This name which he chose to describe his ministry became so important to the early churches that they used it for the collection of books which described that ministry. Thus we came to have the New Covenant, or as we more commonly call it, the New Testament. The two terms are identical, just being different translations of the same expression.

VI   Individual Destiny

The last aspect of the future hope of the Old Testament has to do with the ultimate destiny of the individual. We have seen that a great deal in Israel's future hope had to do with a restored nation. As long as the idea of corporate personality was central to their thinking, this aroused no problem, for the individual could share in that coming kingdom through being a part of the nation, even though he might not personally survive to see it.

But there was more and more of a turn toward individualism, and the concept of corporate solidarity was no longer the whole picture. It was this which made salvation increasingly an individual matter. Furthermore, as long as life was hemmed in by birth and death, there was a growing problem for the individual with the understanding of God's justice and love. As the Hebrews began to struggle with this problem, God was ready with a new revelation.

Death and the Future. We have seen that from the first, the Old Testament had little concept of any kind of existence after death. All that was really left of a man was a shade or a shadow. Furthermore, at death, the dead went down to Sheol, the abode of the dead.

Sheol was pictured as a realm of darkness and decay, with no hope at all for those who were there. It was sometimes even portrayed as an insatiable monster ever ready to swallow humanity. Thus Habakkuk described a greedy man by saying,

> His greed is as wide as Sheol;
>> like death he never has enough (Hab. 2:5).

And the author of Proverbs admonished,

Three things are never satisfied;
> four never say, "Enough":
Sheol, the barren womb,
> the earth thirsty for water,
> and the fire which never says, "Enough" (Prov. 30:15-16).

Furthermore, in Sheol there no longer were any social or moral distinctions. Job longed for it, crying,

> There the wicked cease from troubling,
>> and there the weary are at rest.
> There the prisoners are at ease together;
>> they hear not the voice of the taskmaster.
> The small and the great are there,
>> and the slave is free from his master (Job 3:17-19).

In Sheol, all hope was gone. As long as there was life, there were opportunities. After death, there was nothing.

But he who is joined with all the living was hope, for a living dog is better than a dead lion. For the living know that they will die, but the dead know nothing, and they have no more reward; but the memory of them is lost. Their love and their hate and their envy have already perished, and they have no more for ever any share in all that is done under the sun (Eccl. 9:4-6).

The greatest tragedy of all was that in Sheol there could neither be fellowship with, nor worship of, God.

> For in death there is no remembrance of thee;
>> in Sheol who can give thee praise? (Ps. 6:5).

Those in Sheol were described as knowing nothing of God's goodness or of his greatness.

> Dost thou work wonders for the dead?
>> Do the shades rise up to praise thee?
> Is thy steadfast love declared in the grave,
>> or thy faithfulness in Abaddon?

> Are thy wonders known in the darkness,
>> or thy saving help in the land of forgetfulness?
>> (Ps. 88:10-12).

At the same time, the shades or shadows in Sheol do bear some kind of resemblance to their living bodies. Thus Ezekiel could describe dead warriors as being recognized by their weapons of war (Ezek. 32:27). Further, the witch of Endor saw an old man and his robe which was identified by Saul as Samuel (1 Sam. 28:14).

Yet Sheol was not really outside God's realm. Thus when Amos announced the destruction which God would visit upon Judah, he assured them that there would be no escape, not even in Sheol.

> Though they dig into Sheol,
>> from there shall my hand take them;
> though they climb up to heaven,
>> from there I will bring them down (Amos 9:2).

And the psalmist knew that even in Sheol he could not escape the pursuit of God.

> Whither shall I go from thy Spirit?
>> Or whither shall I flee from thy presence?
> If I ascend to heaven, thou art there!
>> If I make my bed in Sheol, thou art there! (Ps. 139:7-8).

Sheol did begin to be seen as a place of punishment, even though all men went there. This concept arose through the idea of God sending men there before their time. So the psalmist pleads with God about his enemies,

> Let death come upon them;
>> let them go down to Sheol alive;
>> let them go away in terror into their graves (Ps. 55:15).

But still, Sheol was just the abode of the dead. The only real punishment there was going sooner rather than later.

So, for most of the Old Testament, death was the end. Even in Jesus' lifetime the Sadducees still believed that there was no life after death. But this was not the whole story. In this picture of darkness, the light of God began to shine with a hope of something more than extinction after death.

Resurrection and Life After Death. To complete the story, we must consider the first glimmers of hope that were given to Israel. Some of these are little more than a hint. Others are more pointed, but still limited.

We must note that there are several passages which we delight to quote as evidence of life after death which just do not teach what has been suggested. A case in point is the twenty-third Psalm. There the psalmist said,

> Surely goodness and mercy shall follow me
> all the days of my life;
> and I shall dwell in the house of the Lord
> for ever (Ps. 23:6).

Unfortunately, this is a mistranslation. The Hebrew literally says, "I shall dwell in the house of the Lord for length of days." All the psalmist was expressing was a confidence that he would be with God as long as he lived. (Note that the New Testament message has clearly given us a full picture of life after death. For the Christian to use this in stating his confidence that God will never abandon him in this life or the next is not incorrect. But we must recognize that it did not have this meaning in the Old Testament.)

However there are positive statements within the Old Testament which we must consider. The first passage which may give some sort of hint records the words of Hannah. She was bringing her son, Samuel, to serve at Shiloh. There she said to Eli,

> For this child I prayed; and the Lord has granted me my petition which I made to him. Therefore I have lent him to the Lord; as long as he lives, he is lent to the Lord (1 Sam. 1:27-28).

The key here is the word, *lent*. To lend something is to expect to get it back. Yet Samuel was lent for "as long as he lives." In the normal order of things, the mother would die before her son. Yet she seems to have been expressing a hope for some kind of reunion after death. Whatever her hope was, no one picked up on it for a while.

Job afforded two glimmers of hope. He reached out to this hope when he said,

> For there is hope for a tree,
> if it be cut down, that it will sprout again (Job 14:7).

> But man dies, and is laid low;
>> man breathes his last, and where is he? (Job 14:10).

Pondering the fact that a tree had more hope of life than a man, Job was forced to ask the question of the ages.

> If a man die, shall he live again?
>> All the days of my service I would wait,
>> till my release should come (Job 14:14).

Job had a glimmer of the truth in response to his question, for he said, "Thou wouldest call, and I would answer thee" (Job 14:15). But all he had was a glimmer. It was too much for him and he apparently gave up the idea, saying,

> But the mountain falls and crumbles away,
>
> . . . .
>> so thou destroyest the hope of man (Job 14:18-19).

Reaching for the stars, Job finally stumbled back to earth.

But he had another divine insight. He again was led to reach for the stars. This time, he held on. Out of the depths of despair, he finally cried out,

> For I know that my Redeemer lives,
>> and at last he will stand upon the earth;
> and after my skin has been thus destroyed,
>> then from my flesh I shall see God,
> whom I shall see on my side,
>> and my eyes shall behold, and not another (Job 19:25-27).

In this case, Job was absolutely certain that not only would he be conscious after death, he would personally see God taking his part and vindicating him. What a wonderful sight for the poor sufferer! But even here, there is some question of whether Job was just viewing life after death or actually seeing a resurrection.

The Book of Isaiah offers yet another insight. Here we are given a clear view of a limited resurrection for the righteous only. Thus speaking of the wicked, we are told,

> They are dead, they will not live;
>> they are shades, they will not arise;
> to that end thou hast visited them with destruction
>> and wiped out all remembrance of them (Isa. 26:14).

But there was a different future for the righteous.

Thy dead shall live, their bodies shall rise.
O dwellers in the dust, awake and sing for joy!
For thy dew is a dew of light,
    and on the land of shades thou wilt let it fall (Isa. 26:19).

We must remember that the Hebrew conception of personality needed a bodily resurrection to be fully meaningful. This is the first absolutely certain statement that there would be a revival of bodies. Yet even here it was quite limited—only those who belonged to God. This most likely was intended to refer only to the righteous.

Daniel saw a larger resurrection. But it, too, was still limited. There we are told, "And many of those who sleep in the dust of the earth shall awake, some to everlasting life, and some to shame and everlasting contempt" (Dan. 12:2). Here the resurrection was limited to the very good and the very bad. Some were resurrected to life and others to contempt (whatever was included in that).

Suffice it to say that the Old Testament was beginning to move in a very definite way to the concept which blossomed in the New Testament. Ultimately, it was the resurrection of Jesus which gave full meaning to resurrection and to life after death. It was he who gave the answer of the ages to the question of Job, saying, "Because I live, you will live also" (John 14:19). In that promise lies the ultimate victory. "Thanks be to God, who gives us the victory through our Lord Jesus Christ" (1 Cor. 15:57).

9
Worship
in the
Old Testament

INTRO

Most worship, both ancient and modern, is difficult for an outsider to comprehend fully. The reasons for this are not difficult to understand. Worship is an approach to God made by an individual or a group. As such, it is deeply personal and always has an emotional dimension which is quite difficult, if not impossible, to describe, even in a face-to-face conversation. It is even more difficult to write about.

Even though they worship the same God and serve the same Savior, it is quite difficult for a Catholic and an Evangelical to understand each other's worship. Since this is true, even though they share the same national culture and are in the same religious tradition, how much more difficult it becomes when the barriers are multiplied. Between the modern Christian and the ancient Hebrew there are the barriers of time, culture, geography, and language, to mention only a few. It is no wonder then that we generally find the worship of the Old Testament quite meaningless. In an attempt to discover meaning, we sometimes force upon that ancient worship our contemporary meanings. But this still leaves us just as ignorant of what it really meant to them.

Yet the people of the Old Testament were the people of God. They did receive a significant revelation from him. Their approach to God through worship should be worth understanding, if we are willing to make the effort. For whether we are aware of it or not, in spite of the barriers which separate those saints from us, our worship is a direct descendant of theirs. Thus, if we can grasp something of the forms and meaning of their worship, it will help us understand how New Testament worship developed as it did.

The Nature of Old Testament Worship

Like all worship, both ancient and modern, the worship of the Old Testament had two basic focal points around which it revolved: form and meaning. Insofar as form is concerned, there was a certain ritual through which the worship participants went, whatever the actual worship ceremony. The rituals were quite definitely prescribed and the worshiper was expected to observe them precisely as they were set forth. It was because of Israel's failure to observe the ritual properly that Malachi called his people to account.

A son honors his father, and a servant his master. If then I am a father, where is my honor? And if I am a master, where is my fear? says the Lord of hosts to you, O priests, who despise my name. You say, "How have we despised thy name?" By offering polluted food upon my altar. . . . When you offer blind animals in sacrifice, is that no evil? And when you offer those that are lame or sick, is that no evil? Present that to your governor; will he be pleased with you or show you favor? (Mal. 1:6-8).

At the same time, there was a meaning to the ritual and to the entire worship service which went far beyond the ritual itself. It was due to the fact that much of the popular worship had become a meaningless ritual, performed without thought, that other prophets also thundered their message to Israel. The people had been going through the forms of worship but these were unaccompanied by righteousness or repentance. Thus Amos cried in utter dismay,

I hate, I despise your feasts,
  and I take no delight in your solemn assemblies.
Even though you offer me your burnt offerings and
    cereal offerings,
  I will not accept them,
and the peace offerings of your fatted beasts
  I will not look upon.

> Take away from me the noise of your songs;
>   to the melody of your harps I will not listen.
> But let justice roll down like waters,
>   and righteousness like an ever-flowing stream
>   (Amos 5:21-24).

In the same vein, Micah asked,

> With what shall I come before the Lord,
>   and bow myself before God on high?
> Shall I come before him with burnt offerings,
>   with calves a year old?
> Will the Lord be pleased with thousands of rams,
>   with ten thousands of rivers of oil? . . .
> He has showed you, O man, what is good;
>   and what does the Lord require of you
> but to do justice, and to love kindness,
>   and to walk humbly with your God? (Mic. 6:6-8).

So both form and meaning were important. It was never a case of either one or the other, but a case of both one and the other. This is still true of all worship.

Our usual failure to understand Old Testament worship properly is usually due to the fact that we do not direct our attention to both dimensions of it. If we are really going to come to grips with it, we must approach it from both directions. We must grapple with both ritual and meaning.

II. The Meaning of Old Testament Worship

The ritual of the Old Testament was the sacrificial system. Our primary sources for its understanding are Leviticus, and the ritual sections of Exodus, Numbers, and Deuteronomy. Numerous passages in the rest of the Old Testament also shed light on the problem.

But to try to understand the worship strictly from the standpoint of the sacrificial system is like trying to understand the worship of a modern church by reading a collection of Sunday bulletins. This gives only the form, the bare bones of what was intended to be a meaningful celebration. To add the meaning to this form, we turn primarily to the Book of Psalms. This was the hymnbook and the liturgy of Israel's worship. The prophets also shed some light on the meaning of worship. Putting this material together with the sacrificial system gives a rich, full picture of Old Testament worship as it was intended to be.

The worship of the Old Testament was primarily an expression of Israel's love for God. It was an outward expression of all the inner emotions and commitments which Israel had for the God who had redeemed them. The major content of Israel's worship was set to music. The psalms were all primarily meant to be sung. Whether they were sung by the priests, the Levitical choirs, or the people, is immaterial for our purposes. However, it is of significance that they were put to music.

It is an obvious fact in contemporary life that the music of a worshiping congregation really tells more about their faith than anything else. It also propagates the faith better than most other forms of worship. Few people long remember sermons, but the songs that touch their hearts remain with them. The typical worshiper could quote far more verses of hymns than he could verses of Scripture. To really know what any people believe, all we have to do is listen to their favorite hymns. (It is for that reason that we must be so careful that the songs we sing are biblically and theologically sound.) It would appear that music was at least as important in expressing the worshiping faith of Israel as it is today.

We perhaps also ought to note that the dance was a significant part of Israel's worship. This is found on numerous occasions in Israel's history.

David went and brought up the ark of God from the house of Obed-edom to the city of David with rejoicing; and when those who bore the ark of the Lord had gone six paces, he sacrificed an ox and a fatling. And David danced before the Lord with all his might. . . . So David and all the house of Israel brought up the ark of the Lord with shouting, and with the sound of the horn (2 Sam. 6:12-15).

The psalms themselves urged Israel to dance before God, as a means of praising him.

Let them praise his name with dancing,
    making melody to him with timbrel and lyre! (Ps. 149:3).

Praise him with timbrel and dance;
    praise him with strings and pipe! (Ps. 150:4).

Furthermore, when Jeremiah joyously announced the

glorious redemption with which God was going to bless his people, he described what their reaction was going to be.

> Then shall the maidens rejoice in the dance,
>   and the young men and the old shall be merry.
> I will turn their mourning into joy,
>   I will comfort them, and give them gladness for
>   sorrow (Jer. 31:13).

But the primary expression of Israel's worship to God was in song. Here is where we find the best expression of their approach to God. In the Psalms, we note that the basic characteristics of Israel's worship can be collected in a number of different categories. I have chosen six. It could obviously be done differently.

Regardless of how many different characteristics you might identify in Israel's worship, without question the basic characteristic of Israel's worship was exuberant joy. Israel enjoyed God, their fellowship with him, the blessings from him, and even the rebukes by him. They rejoiced in what he had done for them.

> Bless the Lord, O my soul;
>   and all that is within me,
>   bless his holy name!
> Bless the Lord, O my soul,
>   and forget not all his benefits,
> who forgives all your iniquity,
>   who heals all your diseases,
> who redeems your life from the Pit,
>   who crowns you with steadfast love and mercy,
> who satisfies you with good as long as you live,
>   so that your youth is renewed like the eagle's
>   (Ps. 103:1-5).

They also rejoiced simply in what God was, in his very nature.

> Bless the Lord, O my soul!
>   O Lord my God, thou art very great!
> Thou art clothed with honor and majesty (Ps. 104:1).

Regardless of what else was involved in their worship, the note of joy was always there. Even from the depths of deepest sorrow, there was still this note of joy. It was not a false joy, nor even a superficial joy, but it was joy nonetheless. They knew how to rejoice with God, even through their tears. Thus, from the depth of sin, the Hebrews cried,

> For thy name's sake, O Lord,
>   pardon my guilt, for it is great (Ps. 25:11).
> The friendship of the Lord is for those who fear him,
>   and he makes known to them his covenant (Ps. 25:14).

Certainly this note of joy in worship was carried over into the New Testament with an even greater depth of meaning. It not only expressed the joy of the Christians, but served as a witness to the non-Christians. Thus when Paul and Silas had been arrested, beaten, and imprisoned in Philippi, we are told that "about midnight Paul and Silas were praying and singing hymns to God, and the prisoners were listening to them" (Acts 16:25). Further, when Paul was in prison at the end of his ministry, awaiting execution, he wrote to that church in Philippi:

> Rejoice in the Lord always; again I will say, Rejoice. Let all men know your forbearance. The Lord is at hand. Have no anxiety about anything, but in everything by prayer and supplication with thanksgiving let your requests be made known to God. And the peace of God, which passes all understanding, will keep your hearts and your minds in Christ Jesus (Phil. 4:4-7).

The deep note of abiding joy should be present in all true worship. God is good. To be with him is good, whatever the events of life.

Closely related to the concept of rejoicing in God is the second characteristic of Israel's worship. That was praise. His praise was continually upon their lips. Further, they expected all creation to praise him.

> Praise the Lord!
>   Praise the Lord from the heavens,
>   praise him in the heights!
> Praise him, all his angels,
>   praise him, all his host!
> . . . .
> Praise the Lord from the earth,
> . . . .
> Kings of the earth and all peoples,

> princes and all rulers of the earth!
> Young men and maidens together,
>   old men and children!
> Let them praise the name of the Lord,
>   for his name alone is exalted;
>   his glory is above earth and heaven.
> He has raised up a horn for his people,
>   praise for all his saints,
>   for the people of Israel who are near to him.
> Praise the Lord! (Ps. 148:1-14).

They praised him for his loyalty to his covenant, even when
Israel was rebellious.

> Praise the Lord!
>   O give thanks to the Lord, for he is good;
>   for his steadfast love endures for ever! (Ps. 106:1).
> Both we and our fathers have sinned (106:6).
> He remembered for their sake his covenant,
>   and relented according to the abundance of his
>   steadfast love (106:45).
> Blessed be the Lord, the God of Israel,
>   from everlasting to everlasting!
> And let all the people say, "Amen!"
>   Praise the Lord! (106:48).

This deep note of praise and adoration is also found in full
richness among the early Christians. Following the ascen-
sion of Jesus, the disciples "returned to Jerusalem with
great joy, and were continually in the temple blessing God"
(Luke 24:52-53). The deep note of praise is sounded over and
over again to God for his wonderful gift in Christ. We, too,
should join in the anthem of praise with all the saints of all
the ages.

> Worthy art thou to take the scroll
>   and to open its seals,
> for thou wast slain and by thy blood
>   didst ransom men for God
> from every tribe and tongue
>   and people and nation,
> and has made them a kingdom
>   and priests to our God,
> and they shall reign on earth (Rev. 5:9-10).

This is the new song of the saints. But it is the old note of
praise to God for his greatness.

The third major characteristic of the worship of the Old Testament was thanksgiving. The saints of the Old Testament constantly expressed gratitude to God. As a part of this, we need also to note that they knew how to petition. They laid their requests before God. When his answers came, they expressed their gratitude. Thanksgiving and petition were really two aspects of the same kind of worship in Israel.

> O give thanks to the Lord, for he is good;
>> for his steadfast love endures for ever!
> Let the redeemed of the Lord say so,
>> whom he has redeemed from trouble (Ps. 107:1-2).
> Then they cried to the Lord in their trouble,
>> and he delivered them from their distress (107:6).
> Let them thank the Lord for his steadfast love,
>> for his wonderful works to the sons of men! (107:8).

These two ideas are consistently tied together within the worship of Israel. Thus a psalm allowed the worshiper to cry out in agony, laying his need before God.

> Save me, O God!
>> For the waters have come up to my neck.
> I sink in deep mire,
>> where there is no foothold;
> I have come into deep waters,
>> and the flood sweeps over me.
> I am weary with my crying;
>> my throat is parched.
> My eyes grow dim
>> with waiting for my God (Ps. 69:1-3).

But the worshiper rested in the assurance of God's answer. Thus he also expressed his thanksgiving even before the response from God.

> I will praise the name of God with a song;
>> I will magnify him with thanksgiving (Ps. 69:30).
> For the Lord hears the needy,
>> and does not despise his own that are in bonds (Ps. 69:33).

This deep note of thanksgiving was also carried over into the worship of the New Testament. Again, we should note that the connection between petition and thanksgiving was still made. So Paul advised the Philippians, "Have no anxiety about anything, but in everything by prayer and supplication with thanksgiving let your requests be made known to God" (Phil. 4:6). However, for the Christian there are even more reasons for expressing thanksgiving. There is the note of thanksgiving for the victory over death.

> The sting of death is sin, and the power of sin is the law. But thanks be to God who gives us the victory through our Lord Jesus Christ (1 Cor. 15:56-57).

There is also the note of thanksgiving for the victory over sin.

> But thanks be to God, that you who were once slaves of sin have become obedient from the heart to the standard of teaching to which you were committed, and having been set free from sin, have become slaves of righteousness (Rom. 6:17-18).

But the ultimate note of thanksgiving was always reserved for Jesus himself. He is God's greatest gift. Thus Paul exclaimed, "Thanks be to God for his inexpressible gift!" (2 Cor. 9:15).

There was a major dimension to Israel's worship which is seldom, if ever, found in contemporary worship. This is usually categorized as lament. The Old Testament recognized that there are many experiences in life which bring grief. These need to be brought to God and laid before him. There was the deep agony of the guilty sinner, laying his guilt before the only one who could help, God.

> Have mercy on me, O God,
>   according to thy steadfast love;
> according to thy abundant mercy
>   blot out my transgressions.
> Wash me thoroughly from my iniquity,
>   and cleanse me from my sin!
> For I know my transgressions,
>   and my sin is ever before me.
> Against thee, thee only, have I sinned,
>   and done that which is evil in thy sight,
> so that thou art justified in thy sentence
>   and blameless in thy judgment (Ps. 51:1-4).

The psalmist, however, knew that there were other experiences which brought heartache and despair. There was the anger of a man whose enemies slandered him.

> O men, how long shall my honor suffer shame?
>   How long will you love vain words, and seek after
>   lies? (Ps. 4:2).

Further, the agony of sickness and the prospect of death could also bring forth a lament.

> Be gracious to me, O Lord, for I am languishing;
>   O Lord, heal me, for my bones are troubled.
> My life also is sorely troubled.
>   But thou, O Lord—how long?
> Turn, O Lord, save my life;
>   deliver me for the sake of thy steadfast love
>   (Ps. 6:2-3, author's translation).

In addition, there was the grief over the physical attack of enemies. This gave rise to a plea for help.

> O Lord my God, in thee do I take refuge;
>   save me from all my pursuers, and deliver me,
> lest like a lion they rend me,
>   dragging me away, with none to rescue (Ps. 7:1-2).

But the ultimate grief sprang from the sense that the worshiper had been forsaken by God himself.

> How long, O Lord? Wilt thou forget me forever?
>   How long wilt thou hide thy face from me?
> How long must I bear pain in my soul,
>   and have sorrow in my heart all the day? (Ps. 13:1-2).

Jesus had no words of condemnation for those who came to God in agony. Rather, he offered a message of comfort. He promised, "Blessed are those who mourn, for they shall be comforted" (Matt. 5:4). Furthermore, Jesus himself expressed this kind of sorrow and took it directly to the Father. In the darkness of his soul, he went to Gethsemane. There, "he began to be sorrowful and troubled. Then he said to them, 'My soul is very sorrowful, even to death' " (Matt. 26:37-38).

It is a poor relationship with God which does not allow the opportunity to express the deepest hurt of the human heart. We have deprived most people of this experience in our contemporary worship by putting a false front of smiles on a heart which is in agony. May God forgive us for this.

The fifth category of worship which was present in the Old Testament was that of teaching, or recitation. The Hebrews used their songs to teach about the great acts which God had performed in their past. They recited the major events of their history, hiding none of the sordid details. But neither did they hide the graciousness of God. Rather, they proclaimed it. Thus they sang of the Exodus and the wilderness experiences (Pss. 78; 106).

They also taught through their songs of the quality of life which a godly man should have.

> Blessed is the man
>   who walks not in the counsel of the wicked,
> nor stands in the way of sinners,
>   nor sits in the seat of scoffers;
> but his delight is in the law of the Lord,
>   and on his law he meditates day and night (Ps. 1:1-2).

Other things were also taught, such as the wonder of and love for God's Word, or the sustaining power and presence of God (Pss. 19:7-9; 119; 23).

That this emphasis was also carried over into the New Testament is quite obvious. Paul had too much to say about the teaching ministry of a church for us to think otherwise. Further, almost every sermon recorded in the Book of Acts had a teaching dimension. Clearly, worship should continue to teach.

The sixth category of Old Testament worship experiences was quite different from the first five. Old Testament worship also provided for the expression of hostility and open hatred for the worshiper's enemies. Thus they could cry out in bitterness,

> Let their own table before them become a snare;
>   let their sacrificial feasts be a trap.
> Let their eyes be darkened, so that they cannot see;
>   and make their loins tremble continually.
> Pour out thy indignation upon them,
>   and let thy burning anger overtake them.
> May their camp be a desolation,
>   Let no one dwell in their tents (Ps. 69:22-25).

We could multiply examples, but this one will suffice.

It is quite useless to point out the fact that this is far below the attitude of Jesus, who prayed: "Father, forgive them; for they know not what they do" (Luke 23:34). Of course it is! It is also a far cry from the great prayer of Moses, who sought not vengeance but mercy for his people (Ex. 32:32).

This is one aspect of Israel's worship which was not carried over into the New Testament. At the same time, we need to acknowledge that there is a great deal of hatred in the human heart. What better place is there to take it than to God? (It just might be that if we were more open to God with our anger, there might be less church fights and splits.)

So the nature of Old Testament worship was both rich and full. It was also open and honest. They expressed to God what they actually felt. God was never threatened by Israel's honesty. He will not be threatened by ours. They went to God with their hostility and their laments. But they also went to him with their praise and their thanksgiving. They used their worship to teach the great truths of their faith. But through it all, they met God in worship with an exuberant joy. So they could sing with an honest excitement,

> I was glad when they said to me,
> "Let us go to the house of the Lord!" (Ps. 122:1).

But, as we noted at the beginning, this was only part of Israel's worship. Their songs gave it meaning. But it was their sacrificial ritual which gave it form.

III. The Form of Old Testament Worship: The Sacrificial System

The Old Testament sacrificial system furnished the ritual for Old Testament worship. It also made a major impact on the Hebrew conception of salvation and forgiveness. However, the study of the sacrificial system can be quite frustrating. We are so far removed from the cultures which practiced sacrifice that it frequently appears to be beyond our comprehension. Further, the ancient sacrificial rituals are so far short of the revelation of God in Jesus that we often question whether it is worth the effort to try to understand them.

However, sacrifice was important to Israel. Thus it is

important for us to try to grasp its basic rudiments. The first reason for its importance to us lies in the fact that a good bit of the New Testament understanding of worship and of the ministry of our Lord arose from the images of the sacrificial system. The second reason rests in the fact that it was the worship ritual of a people who were expected to be holy because they belonged to a holy God. The concepts of God's and Israel's holiness were central to the sacrificial system. Any attempt to try to understand it apart from the concept of holiness is doomed to failure. The third reason for the importance of studying the sacrificial system is that it sets forth a deep awareness of the horror of sin, as well as an awareness of the overabundant grace of God in forgiveness. The fourth and least important reason is that the sacrificial system was Israel's celebration of religion and life in the presence of the Author of all life. This is true, even though the entire mechanism of sacrifice appears quite gruesome to most contemporary minds.

Roots of the Sacrificial System. Israel did not develop in a vacuum. All the nations which surrounded her practiced sacrifice. It was the accepted way both of expressing religious fervor and of worshiping. There was apparently a common background for all ancient sacrificial systems. The ancient background of these systems seems to indicate that most sacrifices had one or more of the following roots.

First, there was the idea of feeding the deity. Thus in the Gilgamesh Epic, in the story of the Flood, the gods were about to starve to death due to the fact that sacrifices were no longer being offered. When the first sacrifice was offered after the Flood, the gods gathered around like flies, because they were so hungry. Although this idea was obviously common throughout the ancient Near East, there is no evidence that the Old Testament ever had this view of sacrifice. To the contrary, Israel was told,

> If I were hungry, I would not tell you;
>   for the world and all that is in it is mine.
> Do I eat the flesh of bulls,
>   or drink the blood of goats? (Ps. 50:12-13).

Second, sacrifices were also considered by ancient men to be gifts to the deity. It is quite apparent that this idea ran deep in the heart of the Old Testament.

3   Third, sacrifices were considered to bring about communion between the worshiper and his god. Many sacrifices required the worshiper to eat a meal at the shrine or
temple. In the ancient world, people who ate together, or at
least shared salt at a meal, were bound by ties of brotherhood. The ancient story of Ali Baba points up this idea.
When the servant girl noticed that the robber chieftain ate
no salt, she immediately became suspicious. To the Hebrews, eating in the house of God effected a special relationship of peace between themselves and God. This may also
have a very specific bearing upon the meaning of the Lord's
Supper as taught in the New Testament.

4   The fourth root for ancient sacrifice is found in the idea of
released life. Since all life was God's gift, the firstborn was
peculiarly God's, indicating that the race or family was being continued. Life was released from a chosen victim to
give back to God that which was peculiarly his. The sacrifice was not so much for offering a dead carcass to God as it
was for offering him the life which was present in the
blood. This concept of released life may also have had a real
impact upon the New Testament's understanding of the
sacrifice of Jesus.

Although numerous interpreters have sought to demonstrate that one or more of these ideas was *the* original root
of the Old Testament sacrificial system, it appears that no
single idea is really adequate to explain the entire system.
Rather, it is probably nearer the truth to suggest that each
of these, with the exception of the idea of feeding God,
played a part in the origin and growth of the system.

Our major concern must be with the system as Israel
practiced it, not with its ancient roots. Two things quickly
become obvious in any study of Israel's sacrifices as com-
pared with the rituals of her neighbors. First, the forms of
sacrifice were quite similar and frequently identical. That
is only to be expected. Israel had to start where she was. On
the other hand, the covenant faith of Israel gave a significantly different meaning to the rituals. That the systems
were quite similar is obvious both from the ancient documents as well as from the constant problems which the
prophets had with the paganizing of Israel's worship. The
assimilation of the worship of the Baals of Canaan with the
worship of the God of Israel was never any problem, insofar

as the ritual was concerned. It was done quite easily. Israel's problem was that they confused the meaning behind the rituals. But it is the rituals themselves which demand our attention here. We could give a very great deal of space to a detailed analysis of all of Israel's sacrifices. For this kind of study you would be well advised to consider a detailed commentary on Leviticus. For our purposes, we will rather turn to five major categories or classes of sacrifice,

B -   ***The Communion Meal or the Peace Offering.*** The Hebrews, as we have noted, placed great significance upon a meal. Whenever guests came, a fatted calf, a lamb, or a kid was slaughtered and a meal was eaten to effect peace between the host and his guests (Gen. 18:7; 1 Sam. 28:24; 2 Sam. 12:4). It was this background which gave meaning to the communion meal offering or slaughter offering of Israel. In its Old Testament form, the animal was usually eaten by the worshiper. The blood was offered to God upon the altar. Israel was commanded to "eat before the Lord your God, and you shall rejoice, you and your household" (Deut. 12:7). They were considered to be the guests of God at this meal (Zeph. 1:7).

Further, this meal was considered to bring about peace between the worshiper and God. As such, it also included both the sin and guilt offerings. The offering came to be called simply a peace offering. Those who participated in this meal became friends simply by participating. The meal established communion to such a degree that all participants were considered to be members of a family. The Passover was the supreme example of this, reconstituting the relationship which had been sealed between God and Israel, both in Egypt and at Sinai.

This kind of sacrifice reinforced and undergirded the family ties which bound Israel together. It also probably served as the basis for the later prophetic images of Israel as the son or bride of God. Above all, it certainly set the basis for the idea of peaceful relationships between God and Israel. The ideal relationship for which both God and Israel longed was one of peace between them.

C -   ***Devotion of the Firstborn.*** A second major kind of sacrifice in Israel was based upon the concept that every firstborn male belonged to God in a very peculiar way. From the earliest days of the covenant, Israel was told,

The first-born of your sons you shall give to me. You shall do likewise with your oxen and with your sheep: seven days it shall be with its dam; on the eighth day you shall give it to me (Ex. 22:29-30).

But this was not a command for child sacrifice, for the first-born was to be redeemed and another offering made in its place (Ex. 13:13; 34:20).

This peculiar relationship between the firstborn and God added a special meaning to God's statement that Israel was his firstborn. It also served as the justification for the death of the Egyptian firstborn. Since Egypt would not release God's firstborn, they must give up their own.

> Thus says the Lord, "Israel is my first-born son,
> and I say to you, 'Let my son go that he may serve me';
> if you refuse to let him go, behold, I will slay your first-born son" (Ex. 4:22-23).

Again, the specific sacrifice of the firstborn was a communion meal. Clean animals were actually sacrificed. Unclean animals had a substitute made for them. Humans were redeemed. But the end result was the gift of life through the blood poured upon the altar, and the establishment of peace between the worshiper and God.

The Gift Offering. Another major category of sacrifices was the gift offering. It took a number of different forms, but the end result was always the same, that of presenting a gift to God. The major technical difference between this and the two preceding offerings was that here, God was given the entire offering; it was a "whole" offering. At times in Israel's history, the term appears to have been applied only to a grain offering. At other times it was applied to any offering which was totally given to God.

This offering expressed the homage which the worshiper paid to God. It also was given as a tribute, or as an expression of thanksgiving. Further, it was given in fulfillment of a vow. In every instance, it was an offering which was freely made. It came out of the overflow of the worshiper's love for God.

However, even though the gift offering was not required, but freely given, it was carefully regulated. If the worshiper was going to make a gift to God, it had to be done on

God's terms. Thus Israel was condemned for giving to God what was deformed.

> When you offer blind animals in sacrifice, is that no evil? And when you offer those that are lame or sick, is that no evil? . . . You bring what has been taken by violence or is lame or sick, and this you bring as your offering! Shall I accept that from your hand? says the Lord (Mal. 1:8-13).

A gift to God was expected to be the best that the worshiper had, in order to honor God. Anything less than the best was an affront and an insult. It still is.

E - **The Day of Atonement.** For its theological significance, perhaps the most significant sacrifice of ancient Israel was the great Day of Atonement. This was a sacrifice and a ritual performed once a year by the high priest for the benefit of all Israel. It is rightly considered the highest point of the Old Testament sacrificial system.

The purpose of this sacrifice was to take care of cleansing all the sins which had not been taken care of in the confessions of the communion meal and peace offerings. It was intended to insure the maintenance of right relations between Israel and God. On this day, there were two sacrificial victims. One was actually slaughtered upon the altar and the other was sent out into the wilderness, bearing (symbolicly) the sins of the nation (Lev. 16:15,21).

The major New Testament development of this ritual is set forth in Hebrews 9:6-28. There Christ is portrayed both as the High Priest and the sacrificial victim. Further, although this is not stated there, it is implied that he also is to be understood as being the victim who carried our sins into the wilderness.

Be that as it may, for Israel, this day was the high point in their ritual with regard to cleansing from sin. They were sure that no man or nation could serve God while he was living with unforgiven sin. This is still true.

F - **Private Sacrifices.** Each of the categories of sacrifice which we have considered was primarily a corporate sacrifice. Made either by a family or the nation as a whole, these sacrifices were offered to God and the benefits were considered to fall upon the group. But Israel also had quite an elaborate ritual for private sacrifices.

Men had always felt the desire to make personal, private

sacrifices. Thus Cain and Abel brought personal sacrifices to God, long before any such ritual had been commanded or established (Gen. 4:3-4). Throughout Israel's early days, there is abundant evidence of such sacrifices. They were intended to honor God, to appeal for help, to express thanksgiving, and to find cleansing.

Each of these found their place in Israel's later ritual. The freewill offering was perhaps the most common. Not only did the Law codify it, the prophets regularly referred to it. It appears that it was generally offered to God as a token of appreciation for some blessing received.

Closely related to this was the thank-offering. This was a bit more structured, and was usually associated with one or more regular events in Israel's ritual of festivals. This was regularly associated with the bringing of tithes and the produce from the ground. Those commanded offerings, when brought, indicated the goodness of God. There were no tithes nor firstfruits from the ground unless God had bestowed blessings. The worshipers frequently brought an extra gift in expression of gratitude.

The individual Israelite also frequently made a vow-offering. Typical of this was the experience of Jacob.

Then Jacob made a vow, saying, "If God will be with me, and will keep me in this way that I go, and will give me bread to eat and clothing to wear, so that I come again to my father's house in peace, then the Lord shall be my God, and this stone, which I have set up for a pillar, shall be God's house; and of all that thou givest me I will give the tenth to thee" (Gen. 28:20-22).

Although the vow-offering was not commanded, once the vow was made, the offering became obligatory.

We could have considered these offerings in far greater detail. We could also have enlarged the categories of sacrifice to include a number of other divisions. For our purposes, our concern is with the general characteristics of all offerings rather than with the specific details of each offering.

The Teachings of the Sacrificial System

To the ancient Hebrews, sacrifices gave the basic form to their worship. We must never forget this. But the sacrificial system has passed out of existence. The question arises as to whether or not there is anything which endures. Did the sacrificial system of the Old Testament merely exist for a time and then pass away? The answer to that is a resounding no! There was an enduring message to the sacrificial ritual of the Old Testament. It spoke to ancient Israel and it still speaks to us.

First, the basic sacrificial ritual was concerned with restoring or maintaining right relations between the worshiper and God. As the worshiper became increasingly aware of the holiness of God and of his own sin, there was a necessity of finding some way whereby the creature and his Creator might have communion together. The communion emphasis faded more and more into the background, however, and the emphasis upon peace came to the forefront. The primary intent was to make it possible for the worshiper to dwell with God without fear of judgment and without the burden of guilt.

This brings us to the second major feature: throughout the Old Testament history, Israel's worship became more and more concerned with atonement and rescue. As we have noted before, these words never seemed to imply that God paid anything for Israel's sin. The emphasis fell upon the fact that God "covered" her sin, rescuing her from her guilt. Again, the focus appears to be the removal of guilt or unholiness by covering it. Only God can cover sin so that he cannot see it. The Hebrews frequently tried to cover their sin for themselves. This always failed. Again, the ultimate purpose of the atonement or the rescue was the restoration of right relations. The sin was not covered simply that it might be hidden. The sinner was never rescued simply that he might be free. In both instances, the end result was that the sinner might once again enjoy the presence of God.

Since the central thought of the sacrificial system was the restoration of right relations, and since this was accomplished by the atonement or rescue of the sinner by God, the main thought of the system for the worshiper was obedience. He was expected to be loyal to God and to express that loyalty in total obedience. The only external way the worshiper had of being sure that this ritual would accomplish his objectives was to obey it to the letter. We have been highly critical of the Pharisees for their hostility toward Jesus and for their unloving attitude. At the same time, they were perhaps the most moral people who ever lived. They were intensely concerned with doing what God said exactly as he said it. (It does not necessarily follow that obedience to the law breeds a pharisaical spirit.)

4 The fourth significant teaching of the sacrificial system had to do with penitence, or repentance. The demand for obedience caused the worshiper to see how far short he had fallen in disobedience. Through the observance of his ritual, the ancient worshiper became aware of the ultimate sacrifice required by God.

> The sacrifice acceptable to God is a broken spirit;
> a broken and contrite heart, O God, thou wilt not
>   despise (Ps. 51:17).

The ritual of the Day of Atonement further emphasized this. There we were told, "And Aaron shall . . . confess . . . all the iniquities of the people of Israel" (Lev. 16:21). The priest's confession of the sins of the people would have been meeaningless if the worshipers had not been participating in spirit. It was the attitude of the worshiper which ultimately made the ritual valid.

However, we must not forget that there was an objective potency in sacrifice, as far as the Old Testament was concerned. There was no thought of magic in it. It was not some kind of ancient voodoo which Israel practiced. Rather, the power of the sacrificial system rested solely in the grace of God. It worked because God made it work. The full and final message of the prophets was that the sacrificial system did not work just because God was offered acts of penitence, or because the worshiper was obedient in its ritual. The animal victim did nothing for the worshiper unless and until God drew near. Thus, in the last analysis, it was always God who drew near to redeem and to save at the moment of sacrifice. This is still true.

The last word which we must consider about the Old Testament sacrificial system was that it was limited to unwitting sins. It was not effective for sins "with a high hand."

If one person sins unwittingly, . . . the priest shall make atonement before the Lord for the person who commits an error, when he sins unwittingly, to make atonement for him; and he shall be forgiven. . . . But the person who does anything with a high hand, . . . that person shall be cut off from among his people (Num. 15:27-30).

It is quite difficult to know exactly what the difference is between the unwitting sin and the high-handed sin. It is obvious that the sacrificial system had its limits. There was no sacrifice prescribed for the murderer or the adulterer. In such cases, the only hope was to throw oneself upon the mercy of God. But this is precisely where the worshiper had always had to rest.

Suffice it to say that the sacrificial system focused its primary attention upon ritual sins. Moral sins were generally beyond its powers to save. But they were never beyond God's powers to save.

It is precisely at this point that we see the New Testament fruit from this root. For Jesus became our sacrifice. The major emphasis upon this is found in the Letter to the Hebrews.

And every priest stands daily at his service, offering repeatedly the same sacrifices, which can never take away sins. But when Christ had offered for all time a single sacrifice for sin, he sat down at the right hand of God (Heb. 10:11-12).

The high priest in ancient Israel never got to sit, for he was never through sacrificing. But Jesus could sit when he offered his sacrifice. It was all done. He was through!

It is obvious that the early Christians continued to participate in the regular ritual of the Temple. Thus we are told that "Peter and John were going up to the temple at the hour of prayer" (Acts 3:1). And Paul was arrested when he went to the Temple with some men who were making a vow offering (Acts 21:23-26).

But ultimately, they realized the full implication of what Christ had done for them, as God opened their minds. Thus Paul wrote:

For he is our peace, who has made us both one, and has broken down the dividing wall of hostility, by abolishing in his flesh the law of commandments and ordinances, that he might create in himself one new man in place of the two, so making peace, and might reconcile us both to God in one body through the cross (Eph. 2:14-16).

Jesus had become the peace offering himself, effecting communion and fellowship between God and man and between Jew and Gentile. Further, by becoming the ultimate sacrifice, he put an end to the sacrificial system for Christians.

Paul further proclaimed that Christ had established this peace by becoming the sin offering for us. Since he himself had not sinned, he was without blemish, the perfect sacrifice (2 Cor. 5:21). When he made the perfect sacrifice, the old covenant with its sacrificial system was replaced by the new covenant in Christ Jesus.

Yet at the same time, worship must go on. In fact, the worship of the Christian should be more meaningful than any Old Testament worship ever was. The principles of worship remain the same. The ritual has been changed. So Christians were advised to find new ways of fulfilling the old meanings.

I appeal to you therefore, brethren, by the mercies of God, to present your bodies as a living sacrifice, holy and acceptable to God, which is your spiritual worship (Rom. 12:1).

Lest there be any misunderstanding, Paul pointed out in detail the kinds of things he expected to be done in this living sacrifice (Rom. 12:6-20). The ultimate purpose of the sacrificial system had been to give ancient men a means of overcoming and defeating the evil in their lives. But it is Christ who makes it possible for us to fulfill this goal of the Christians' sacrifice: "Do not be overcome by evil, but overcome evil with good" (Rom. 12:21).

10
The Servants of God

There are a number of active verbs which the New Testament uses to describe what Christians should be doing in the world. We are expected to witness, to serve, to evangelize, to minister, to proclaim, to heal, to work, and numerous other such actions. Each of these, along with countless other such concepts have their root in the Old Testament. The fact is that God chose to carry out his work in the world through human servants. As we see who these servants were in the Old Testament and how they related both to God and man, we gain new understandings as to what our tasks and relationships should be.

It is obvious that each of the persons in the Old Testament who were servants of God were individuals. As such, each one brought the unique dimensions of his own personality and religious experience into the service of God. At the same time, many of these persons fulfilled similar ministries, so that we can identify them by the kinds of tasks which they were given by God. Further, as we shall see, even across the lines separating the various categories, there are common characteristics. It is both the unique features of each individual's service of God as well as the common characteristics which shall help us to understand our own ministries for and service of God.

1. The Patriarchs as Servants

The people of the Old Testament regularly looked back to Abraham, Isaac, and Jacob as the founding fathers of their racial and religious heritage. Three such different men could hardly be found. Yet, each in his own way was an example of faithful service to God.

Abraham was the pilgrim of faith who responded to a God whom he did not know to go to a land of which he had not heard.

> Now the Lord said to Abram, "Go from your country and your kindred and your father's house to the land that I will show you.
> So Abram went, as the Lord had told him (Gen. 12:1,4a).

It is immaterial to point out that many Amorites were migrating from the Mesopotamian Valley to Canaan at this time in history. They were a people on the move. But Abraham was moving in response to God's call. As an illustration of this, consider the fact that there were many people who moved from the eastern United States to California in the winter of 1974-75. My family and I also moved then. But there was a difference. I moved there in direct response to the call of God to teach at Golden Gate Baptist Theological Seminary. What Abraham did was not different from what many of his contemporaries did. Why he did it was altogether different.

Many other details of Abraham's life could be considered. They are all important. But the prime characteristic which the New Testament writers recalled was that he was a man of faithful obedience (cf. Rom. 4:1-3). At the same time, the Bible does not gloss over Abraham's humanity. His weaknesses clearly show through. In spite of these, his faithful obedience allowed him to be used by God.

Isaac had the misfortune of being sandwiched between a great father and a great son. He was quiet, retiring, and made a much lesser impact upon Israel's memory than his father or his son. To understand him, we must consider his near-sacrifice at Moriah (Gen. 22:1-14). As he accompanied his father, he surely realized that he was about to be sacrificed. When God delivered him, the experience had to make a profound impact upon him and his relationship to God. He

apparently developed a quiet, introspective life, with a deep
sense of devotion to the God who had saved him. When the
Genesis writer later recorded, "And Isaac went out to medi-
tate in the field in the evening" (Gen. 24:63a), it was said in
such a way as to indicate that this was a repeated characteristic of his life. Again, it is obvious that Isaac was human,
with human weakness. But he also was a man of quiet reverence who passed on the faith of his father. Even though
both of his sons seemed to have ignored their father's faith
in their youth, yet it made an impact upon them in their
later years.

The third of the patriarchs whom we shall consider is Jacob. He was the confidence man. Always out to turn every
situation to his advantage, his first thought always seemed
to have been, "Is it good for me?" Selfish, scheming, and
deceptive, he regularly sought to advance himself by taking advantage of others' weaknesses. He treasured the
family heritage without wanting the relation with God. But
when he got into situations beyond his own manipulation,
he was suddenly open to the voice of God. Over the years,
his experiences with God developed until he could say after
the night at the Jabbok, "I have seen God face to face, and
yet my life is preserved" (Gen. 32:30). In that night of wres-
tling with the angel of God, both Jacob's name and nature
had been changed. He was never the same after that experience. That experience was one of traumatic and dramatic
conversion.

It made such an impact upon him and upon Israel's memory of him, that the psalmists could later sing:

> God is our refuge and strength,
> a very present help in trouble.

> The Lord of hosts is with us;
> the God of Jacob is our refuge.

> The Lord of hosts is with us;
> the God of Jacob is our refuge (Ps. 46:1,7,11).

A sure basis of their hope in God was the fact that God could
and did use a man like Jacob. If God could transform and use
Jacob, he could do the same with anyone. He still can. He is
a transforming, redeeming Savior.

The servanthood of the patriarchs shows us that God can

use the giant of faith or the chief of sinners. He can take the quiet man, the schemer, or the one quick to follow, and use each of them to accomplish his will and purpose. Human weakness merely allows him the opportunity to show the abundance of his power and grace, as well as the all-sufficiency of his love.

These things show up at the heart and center of the gospel message. It was good news that God could make saints out of sinners. It still is.

II. The Judges as Servants

Of quite a different sort were the people we have come to know as the judges. These were people who became leaders of Israel in a time of crisis because they had certain gifts or abilities which enabled them to meet the needs of the moment. There are four of these whom we shall consider.

Deborah is identified as a prophetess who "was judging Israel" (Judg. 4:4). As the term, "judge," is used, it does not refer to a legal position, but to one who had become Israel's leader in a crisis situation. Deborah was the leader behind the military man who delivered the northern tribes from oppression by Canaan.

It is important to note that here was a woman in a position of leadership who was also a prophetess for God. The fact that this was true in Israel while no one seems to have been surprised is extremely informative. In spite of all Israel's emphasis upon the prominence of men, there was the recognition that God could and did raise up women as his servants. Not only was this accepted by Israel, they also accepted the fact that the military general, Barak, showed up as timid and reluctant beside her commitment. When called to lead his army forth,

> Barak said to her, "If you will go with me, I will go;
> but if you will not go with me, I will not go" (Judg. 4:8).

That women could share in positions of leadership as God's servants was further emphasized in the New Testament. Paul commended to the church in Rome a woman named Phoebe, who is identified as "a deaconess of the church at Cenchreae" (Rom. 16:1). He also sent greetings to Prisca, a woman whom he described as a fellow worker

(Rom. 16:3). It is obvious that God raises up whomsoever he will to be his servant.

Deborah showed up as forthright and courageous. Gideon, on the other hand, was quite different. Anything but courageous, he was hiding in a winepress to thresh his grain (Judg. 6:11). When assured that God was with him and his people, he wanted to see a miracle, unable to accept the announcement on faith (Judg. 6:13). Addressed as a "mighty man of valor" (v. 12), he responded,

Pray, Lord, how can I deliver Israel? Behold, my clan is the weakest in Manasseh, and I am the least in my family (Judg. 6:15).

Ultimately, he challenged God with two tests of the fleece and the dew (Judg. 6:36-40). It is worth noting that Gideon did not present these tests to find out God's will for him. He already knew that. What he apparently was trying to do was to avoid God's call by presenting two impossible situations. He was no willing volunteer but a most reluctant draftee. Yet, even so, in the end he did do God's will and did become an obedient servant, no matter how reluctantly.

Samson was still a different kind of judge. Sensual, selfish, playing with sin, his service of God was almost forfeited by his own lust. He took God for granted. Perhaps the most tragic verse in all the Bible describes the end of his dalliance with Delilah. When she aroused him from his sleep the last time, we are told that

He awoke from his sleep, and said, "I will go out as at other times, and shake myself free." *And he did not know that the Lord had left him* (Judg. 16:20, italics mine).

Further, at his death, Samson is presented as seeking vengeance for himself, not as serving God. Yet, God used Samson in spite of himself to bring deliverance to Israel from the Philistine oppression. One of the wonders of God's sovereignty is that his servants can forfeit their call, yet still be used to accomplish his purposes. We tend to remember Samson for his strength, yet it was his weaknesses which destroyed him. However, it was his weaknesses which allowed God's power to be seen most clearly.

The fourth judge to be considered is Samuel. Not normally considered as a judge, he actually bridged the gap between the periods of the judges and the monarchy. He is known most commonly as a prophet, yet we are told of him that "Samuel judged Israel all the days of his life" (1 Sam. 7:15). Dedicated to God from the earliest days of his youth, he was a giant in faithful obedience. At the same time, he, too, had his weaknesses. But it was for his strengths that he was remembered.

He was a man who listened to God and proclaimed what he heard faithfully to his people (1 Sam. 3:19 to 4:1a). His response to God as a child had apparently become the pattern of his life. As a child, he had said to God, "Speak, for thy servant is listening" (1 Sam. 3:10, author's translation). Leading his people, he appeared as a stern, austere figure. When his people pled for a king, he felt personally rejected. God forced him to get things back in the proper perspective when he said, "They have not rejected you, but they have rejected me from being king over them" (1 Sam. 8:7). There is a real tendency on the part of God's servants to exalt their own position in God's economy. It was to emphasize this that Jesus said,

Truly, truly, I say to you, a servant is not greater than his master; nor is he who is sent greater than he who sent him (John 13:16).

The judges point out to us that God's servants are people who are called to use their God-given talents to accomplish God's will in the world. Historians frequently debate over whether it is important events which call forth great people or whether it is great people who make their time important. The biblical writers would say that both statements miss the mark. Rather, it is God who prepares his servants with the abilities to meet the needs of their moment in history.

The servants may be moved either by courage or cowardice. God uses his servants' abilities when they respond in faith. But if they respond in disobedience, God can still use them to accomplish his will. Such is the sovereign grace of God. With us, or in spite of us, his purposes will ultimately be fulfilled. This is true even when we lack the vision of faith to understand what he is doing.

III. The Prophets as Servants

We have already considered the prophets both in the treatment of revelation (ch. 1) and in the treatment of God's call of individuals (ch. 4). In addition, the messages of the prophets have had a significant impact in almost every aspect of the Old Testament faith with which we have dealt.

But the prophets were more than spokesmen or theologians. They were servants of God. One of the more common titles applied to these men is that of servant.

Surely the Lord God does nothing,
without revealing his secret
to his servants the prophets (Amos 3:7).

You have neither listened nor inclined your ears to hear, although the Lord persistently sent to you all his servants the prophets (Jer. 25:4).

They did not heed my words, says the Lord, which I persistently sent to you by my servants the prophets (Jer. 29:19).

To the prophets, the concept of servanthood apparently revolved around three basic ideas. To them, it was imperative to know what God expected. The servant must know what is his Master's will. Whether it was revealed on God's initiative or in response to the prophet's prayer, the end was the same. The prophetic servant ultimately knew what God expected or demanded.

The second basic concept was directly related to the first. The prophet obeyed the will of God. Whether this involved continuing to love his unfaithful wife, as in Hosea's case (Hos. 3), neither marrying nor having a family, as in Jeremiah's case (Jer. 16:1-2), or refusing to grieve over the death of his wife, as in Ezekiel's case (Ezek. 24:15-18), in every instance the prophetic servant was expected to obey God's command.

Furthermore, the prophetic servant of God was expected to proclaim God's will to his people. Thus Ezekiel was told,

So you, son of man, I have made a watchman for the house of Israel; whenever you hear a word from my mouth, you shall give them warning from me (Ezek. 33:7).

Also, when Amos was ordered by the priest of Bethel to go proclaim his message in Judah, he responded,

> The Lord took me from following the flock, and the Lord said to me, "Go, prophesy to my people Israel." Now therefore hear the word of the Lord (Amos 7:15-16).

It is absolutely essential, if we are to understand the ministries of the prophets, that we remember that they were servants of God. They were not merely spokesmen of the divine word. They were expected to obey it themselves. It was probably as an outgrowth of this idea that James wrote, "Be doers of the word, and not hearers only, deceiving yourselves" (Jas. 1:22). It is imperative that the servant of God be one who not merely knows and proclaims God's Word, but also obeys it.

Furthermore, one of the fundamental concepts of the New Testament is that Jesus was not simply God incarnate (God in flesh) but that he is also God's Word incarnate. "And the Word became flesh and dwelt among us" (John 1:14). In a very real sense, the servanthood of the prophets was a foreshadowing of this. For as they obeyed God's will, his Word was enfleshed in their lives. Thus they not merely proclaimed the divine Word, they lived it out in actual deeds.

IV. The Priests as Servants

In a very real sense, the verb "to serve" is more characteristic of the priests in the Old Testament than the title of "servant." Yet, one who serves is in fact a servant. The priests were especially consecrated to serve God in the worship. There was a very precisely prescribed ritual which was used for setting them apart for this service. This was so from Israel's earliest days.

> Now this is what you shall do to them to consecrate them, that they may serve me as priests. . . . Aaron also and his sons I will consecrate, to serve me as priests (Ex. 29:1,44).

It is quite obvious, however, that even though it was Israel who performed the ritual, it was God who actually set the priests apart for service.

Furthermore, whereas in the prophet's case, he was to live out God's Word in daily life, in the priest's service he was to lead the people in approaching God in worship.

It matters not that some priests failed to show forth an understanding of the real meaning of worship. There were also many false prophets. The point here is that the priest was a special servant of God, leading the people to God. Even when Aaron failed so abysmally in the episode of the golden calf (Ex. 32), there was never any question but that it was the man who failed. The office was still that of God's servant. When the priest functioned at his highest and best, his divine service was a blessing to the people. Then they were genuinely aware of God's presence in their midst (Lev. 9:22-23).

Probably the greatest service which the priests rendered was at the great Day of Atonement. There, the high priest entered into the holy of holies to make annual atonement for the sins of Israel (Lev. 16:3). It was this particular service of the priesthood which became most meaningful in its New Testament development. The entire Letter to the Hebrews develops the idea that Jesus had become God's High Priest. In this function, he is our High Priest, offering atonement for our sins.

Since then we have a great high priest who has passed through the heavens, Jesus, the Son of God, let us hold fast our confession. For we have not a high priest who is unable to sympathize with our weaknesses, but one who in every respect has been tempted as we are, yet without sin. Let us then with confidence draw near to the throne of grace, that we may receive mercy and find grace to help in time of need (Heb. 4:14-16).

This also has a bearing upon the fact that the New Testament describes all Christians as priests. We are to be "a royal priesthood" (1 Pet. 2:9). As such then, we are to be servants of God, leading people into his presence.

The Kings as Servants

The relationship which existed between the kings of Israel and God has been the subject of a great deal of close scrutiny and much debate in recent years. A great deal of this debate still remains unsettled. However, one thing looms very large: the king was a special servant of God in Israel. We do not normally think of political leaders as di-

vine servants. Our culture has marked a major division between church and state. This is so strong that it has almost
become a proverb that "religion and politics do not mix."
The Old Testament kings would have found such a statement either ridiculous or incomprehensible. This would
have been so even among the so-called godless kings. Whatever their faith, it was totally involved in their kingship.

It was this attitude which marked the major difference
between the kings of Israel and those of other ancient Near
Eastern countries. The king was always God's servant in
Israel. This was fundamental to the very rise of kingship.
The king was selected by God. As might be expected, this
was true of the first king, Saul (1 Sam. 9:15-18). But it was
equally true of his successor, David (1 Sam. 16:1-13).

Even more important, the king was not above the law. He
was expected to be obedient to God. In almost no other nation of the ancient world was the king subservient to the
law. Thus when Ahab longed for Naboth's vineyard, he
dared not take it even though he had the power (1 Kings 21).
Possessing the power, he did not possess the right, and he
knew it. Jezebel, the daughter of the Phoenician king, could
not understand such an attitude. She seized the land with
no qualms.

Furthermore, no other ancient Near Eastern king would
have had a second thought about adding another man's wife
to the royal harem. Yet David tried to cover it up. But when
he was confronted by his deed, he acknowledged his sub-
servience to the law of God (2 Sam. 11 and 12).

The king, then, served God through his obedience to the
law of God. But he also served God by being a shepherd to
God's people. When Micaiah predicted the death of Ahab, he
described it by saying, "I saw all Israel scattered upon the
mountains, as sheep that have no shepherd" (1 Kings
22:17). The concept of shepherd had a rich meaning for the
people of Israel. Whatever a shepherd did for his sheep, the
king was expected to do for his people. The term was
further enriched by the thought that God was the supreme
Shepherd for Israel. The king was to be in a human way
what God was divinely to his people.

But the Old Testament was quite clear as to what the servanthood of the king did not involve. He was not a priest.

The author of Chronicles is quick to point out that good king Uzziah was punished for seeking to function as a priest (2 Chron. 26:16-21). Saul was also rebuked for acting as a priest, offering sacrifice at Gilgal (1 Sam. 13:8-14).

The concept of the servanthood of the king underscored the fact that human government is to be subservient to God. Paul developed this idea further in writing to the church in the center of the Roman empire.

Let every person be subject to the governing authorities. For there is no authority except from God, and those that exist have been instituted by God (Rom. 13:1).

Jesus also identified with this thought when he was on trial before Pilate.

Pilate therefore said to him, "You will not speak to me? Do you not know that I have power to release you, and power to crucify you?" Jesus answered him, "You would have no power over me unless it had been given you from above" (John 19:10-11).

Human rule is ordained of God. But the ruler is always responsible to God.

Let us clearly note that there is a difference between a political leader being responsible to be a servant of God and the establishment of any religion as the official religion of a modern state. But this does not negate the responsibility of the leader. It never did. First and foremost, government is not so much to rule as to serve. Those who govern forget this to their peril.

VI. Miscellaneous Servants

The Old Testament concept of servanthood is incomplete without a consideration of those who do not fit into any specific category. There are clearly those who were God's servants who were neither patriarchs, judges, prophets, priests or kings.

There were the people of Israel. The nation itself was to be God's servant. As such, they were to be obedient, faithful, and loyal in their loving service to him. As we noted in our consideration of God's choice of Israel, they were chosen to serve him, both individually and collectively. As his

servants, they were to bring forth the fruit he expected
from them. Isaiah castigated them for their failure at this
point.

> My beloved had a vineyard
>   on a very fertile hill.
> He digged it and cleared it of stones,
>   and planted it with choice vines;
> he built a watchtower in the midst of it,
>   and hewed out a wine vat in it;
> and he looked for it to yield grapes,
>   but it yielded wild grapes (Isa. 5:1-2).

> For the vineyard of the Lord of hosts
>   is the house of Israel,
> and the men of Judah
>   are his pleasant planting;
> and he looked for justice,
>   but behold, bloodhsed;
> for righteousness,
>   but behold, a cry! (Isa. 5:7).

The nation is specifically identified as God's servant in the
vision of the great redemption.

> But now hear, O Jacob my servant,
>   Israel whom I have chosen! . . .
> Fear not, O Jacob my servant,
>   Jeshurun whom I have chosen (Isa. 44:1-2).

Unfortunately, Israel seems regularly to have forgotten
that they were to be God's servants. All too often, the people
seem to have felt that it was the other way around. Instead
of serving God, they seem to have expected God to serve
them.

Although Israel was specifically and specially to be God's
servants, foreign nations and kings were also the servants
of God, even when they did not know him. Such was his sovereign power that he could use them to accomplish his divine purposes. It was within this concept that Jeremiah
proclaimed to Judah,

Now I have given all these lands into the hand of Nebuchadnezzar, the king of Babylon, my servant, and I have
given him also the beasts of the field to serve him (Jer.
27:6).

Even though the king of Babylon had probably never heard of the God of Israel, he was a servant of that sovereign Lord just the same. This is even more clearly noted concerning Assyria.

> Ah, Assyria, the rod of my anger,
> the staff of my fury!
> Against a godless nation I send him,
> and against the people of my wrath I command him,
>
> . . . .
>
> But he does not so intend,
> and his mind does not so think (Isa. 10:5-7).

Thus we may say that, in the final consideration, the servants of God are those through whom God accomplishes his will. It is far better if those servants are responding in obedient faith to the divine Word. It is better still if they are courageous and loyal. But under all circumstances, the ultimate will and purpose of the sovereign God of Israel will be accomplished by his servants.

The point which the New Testament makes of this is that God has chosen to accomplish his will on earth through human agents. He has given his servants diverse tasks to accomplish. Jesus warned that "no one can serve two masters" (Matt. 6:24). But, implied in that warning is the fact that every man must serve one master. Paul further developed the thought by warning that we will either be servants (slaves) to sin or servants (slaves) of God (Rom. 6:20-22).

Further, we are called to serve both within and without the community of believers. Each of us has different services to render. But the goal is always the same. Within the community of believers, our service is that

some should be apostles, some prophets, some evangelists, some pastors and teachers, to equip the saints for the work of ministry, for building up the body of Christ, until we all attain to the unity of the faith and of the knowledge of the Son of God (Eph. 4:11-13).

Outside of this community, our service is perhaps best stated in the Great Commission.

Go therefore and make disciples of all nations, baptizing them in the name of the Father and of the Son and of the

Holy Spirit, teaching them to observe all that I have commanded you (Matt. 28:19-20).

We must never forget that from first to last, we are the servants of Christ. This New Testament fruit was especially obvious in the self-concept of the rabbi, Saul of Tarsus. He identified himself as a servant to the congregations at Rome and Philippi (Rom. 1:1; Phil. 1:1). But more importantly, Jesus himself admonished his disciples to become the servants of all (Mark 9:35). It is his will that we should be servants. That was enough for the disciples. It should be enough for us.

11
Beyond the Old Testament

The story of human history has not ended. It does not matter to which period or era we direct our attention, there is always more beyond. The same is true of the divine revelation as found in the Old Testament. It did not end. Neither the history of Israel nor the revelation of God ended when the Old Testament was completed. There was significantly more beyond its pages. It is to this which we now direct our attention.

Specifically, there are two questions which we must answer, if we can. First, what happened to the faith of Israel following the end of the Old Testament? The second question may have an answer which is quite similar or widely divergent. It is, what happened in the divine revelation following the end of the Old Testament?

The Movement to a Religion of the Law

It is quite obvious that the Judaism which confronted Jesus in his life or which is found in our contemporary world is somewhat different from the faith of Israel which we have seen in the pages of the Old Testament. In trying to understand how and why it changed, we could make a very lengthy and detailed study. That is beyond the scope of this brief treatment. However, there are some features which are worthy of our consideration.

Mainstream Judaism in Jesus' Day Perhaps the most significant feature of the religion of the Hebrew people in Jesus' lifetime was the synagogue. This was the center of worship and of training in the faith. Yet, there is no mention of it in the Old Testament.

The synagogue apparently had the beginnings of its development among the exiles and scattered refugees during the Exilic period. They needed a place or places to worship, since they were isolated from their land and since the Temple had been destroyed. It was in response to that immediate need of a place to carry on their worship and through which to teach their faith that the synagogue arose.

After the return and the rebuilding of the Temple, the people apparently still felt a need for local places where they could gather for worship and study. However, the synagogue never became a major feature in Israel's religion until the Maccabean era. By the close of this era, the synagogue had attained a place of significance in their religious observance and so it has continued to be over the years.

Without question, the synagogue played a major part in the worship of Jesus. Following his baptism and temptation,

he came to Nazareth, where he had been brought up; and he went to the synagogue, *as his custom was*, on the sabbath day (Luke 4:16, italics mine).

Clearly, he had a habit of worship and study in the synagogue of his hometown. Furthermore, we note that he regularly chose the various synagogues of Galilee as the places of his personal teaching in the early parts of his ministry (Matt. 4:23; Mark 1:39; Luke 4:15). In addition, the synagogue in Capernaum became one of the major centers of his early ministry (Luke 4:33). It was the synagogue of Judaism which furnished the early pulpit and lectern for Jesus, as well as the site for many of his healing miracles.

Furthermore, Paul also found that the synagogues scattered around the Roman world were the best, first place for him to begin his missionary endeavors (Acts 13:14-15; 17:1-3; 18:4). There he found a people who were familiar with the Old Testament Scriptures, to whom he could begin preaching the good news of Jesus Christ.

Ultimately, however, the synagogues were to reject both the Christian gospel and the Christians themselves. The healing of the man blind from birth had precipitated a crisis in one synagogue, so that the leaders agreed that "if any one should confess him [Jesus] to be Christ, he was to be put out of the synagogue" (John 9:22). Further, Jesus warned his disciples that their message would be rejected and that they would be "beaten in synagogues" (Mark 13:9).

The reason for this violent reaction of the synagogues to the Christian message was that Israel had moved to a religion of the Law. The Pharisees had become the dominant party of the day. In all fairness, we should note that there probably was never a group of people who were more morally upright than these. They were meticulous in the keeping of the Law. But by becoming so engrossed in keeping the Law, the living faith of their fathers had passed out of existence. They had lost the spirit of joy and excitement. Their religion had become a burden. It was this burden of Pharisaism which Paul ultimately cast off when he came to know Jesus Christ as Lord.

It is well to note that even though they were the leading party in Judaism in Jesus' day, the Pharisees were never a numerous people. Most of the Jews who were contemporary with Jesus had no time or interest in such things. For the overwhelming majority of the people, they participated in the synagogue worship, going quietly about their lives. The mainstream of the people seem to have had a very practical approach to their faith. God was good. Sin was real. Life was difficult. The Law was a hedge about their lives to protect them. They did not involve themselves generally in the debates between the leaders over the resurrection or over the collaboration with their Roman rulers. They longed for a deliverance from political oppression by a military messiah.

But if the majority of the people were not concerned with the finer nuances of the Law, the Pharisees and the Sadducees were. The Sadducees were an even smaller, but more influential group than the Pharisees. They were generally both more wealthy and more politically prominent. The Pharisees hated the Romans and refused to collaborate in any way. The Sadducees sought to accommodate themselves to the Roman rule and consequently received a significant amount of temporal authority in their land. The Pharisees believed in a resurrection. The Sadducees believed in no resurrection, holding that both rewards and punishments were meted out in this life. (It is easier to believe this when you are both wealthy and powerful.) The Pharisees were frequently involved in intrigues aimed at the overthrow of Rome and the acclaiming of a messiah. The Sadducees sought to make the best of the world as it was.

Generally, these two groups were at each others' throats. Their arguments were theological. The basis of them was a quest for power. One of the few things which united them was their opposition to Jesus. Both parties recognized him as a threat to their cherished beliefs and to their way of life. So he was. Life must change when Jesus comes.

However, it is imperative that we should note that regardless of how the Law was interpreted, there was no disagreement among the people, the Pharisees, or the Sadducees that the Law was the ultimate authority for their lives. It had come from God and was the final guide for living. The rabbis and the scribes might debate its application. There was no question but that it did apply. Life was governed by the Law for the Judaism of the first century AD.

B. ***The Qumran Community.*** Along with the development of Judaism in this direction, there was another parallel development to which we must also give some attention. Along the western shore of the Dead Sea, the ruins of a monastery have been found which is known as the Qumran community. It has been identified as belonging to the Essenes, a sect of Judaism. Although this is not at all certain, it appears to be quite probable. It is from this group that the manuscripts known as the Dead Sea Scrolls have come.

These people withdrew from the society of their day, living an ascetic and a celibate life. Since they were celibates, the only way for growth was by attracting converts. They, too, emphasized the Law as the basis for their lives. They had a very rigorous manual of discipline under which they lived and by which they governed themselves. There are two major features of importance in their lives which are important for our study. First, they were concerned with the preservation of their sacred scriptures. This concern gave to contemporary biblical scholarship the large number of manuscripts and fragments which we have called the

Dead Sea Scrolls. (These have been briefly considered in our discussion of the biblical text in the "Introduction.") In addition to the many biblical manuscripts which they preserved, they also left numerous scrolls setting forth the teachings of their community. Many of their teachings are quite similar to those of Jesus and the New Testament. The relationship between Jesus and the Essenes opens an entire area of study in itself.

The second consideration of major importance for us is the development of their messianic hope. Within the post-Old Testament period, there was a belief developed among some circles of Judaism that there were going to be two messiahs. One of these would be the offspring of David, who would reign as a King. The other messiah was expected to be a descendant of Aaron, who was expected to be the great high priest. This concept of two messiahs took on a major significance among the inhabitants of Qumran.

This becomes especially important in relationship to the ministry of John the Baptist. John grew up in the wilderness of Judea (Luke 1:80;3:2). This region included the area around Qumran. It is quite possible that John spent some time among these people. It appears highly probable that he was familiar with their teachings, especially in the light of much of his own preaching.

This may shed some significant light upon the problem of John after he had been arrested and cast into prison. John seemed to have been quite certain at Jesus' baptism that he was to be God's Messiah. Yet, from his prison, John later queried, "Are you he who is to come, or shall we look for another?" (Matt. 11:3). It is possible to understand John's rising doubts, since he was shut up in prison. This is especially so if he were expecting Jesus to be a political Messiah who would overthrow the hated Roman rule.

But, if John was familiar with the teachings of Qumran concerning the two messiahs, his question might have had a theological point rather than have been expressing a wavering faith. In that light, John's question could have been, "Are you the only one who is coming, or is there another in addition to yourself?" If this is what John intended, it adds a much more profound significance to his question.

But whether this is correct or not, the community of Qumran was quite legalistic. Thus, on every hand, the religion of Israel in Jesus' day had become a religion of the Law. But it is imperative to note that this was not the only development which the Old Testament took.

〃 The Movement Toward Christianity

While the Old Testament is the Bible of Judaism, it is also the Bible of Christianity. As we have noted throughout this book, the roots of faith which are so deeply planted in the soil of the Old Testament bore frequent flowers in the faith of the New Testament.

Thus we can pointedly claim that the Old Testament led directly to Christianity. It laid the foundation upon which the New Testament was built. The very first book in the New Testament begins by connecting Jesus with Abraham (Matt. 1:1-17). On almost every page, in almost every chapter, the Gospel of Matthew is anchored to the Old Testament. There is almost a recurring refrain.

All this took place to fulfill what the Lord had spoken by the prophet(Matt. 1:22).

So it is written by the prophet (Matt. 2:5).

This was to fulfill what the Lord had spoken by the prophet (Matt. 2:15).

Then was fulfilled what was spoken by the prophet Jeremiah (Matt. 2:17).

That what was spoken by the prophets might be fulfilled (Matt. 2:23).

But the New Testament does far more with the message of the Old than merely proof text it, citing specific passages which serve to confirm or to illustrate it. The very essence of the New Testament message is that it is the final revelation of God which was begun in the Old Testament. Jesus himself acknowledged the authority of the Old Testament and established its authority for Christians. He warned his disciples against the folly of casting the Old Testament away, saying, "Think not that I have come to abolish the law and the prophets; I have come not to abolish them but to fulfil them" (Matt. 5:17). In so doing, he contrasted the legalistic development of the Judaism of his day with the development which he was making by saying, "Unless your righteousness exceeds that of the scribes and Pharisees, you will never enter the kingdom" (Matt. 5:20). Furthermore, after his resurrection, Jesus still pointed to the Old Testament as the book which was the basis for their knowledge and faith. "Beginning with Moses and all the prophets, he interpreted to them in all the scriptures the things concerning himself" (Luke 24:27).

The early Christians had no intention of separating themselves from the faith of Israel. The early disciples were daily in the Temple, participating in the regular worship (Acts 2:46). This was apparently continued until the Jewish leaders themselves banned the disciples from this worship. Even then, we find Paul still worshiping in the Temple at the time of his final arrest (Acts 21:26-28). When the Temple and the synagogues were finally closed to them, they still held on to the Old Testament. It was the basis for their faith. It should be so for ours.

There was no question in either Jesus' mind or in those of the apostles but that the New Testament was the fulfillment of the Old. It still is.

12
How Do You Interpret the Old Testament?

The Old Testament, as we have pointed out, has been the object of a great deal of misunderstanding and an even greater amount of misinterpretation. But we must clearly understand that the greatest mistreatment is to ignore it. Even if some interpreters have misunderstood it or misinterpreted it, at least they were seeking to discover what God was saying through its pages. The greatest failure on the part of most Christians is that we do not even make the effort. It is not so much that we have tried to interpret it and found its message lacking the full New Testament development. Rather, we have found it difficult to understand and therefore have made no effort at all. Yet it is of this very book that Jesus said,

You search the scriptures, because you think that in them you have eternal life; and it is they that bear witness to me (John 5:39).

Yet, if we are going to study the Old Testament seriously, we must develop a methodology or technique for doing so. The hit or miss approach has more often missed than hit. It appears to me that there are five basic steps which must be applied in any systematic study of the Old Testament. Each of these must be applied carefully and thoroughly if we are going to be serious in our desire to come to grips with the real message of the Old Testament.

⁀ The Lordship of Christ

As a preliminary to the actual approach to the Old Testament, we must underline our faith commitment to the lordship of Jesus. He is Lord of all of life. He is Lord of the Bible. He is Lord of the Old Testament. The beginning point of interpreting any passage must be our commitment to Christ as Lord. If the passage fails to undergird and enforce that belief, then we have failed to interpret it properly.

Furthermore, the end point of our interpretation must also be the lordship of Christ. He is the fulfillment of the Old Testament, by his own claim. If our study of the Old Testament does not lead us back to Jesus, then we have also failed to study it properly.

This in no way means that every passage in the Old Testament must be seen on the same level as the teachings of Jesus. This is simply not so. But the Old Testament did lead to Jesus. Therefore, if a passage appears to fail to do that, however dimly, then we have failed properly to come to grips with it.

Let us note a significant warning at this point. We must never be guilty of reading something into a passage that is not there. We must not be so eager to find a spiritual truth that we manufacture one. The Old Testament itself lashed out at this kind of interpretation. In the Book of Job, his three friends said much that sounded pious and true. But it was wrong.

The Lord said to Eliphaz the Temanite: "My wrath is kindled againest you and against your two friends; for you have not spoken of me what is right, as my servant Job has" (Job 42:7)

There is no need to read more into a passage than God has placed there. But neither is there any need to take away from a passage the genuine truths which God has placed there. We must probe to the very depths to find the truth of a passage. We dare not force our theology upon it. Neither dare we let our beliefs blind us to what it does say. It is our task, under the lordship of Jesus, to find out exactly what it does say. Either more or less is to compromise with God's revelation. That we must not do.

Step 1: Find Out What the Passage Really Says

In beginning the task of interpretation, we must first determine what the passage in question really says. It is best to translate it for yourself, but most Christians lack the knowledge and skill to do that. Fortunately, that is not an irretrievable loss. In this day and age, there are so many translations of the Bible available, we can come fairly close to the actual passage by comparing various translations.

We need to be aware of the fact that there is a decided difference between a translation and a paraphrase. A translation is an attempt by a person or a group of persons to put the original words of the Scripture into the best words of our language. A paraphrase is the attempt to understand the meaning of a passage and to put it in the words of the author. Paraphrases may be helpful in Bible study. But they are a serious hindrance to trying to find out exactly what a passage really said.

The translator will bring to bear the best evidence of all the ancient manuscripts which are available, in order to try to discover what the original said. He will also bring to bear his best knowledge of the biblical languages and of contemporary languages so that his translation will most nearly approximate the original. Since our own language is changing, words which were adequate a century or even a generation ago may no longer be entirely adequate. It is for this reason that you and I must use several translations, always including the newest and best which are available.

When we study the various translations, we must compare and contrast them until we feel that we have gotten the best understanding of what the original said. It should be obvious that we do not merely pick the translation which most nearly agrees with our own preconceptions. Rather, we are seeking to discover what was actually written.

When this has been completed, then we must make a word study of the key words in the passage. Recognizing that frequently several different Hebrew words are translated by a single English word, and vice versa, a good analytical concordance will be most helpful. This gives the Hebrew word (or words) from which a particular English word was translated. As we study the use of identical words in similar passages, we can get a better understanding of the real meaning of the word. We must also be sure that we understand the real meaning of the English word. A good dictionary is absolutely necessary at this point.

I cannot emphasize enough just how important it is to know as closely as possible exactly what a passage said and what the words in it meant before we go further in any attempt at interpretation. Our interpretation of a passage may be thoroughly done, but if the words with which we are dealing are not what it really said, we will have accomplished nothing. Thus, the first step is always to find out what a passage says. Without this, all else will fail.

Step 2: Establish the Passage's Historical Meaning

Once we have established what a passage says, we are ready for the second step. Here we must determine what the passage meant in its original historical setting. Every passage in the Old Testament was originally written for a particular time and place. It had a message from God to that audience, and we must seek to understand it. Putting a passage against its historical background is difficult and requires diligent and consistent study, as well as a great deal of careful thought.

In order to do this we must bring to bear all the knowledge about the ancient world which we can gather. Here we search the archaeology books, the histories, and the Bible itself. We must be careful in dealing with archaeology books and with histories to recognize that discoveries are constantly being made which change these works. Therefore we need to keep such study going at all times. Good commentaries are also helpful at this point. But beware! Just because someone wrote something in a book does not make it right. It could simply have been wrong, based on insufficient information or research. It could be outdated. Either way, this kind of information can be misleading. Keep your wits about you as you read and study. The more you can learn about the historical periods of the Old Testament and the more you can learn about Israel's culture and that of her neighbors, the better able you will be to understand your passage in its own setting.

For example, the plagues of Egypt have always been of

great interest. But they become extremely meaningful when we realize that each of them was specifically directed at some current religious belief of Egypt. There is new meaning to the entire episode when we realize that God was not merely playing with the Egyptians. The entire series of events was a contest between the gods of Egypt and the God of Israel. In every instance, the gods of Egypt lost. The God of Israel was sovereign Lord!

As we understand the background against which a particular passage is set, we are far more likely to really understand what God was saying to his people. Until we have a degree of confidence as to what the passage meant to the author or speaker and to the recipients, we are not ready to move beyond this step in our interpretation. When we have established its historical meaning, then we can proceed.

Step 3: Discover the Passage's Basic Principle or Thrust

One of the fundamental emphases of the Bible is that God is the God of order, not of chaos. He is the God of meaning, not of nonsense. It is upon this concept that we move to the third step in interpreting a passage. Whatever fundamental meaning a passage may have, it must be rooted in its historical meaning. Its meaning for us today may be different from its ancient meaning But its contemporary meaning must be related to its ancient meaning. It must grow from it.

At the same time, we must be aware that we cannot fail to take this step, finding a passage's thrust. Perhaps the greatest single weakness of much Old Testament study is that it never progresses to this step. Having established a historical meaning, the commentator quits. To stop with the Old Testament would mean that we should never get to the New. To stop with the Old Testament would be to fail to see Jesus at all.

Perhaps the best example of what is meant by discovering a passage's basic principle is found in the Gospel of Matthew. There, in the Sermon on the Mount, we find Jesus' own approach to this problem. In dealing with killing, he went to the fundamental problem of anger (Matt. 5:21-26). In dealing with adultery, he moved to the principle and attacked lust (vv. 5:27-30). In dealing with divorce, he approached the basic problem of marriage. (vv. 31-32). In considering false swearing, he sought out the essential problem of simple truthfulness (vv. 33-37). In dealing with exact and equal justice, he advocated going beyond what could either be demanded or expected (vv. 38-42). Finally, in considering the commandment to love one's neighbor, he set forth the principle of loving one's enemy (vv. 43-48).

In every instance, the underlying principle was discovered and it was set forth with new application, carrying it forward in the same direction in which it originally had been set forth. The new teaching was intimately related to its ancient meaning. But in no instance was it either limited to its ancient meaning or simply lifted up and planted without change into the world of Jesus.

So it is that we must make the same kind of approach to the Old Testament. Having identified the historical meaning, we must search for its principle and the direction in which it was moving. This thrust or direction, then, will guide us in discovering what it means now.

But even this is not yet enough. We must still do more.

Step 4: Apply the Passage to Contemporary Life

Once we have moved from an ancient to a modern meaning for a passage, then we must seek to discover how it applies to contemporary life. This requires a genuine knowledge of what life is about. We must be aware of the joys and heartaches, the problems and potentials, the defeats and victories which we and those about us face every day. God has a message for them and for us. To apply a passage of the Old Testament to contemporary life requires the knowledge of both life and the passage.

Every passage has a "So what?" It is the interpreter's task to find out precisely how the passage relates. There are a number of helpful tools. Steady reading of the newspaper, as well as of the major newsmagazines, coupled with a regular watching of television newscasts or a listening to the radio newscasts will help you to understand both the major and minor crises of our day. This is imperative. But it is not enough, by itself.

This must also be coupled with an intense interest in and a concern for the affairs of people. Listen to those around you. Hear their words and the deeper meanings behind what they say. In short, become an effective empathizer with those about you.

Both of these must also be coupled with an honest attempt to understand your own needs. People are generally pretty similar. We at some time or another have similar fears and doubts, similar hopes and dreams. As we come to understand our world, our neighbors, and ourselves, we shall be best able to apply the passages under study to its needs. God's Word will speak to the human heart. But we must let him use us in applying it. This brings us to the final step in the process of interpreting the Old Testament.

Step 5: Apply the Spiritual Dimension

We began this chapter by referring to the fact that Jesus is Lord of the Old Testament. We have continued it by listing the basic steps in interpretation. But under the lordship of Christ, there is a fifth step which must be applied to the methodology of interpreting the Old Testament. It is God's book with which we are dealing. It is God's Word which we are seeking to interpret. To do this without God would be the height of folly. Therefore we must apply the spiritual dimension to our technique of interpretation.

We must pray for the Holy Spirit to guide us throughout. This is not to be applied only at the end. It must be applied throughout. Jesus, recognizing the limitations of his disciples, said to them,

I have yet many things to say to you, but you cannot bear them now. When the Spirit of truth comes, he will guide you into all the truth. . . . He will glorify me, for he will take what is mine and declare it to you (John 16:12-14).

This is still true.

If we are to be successful interpreters of the Word, we must seek God's leadership through prayer every step of the way. We must lay hold of Jesus' promise that the Holy Spirit will guide us into all the truth, that "he will teach you all things" (John 14:26).

Without praying for the leadership of God's Spirit, we will be seeking to understand God's revelation from our own strength. This will be doomed to failure. It will become merely an intellectual exercise, and not a spiritual pilgrimage. There are riches in the Old Testament which can be mined by the eager student of the Word who is spiritually discerning. They are not hidden. They are available. God has placed them there and he will help us to uncover them. But we must come sincerely and seek diligently. Anything less will fail.

The Old Testament is the root from which the New Testament grew. It was the Bible of the early churches. It has a message for us. I have sought both to highlight the basic emphases of its message as well as to encourage and help you in your further study. But in the last analysis, it will be your own devotion to God and his Word which will determine your use and your study of this magnificent revelation from God. You may ignore it or treasure it. That is between you and God. But remember that it was God who said,

The grass withers, the flower fades;
   but the word of our God will stand for ever (Isa. 40:8).

So be it.

Suggestions for Further Study

Note: this is not an attempt to give a bibliography. Those familiar with the field will recognize my indebtedness to all who have worked in the area. Rather, I am suggesting sources which those unfamiliar with the field may seek out for further study. Throughout, I have used the Revised Standard Version of the Bible except in those places where I have made my own translation for clarity on a particular point. Such places are carefully noted.

Albright, William Foxwell, *From the Sone Age to Christianity.* 2nd ed. New York: Doubleday & Co., 1957. This book is a history of the Old Testament era, primarily based upon the biblical text and the archaeological evidence. An excellent source for those unfamiliar with the field of Old Testament archaeology.

Baab, Otto J., *The Theology of the Old Testament.* Nashville: Abingdon Press, 1949. An older, systematic approach to the subject. The chapter on sin is especially well done.

Bright, John, *The Authority of the Old Testament.* Nashville: Abingdon Press, 1967. An excellent survey of the problem of authority together with good suggestions for arriving at an understanding of authority.

_____ *A History of Israel.* 2nd ed. London: SCM Press, 1972. Probably the most thorough history of Israel ever done. Incorporates the best of contemporary archaeological discoveries.

Eichrodt, Walther, *Theology of the Old Testament.* 2 vols. Philadelphia: Westminster Press, 1961-64. The most thorough, technical Old Testament theology currently in print. It sees the central emphasis of the Old Testament as covenant. Written from the standpoint of German critical research.

Francisco, Clyde T., *Introducing the Old Testament.* Rev. ed. Nashville: Broadman Press, 1977. A good, conservative introduction to the Old Testament written by one of Southern Baptists' best scholars. Contains a brief, section-by-section, book-by-book introduction to the contents of the Old Testament.

Jacob, Edmond, *Theology of the Old Testament*. New York: Harper, 1958. The best brief theology of the Old Testament written. However, it is quite technical. Its viewpoint is primarily that of Eichrodt.

Johnson, Aubrey R., *The Vitality of the Individual in the Thought of Ancient Israel*. Cardiff: University of Wales Press, 1949. An excellent survey of the Hebrew psychology of personality.

Laurin, R. B., *Contemporary Old Testament Theologians*. Valley Forge: Judson Press, 1970. An excellent survey of the methodology and approach of the major Old Testament theologians of the past fifty years.

Mowinckel, Sigmund, *He That Cometh*. New York: Abingdon, 1956. The best, most thorough study of messianic prophecy available. Although written from the Scandinavian approach, it is well worth reading. Its survey of the available biblical material is quite comprehensive.

North, C. R., *The Suffering Servant in Deutero-Isaiah*. Oxford: Oxford University Press, 1956. The best survey of the so-called Servant Songs which is available. Quite thorough and very insightful.

Richardson, Alan, *A Theological Wordbook of the Bible*. New York: Macmillan, 1951. By far the best one volume dictionary of key theological words of the Bible which is available. Traces word and thought development throughout both the Old and the New Testaments.

Robinson, H. Wheeler, *Religious Ideas of the Old Testament*. London: Gerald Duckworth, 1956. An older, but quite readable approach to the key theological ideas of the Old Testament.

Rowley, H. H., *The Biblical Doctrine of Election*. London: Lutterworth, 1950. The best, most thorough treatment of the concept of God's free choice which is available.

Rust, E. C., "The Theology of the Old Testament," *The Broadman Bible Commentary*. Vol. 1. Revised. Nashville: Broadman Press, 1973, pp. 71-86. A brief, but very well done, survey of Old Testament theology.

Snaith, Norman H., *The Distinctive Ideas of the Old Testament*. New York: Schocken, 1964. An excellent technical survey of the essential characteristics of God as found in the Old Testament.

Wright, G. Ernest, *God Who Acts*. London: SCM, 1952. An excellent survey of the Old Testament conception of God as active in history. Brief, but very well done.

Zimmerli, W., and Jeremias, J., *The Servant of God*. London: SCM, 1957. A very well done survey of the entire Old Testament understanding of the Servant of God and its impact upon the mission of Jesus.

Scripture Index